STEPCHILDREN
OF
MOTHER RUSSIA

STEPCHILDREN OF MOTHER RUSSIA

The Story of a Jewish family

Boris Draznin

Schreiber Publishing
Rockville, Maryland

Stepchildren of Mother Russia
Boris Draznin

Published by:
Schreiber Publishing
Post Office Box 4193
Rockville, MD 20849 U.S.A.

Library of Congress Cataloging-in-Publication Data

Draznin, Boris.
  Stepchildren of mother Russia : the story of a Jewish family / Boris Draznin.
    p. cm.
  ISBN 1-887563-90-3
1.   Draznin family. 2.   Jews--Soviet Union--Biography. 3. Medical scientists--Soviet Union--Biography. 4.   Soviet Union--Biography.   I. Title.
DS135.R95D733 2004
947'.004924--dc22

                                                    2004007223

Printed in the United States of America

To my parents,
Nahum and Rosa Draznin

Acknowledgements

"You never know what awaits you in the future." My father used to say. "What you do know is your past from which you draw your aspirations for the future. With that, you have your judgment as to how to transform your dreams into reality. To be able to live your life creatively is both a gift that ought to be cherished and a burden to be carried with dignity."

I thank him and my mother for giving me this gift. I thank my parents and my parents-in-law (Victor and Judith Lerman) for supporting my creative endeavors and guiding me through the labyrinth of life with their invaluable insight. I thank my wife, Elena, who has been the guardian angel of my sanity since 1965.

As far as my writing is concerned, I wish to thank my first medical editor, Joan Goldstein Parker, who helped me with my first professional books in the 1980s; my English language editor, Mac Beckett, whose constant encouragement served as a sweet reword for every chapter written; Michael Merson, my friend and a harsh critic of my style and the content of my prose; and Mordecai Schreiber, whose interest in preserving Jewish history in print goes far beyond the ordinary.

The Draznin and Lerman Families

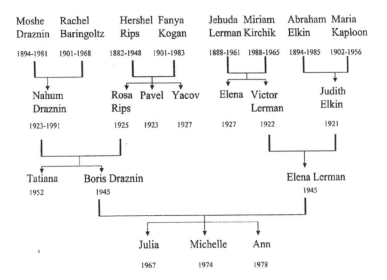

Moshe Draznin	Rachel Baringoltz		Hershel Rips	Fanya Kogan		Jehuda Lerman	Miriam Kirchik		Abraham Elkin	Maria Kaploon
1894-1981	1901-1968		1882-1948	1901-1983		1888-1961	1988-1965		1894-1985	1902-1956

Nahum Draznin		Rosa Rips	Pavel	Yacov		Elena	Victor Lerman		Judith Elkin
1923-1991		1925	1923	1927		1927	1922		1921

Tatiana	Boris Draznin		Elena Lerman
1952	1945		1945

Julia	Michelle	Ann
1967	1974	1978

PREFACE

T he story of my family, which you are about to read, was conveyed to me by my grandparents, parents, uncles and aunts during hours-long conversations, frequently conducted over maps, photographs, old letters and post-cards and saved pages of diaries. I have tried to record all conversations verbatim, or as close to it as human memory would allow, in order to preserve the spirit of the events, most of which I could not have witnessed. In recent years, after conversing with many intellectual Russian Jews, I have finally realized that the story of my family exemplifies the aspirations and struggles of hundreds, if not thousands, of Jews in Twentieth Century Russia.

My family, like many others, made the transition to modern times from the vanished world of Eastern European Jewry, whose tragic fate was so brilliantly depicted in the photographs of Roman Vishniac and on the walls of the Holocaust Museum in Washington, DC. This world, however, was not only about tragedies, death, destruction and accidental survival, but also nurtured the seeds of powerful intellectual growth, professional success and the exemplary lives of new generations of Eastern European Jews. My memoirs and the story of my family depict this miraculous transition.

I apologize if any of the facts or names are not completely accurate, for I am merely a conduit of the information presented to me. Overall, I am deeply grateful to my elders for preserving these facts, these dialogues and these images for me, for my children and for my readers.

CHAPTER ONE

N ahum Draznin's life, as he remembered it, began on a roof. He was actually born in the house of his grandmother, Haya Baringoltz, in the small Ukrainian town of Ovruch, on May 3, 1923, but his own birth had not registered in his memory. His grandma's house was the place where he had spent the first three years of his life, an uneventful infancy, in the care of his mother, Rachel, his father, Moshe, and his grandma, Haya. Not surprisingly, when he grew up, he didn't remember a single day or a single event from this period of his life.

In 1925, Moshe, Rachel and little Nahum moved to a larger town, Zhitomir, a regional center west of Kiev. They stayed there for the next three years, until Nahum was almost six, but, no matter how hard he tried, he couldn't remember anything about his life in Zhitomir, either.

His memory of his life began on the roof of a four-story apartment house on the corner of Chernishevskaya Street and Basseinaya Street in Kharkov, on July 21, 1929. He was six years old. Some people claim to remember much earlier times in their lives, but Nahum didn't, though he could distinguish what he actually remembered from what his parents had told him about his childhood.

At the end of 1928, Nahum's family had moved to Kharkov, the capital of post-revolutionary Ukraine, and a large industrial city some 400 miles east of Kiev and 700 miles south of Moscow. Moshe's childhood friend, Nahum Olshansky, had become one of the top officials of the Ukrainian Communist Party Central Committee, and had offered Moshe a job as his deputy. The job came with a two-room flat on the top floor of a large apartment house in the center of Kharkov. Moshe had gone ahead alone, but, as things settled, six months later, Rachel and Nahum joined him in their new apartment in the capital city of Ukraine.

The apartment house had been built in 1916, of oversized gray bricks. It had four entrances, marked from A to D, and a vast basement that housed the apartment of the janitor, a boiler room with coal-burning stoke-holes that provided hot water for the apartment dwellers and numerous small storage rooms for the people living in the complex. The building was very tall for the city; four stories. The flats had twelve-foot ceilings, and there was an attic, which held a network of hot- and cold-water pipes and a door to the roof.

It was the middle of the summer of 1929 when Nahum and a group of other boys from the apartment house found themselves standing four stories up, on the hot metal roof. This was the first event in Nahum's life that etched itself into his memory, and one that he would never forget.

Summer days in Kharkov are long and hot and humid. The school year ended in the second week of June, and kids from the apartment complex spent their days playing in the back yard, called the "*dvor*." Each apartment house on their street had a *dvor*, but theirs was particularly large and well land-scaped.

Two rows of old apple trees grew down the middle of it, running the length of the building. The apple trees had probably been there before the building was erected. They were relatively short, with dark-brown bark and many thick, strong branches. There were four sturdy trees in each row, proudly displaying their powerful branches, like bodybuilders flexing their accentuated muscles.

Neatly arranged gravel walkways originated from the four back doors of the building, crossing the entire depth of the yard. Wooden benches with curved backs were placed along the walkways and under the trees. Ordinarily, these benches, covered with scraps of peeling green paint, were the domain of the older women who lived in the apartment house.

On the other side of the trees, away from the building and toward the six-foot brick wall, stood two wooden tables with long benches, where men of the apartment complex played cards, dominoes, chess and checkers. To the right of the tables was a large sandbox for small kids to play in, and to the left there was a little exercise station with a couple of benches and a high bar. The rest of the back yard was covered in tall grass that no one bothered to mow and weeds that no one wished to kill.

The back yard was never empty. It seemed as if someone's grandma, "*babushka*," was always there, sitting calmly on one of the benches, as if she were the guardian of the tranquility of the *dvor*.

There were five of them on the roof. Nahum and Leonid Rubenstein, the two youngest, were in the same kindergarten class. Leonid lived on the second floor of the C entrance with his parents and his aunt, his mother's sister. Both women worked at the bakery one block down the street, at the corner of Chernishevskaya and Ivanova streets.

Leonid's aunt was a very short woman with some sort of congenital disease. Her trunk and head were of normal proportions, but her limbs, especially her legs, were short and bowed. She lived with her married sister, and helped with raising Leonid and with various house chores.

No one knew what Felix Rubenstein, Leonid's father, did. He was an older man, in his fifties, and he was almost never at home. Even on the days when he stayed home, he would leave at dawn and return late at night. He never smiled and never talked to anyone, and everyone, including Leonid, was somewhat afraid of his shadowy appearance.

Arkady Pilman was a ten-year-old boy from the D entrance. His father, David Maximovich Pilman, was an officer of the Red Army, and wore a dark-green uniform with a red rhomboid on the collar of his jacket, and tall, black, shiny boots. Arkady's mother, Maria Ivanovna Pilman, was an elementary-school teacher who taught in the neighborhood school. In fact, City School #82 stood immediately across the street from their apartment house. Arkady, tall for his age, with a large tuft of dark, curly hair that he had inherited from his father, was a brilliant kid. He loved to read and, every afternoon, when he and his friends used to gather in the shade of the apple trees, hiding from the burning rays of the blazing, scorching mid-summer Ukrainian sun, he would tell them the stories he had read the previous day.

Or so he claimed. His friends suspected that, on occasion, he probably made up some of these stories, telling his listeners that he had read them in books just the night before.

"One day I'll read all these books myself," thought Nahum, listening intently, enchanted by Arkady's storytelling skills.

Even Yurka Gremko, an oversized thirteen-year-old boy from the ground floor of the B entrance, the worst pupil at City School number 82, liked to listen to Arkady. Yurka was such a bad student that he had had to repeat first, second and third grades. He had not completed any of these grades, and had been allowed to move on only because the school administration could not keep him in the same grade for more than two years.

He was there on the roof as well, towering over his younger and shorter friends in his rugged gray clothes. Yurka lived with only his mother, Varvara Mikhailovna, a cleaner at the regional hospital. For extra income, she also cleaned staircases in their apartment house, helping the janitor.

Yurka had never known his father, but bragged to everyone that his father had been a former hospital director who had died before Yurka was born.

The fifth boy on the roof was Vasily Chernenko, a classmate of Arkady, a quiet, short, muscular, ten-year-old with freckled skin and bushy red hair. Everyone called him "Red," even his parents, Ivan Nikolaevich, a draftsman and Maria Tikhonovna, a nurse, and his twin sister Lana. He was the only red-haired kid in the entire school, and was the subject of perpetual teasing and bullying.

About five weeks before, Arkady's father, David Maximovich Pilman, had bought his son a model airplane. He and Arkady had spent several nights at home assembling this airplane, gluing on the wings, attaching the propeller and painting the fuselage. The results had been spectacular. It turned out to be a beautiful model. Not only the children, but also all the adults of the apartment house had come out to see it, when David Maximovich dressed up in his military uniform and Arkady brought it down and placed it on a table that had been cleared of its domino-players. Admiring this magnificent plane, people asked whether or not it could fly.

"Unfortunately, not," explained David Maximovich. "It doesn't have an engine. It can only glide." The answer was good enough. People touched the model carefully, and three of David Maximovich's friends were even allowed to hold it in their hands. The model was then taken back to the Pilman apartment and hoisted onto a bookshelf, where it proudly displayed its four red stars, one on each wing and one on each side of the tail.

Arkady, however, was not satisfied with having an airplane sitting in his apartment, an airplane that he was allowed to touch only in the presence of his father. He decided to build a similar model, but of larger size, so it could glide over their *dvor*, and maybe even over the city. He shared this idea with his friends and, for the entire week, they collected cardboard, twigs, plywood, veneer and rough paper.

Arkady drew the sketches, and they cut and pasted various parts together until they had built an airplane four feet long and six feet from the tip of the right wing to the tip of the left. Today they were ready to set it gliding.

They had carried it all the way to the roof of the apartment building, and now they assembled around it in a last prelaunch-launch discussion.

"We're gonna push it from the middle," announced Arkady, peering down at the *dvor* over the three-foot guardrail at the edge of the roof, just above the rusty gutter. "We'll lift it, set it on the guardrail and push it on the count of three."

"Hey, guys, what if we put our cat inside?" asked Vasily, suddenly. "As a test pilot."

"Wow! Great idea!" echoed Arkady, visibly upset that he himself had not come up with this brilliant thought. "Go get your cat!"

"It's probably in the garbage dumpster. I need help; I won't catch it alone."

"Good. Yurka and Nahum will help you," agreed Arkady. "Go."

The three of them dashed back downstairs, left hands sliding along the banister as they skipped every other step of the stone-etched staircase. They ran out the back door of the building, to the dumpster in the far left-hand corner of the *dvor*. The dumpster was where the local cats spent their time foraging for food. Most people gave their cats a saucer of milk in the morning, and the rest of the day the cats were on their own, roaming through the neighborhood dumpsters.

The boys tiptoed up to the large, open, metal dumpster, trying not to scare the cats inside. Sure enough, one of them was the gray-and-white longhair of the Chernenkos. Vasily peeked inside and, in a very quiet voice, called it by name. The cat looked up, but didn't move.

"Yurka, you make a lot of noise and pretend to jump in from the left side," said Vasily. "Nahum, you catch my cat from the right side, and I'll cover the front. Let's do it!"

When Yurka jumped up and down on the side of the dumpster, banging it with his boots and screaming, "Pow-Wow!" the cats jumped out, scattering in all directions. Vasily's cat jumped to the right, flying over the side of the dumpster next to Nahum. Nahum tried to catch it in the air, but missed, and could only grab its tail. Screaming, "Meow-w-w!" the cat turned and attempted to free itself from Nahum's hands, scratching his face with its claws.

"Help!" shouted Nahum, hanging onto the tail.

In a split second, Vasily was next to him, grabbing the body of the cat. "I got it! I got it! Let go!" And Nahum let go the tail. Blood was streaming down his cheek from a couple of fairly deep scratches.

"Here, take this," said Yurka, offering Nahum a large sheet of newspaper he had found in the garbage. "It's clean. Apply some pressure to your cheek."

Nahum took the paper and pushed it against the wound, and they started back up to the roof.

On the way back, they met Lana, Vasily's twin sister, who was always trying to be with the boys. She loved to climb trees, scale fences, play soccer, throw stones and play war games—Reds against Whites.

"Red! What are you doing with my cat?" cried Lana, in a high-pitched voice.

"Nothing!"

"But where are you carrying it to?"

"Your cat will be the pilot," replied Yurka.

"Pilot? What do you mean, 'the pilot?' What kind of pilot?" She was running up the stairs just behind Vasily and Yurka and ahead of Nahum, who was attempting to keep pace with the older boys while pressing his dirty, bloody piece of paper against his cheek.

"It will be the pilot of the plane we built," answered Vasily, reluctantly, "but don't tell Mama."

"I won't. I swear, I won't! Where is the plane?"

"On the roof."

"Wow!"

By the time they returned to the roof, Nahum's bleeding had stopped, leaving only a pair of bright red lines on his left cheek and a burning pain in the entire left side of his face.

Leonid greeted them with, "Hey, the pilot is here! And why did you bring *her*?" He jerked his head toward Lana.

"She just came along. Don't worry," said Vasily. He knew most of the boys didn't mind her presence, because of her tomboy behavior.

"Let's lift the plane onto the guardrail," commanded Arkady. "Put your cat in the pilot's seat and hold it there. On the count of 'three,' we'll push the plane, and you'll let the cat go. Understood?"

"Understood!" they all replied, in one voice.

They lifted the plane. Leonid, Nahum, and Lana held it from one side, and Yurka and Arkady from the other. Vasily was standing a step behind Arkady, holding his cat firmly in the pilot's seat.

"One, two," counted Arkady, loudly but slowly, "three!"

Vasily let go just as they pushed the plane off the guardrail. The cat froze in its seat, ears pointed, hair bristling. The plane glided gracefully over the *dvor* toward the fence, and then turned to the left and back over the exercise station, circling around the apple tree, back toward the house. The kids were watching from the roof, standing motionless in a row, clinging tightly to the guardrail. Now the plane circled under the branches of another apple tree, above the heads of three scared grandmas chatting on the bench, glided above the sandbox where a few toddlers played and landed in the weeds in the far right corner of the *dvor*. As soon as the plane hit the ground, the cat jumped out and ran across the *dvor*, to hide behind the dumpster.

"Hooray!" screamed the gang on the roof, and they raced downstairs to their plane.

"What a landing!"

"It didn't even get scratched!"

"Great gliding! Almost two full circles around the *dvor*!" shouted the boys, as they surrounded the plane in the weeds.

"My cat! My cat! The pilot was the best!" added Lana, infected by boys' enthusiasm.

"We need a real pilot, don't we?" asked Arkady, moving his eyes from one friend's face to another.

Leonid immediately volunteered, "I'll glide!"

"I'll do it!" echoed Vasily. "I'd love it!"

"Let's take it back to the roof, and then we'll decide," said Arkady, authoritatively, carefully lifting the fuselage.

They carried it back to the roof, Arkady and Yurka holding the body of the plane, Nahum and Leonid supporting the wings and Vasily holding the tail.

"I think we need the smallest guy to be the pilot," said Arkady when they climbed onto the roof from the attic window. Everyone looked at Nahum, who had the smallest frame. Leonid was of about the same height, but he was a fairly chubby boy, and he knew it. Lana was about a foot taller than Nahum. "Plus," added Arkady, "Nahum was wounded today. He should be rewarded."

Nahum didn't quite know whether he should be happy or run away. He wanted to be the pilot, but he was also afraid of being pushed off the roof of the apartment building in this dinky little plane.

"You're not afraid, are you?" asked Vasily, seeing hesitation on Nahum's face.

"No, I'm not," mumbled Nahum, as his mouth and throat became instantaneously dry.

"Good, let's do it then," added Yurka, and he pushed Nahum toward the plane.

Shaking inwardly, Nahum squeezed his body into the cardboard seat of the plane, and his friends hoisted it and its frightened pilot onto the guardrail. Nahum was afraid to look down. He closed his eyes and clung to the sides of the plane.

"Remember, push him on the count of three," reminded Arkady. He began to count. "One, two." Everyone flexed his or her muscles. "Three!"

It wasn't clear whether the push from the left side, where stood Yurka and Vasily, was stronger, or whether Nahum raised his arms and threw off the plane's balance, but the plane veered to the right almost immediately, and began falling over its right wing.

Instinctively, Nahum moved his body to the left, and that movement corrected their course for just a second. Then the plane twisted to the left and somewhat forward, heading straight into the apple tree. It fell apart upon impact with the tree, while Nahum screamed at the top of his lungs as he went down through the leafy crown of the tree, descending rapidly through the branches.

The thick branches actually saved his life. Two leafy ones that crossed one another finally halted his fall, and he stuck, upside down, right between them, fifteen feet above the ground.

His shirt was torn, his torso, arms and legs were scratched in many places, and drops of bright red blood dripped from his bruised nose onto and through the green leaves of the apple tree.

The plane was destroyed. One wing had fallen next to the bench, and another one had flown over the tree and landed next to the table, almost hitting one of the domino players. The cardboard of the fuselage had been torn into large and small pieces by the branches of the tree as it was making its way down to the ground. The tail was stuck in the crown of the tree, pointing to the sky and proudly displaying the red stars of Russia.

The kids stood frozen on the roof until the scream of one of the women on the bench broke the spell.

"My God! Nahum Draznin fell from the sky!" The kids rushed downstairs as the domino players and the women from the bench ran to the tree.

"Rachel! Rachel!" screamed another of the women, toward the open window on the fourth floor. When Rachel looked down from the window, she added, "Your son is hurt! He is here, stuck in that tree! He just fell off the roof!"

Rachel, brain shocked by the phrase, "Your son is hurt," disappeared from the window and raced downstairs as fast as she could, mumbling in Yiddish *"Vey iz mir, vey iz mir. Oh, mein Gott ! Oh mein Gott!"* When she reached the tree, two men had already pulled back the branches and lowered Nahum to the grass.

His bleeding had stopped, but he was smeared all over with blood. His shirt and pants were torn, and a rough landing on the thick branches had knocked the wind out of him. He lay motionless with his eyes closed until his mother's face, warm and wet with tears, touched his cheek.

"Mama," he said quietly, "Mama," and closed his eyes again.

She lifted his head and chest and hugged him, pressing his face against her breasts. She tried to rise from her knees, but couldn't. She felt weak.

"Let me do it, " said one of the neighbors, and literally pulled Nahum away from her. "I'll carry him upstairs." He walked slowly, carrying Nahum in his arms. Rachel shuffled behind.

"Lucky that he is alive," she heard one of her neighbors say. "Just think of it—to fall from the roof!"

Nahum fell asleep, or perhaps fainted from exhaustion. Next time he opened his eyes, he was in his bed, with his mama, papa and grandma Haya sitting silent, next to his bed.

Nahum smiled.

CHAPTER TWO

Theirs was an exceptional apartment by every standard of Ukraine in the nineteen-thirties. There were two bedrooms, a kitchen, a bathroom, a tiny but separate toilet-room and a short, wide hallway connecting the entrance door with all the rooms in the flat. The smaller bedroom, which had a large balcony, was Moshe and Rachel's. Their double bed stood along the wall in the left-hand corner, a small desk was against the balcony door and Nahum's small bed was along the right-hand wall. The walls were painted off-white, and capped with a foot-wide magenta decorative wallpaper trim that circled the room just below the ceiling.

The second, larger room was at the end of their short hallway, directly opposite the front door. It served as their living room and dining room, and as a bedroom for Haya, Rachel's mother. Her bed was placed along the right-hand wall, with its headboard toward the window. In the middle of the room was their rectangular dining-table, surrounded by six simple, brown, wooden chairs. A glass-doored cabinet that housed the holiday dinner service stood in the corner, and a credenza with a radio, two crystal vases and several framed photographs stood along the wall across from the bed.

The only decoration, not counting the blue-wallpaper runner just below the ceiling, was a wall-mounted wooden clock with a long bronze pendulum and large Roman numerals around its shiny pearl-like face. The clock chimed every fifteen minutes, and a gong beat out the hour.

In the kitchen stood a little wooden table on which were three single-burner Primus stoves. They burned the kerosene that was kept in a large canister hidden under the table. Next to this cooking-table was a sink, and along another wall stood a large cabinet full of pots and dishes. A small, square dining table was pushed against the window opposite the kerosene stoves. There were only two chairs, one on each side of the table.

A small toilet-room in which a tall person with long legs would have had trouble closing the door, was separate from the bathroom, which had a long, deep bathtub under its window, and a small sink.

All the rooms except the largest one had single sixty-watt light bulbs hanging from the ceilings at the ends of long cords, under simple, white lampshades. The largest room had a three-standard lamp with three smaller lampshades covering its light bulbs.

It was a perfect apartment for the Draznins, in every sense of the word. It had enough room for the four of them, big windows, a balcony and a tub in the bathroom. Its only drawback was that it was on the fourth floor, the highest floor of the building, and there was no elevator. But to live in the center of the city and not share an apartment with neighbors was a fantastic deal, and the Draznins considered themselves extremely lucky. For a young couple, the lack of an elevator was not a problem at all, and the older Haya didn't go outside that often, anyway.

Moshe had received this apartment as the newly appointed deputy of his *landsman*, Nahum Olshansky, who was Chief of Operations of the Ukrainian Communist Party Central Committee. Olshansky was about seven years older than Moshe, and he was really a buddy of Moshe's older brother, Aaron, but he had worked with Moshe before, and taken him on as his deputy as soon as the position opened up.

Moshe's responsibilities were straightforward, but not easy. He was in charge of supplying the upper echelon of Communist Party leaders with whatever they needed for their personal lives. He delivered groceries to their homes, provided drivers for them and their spouses, responded to problems with plumbing, electricity, paint and all sorts of repairs in their apartments, took them tickets to concerts and various shows, and did whatever else they and their family members might need.

It was a critically important position. The classless society which the Communists had promised the rest of the country was, in reality, giving birth to a new class of its own privileged members: local, regional and national Party leaders. The Party opened special stores for the leaders and high government officials only, began erecting apartment buildings for the members of the new elite, and began constructing clinics and hospitals for leaders only. It was only natural for the Party Central Committee to employ someone to take care of the Party leaders' daily needs. This function, looking after the private needs of the leadership of the Central Committee of the Ukrainian Communist Party, was assigned to the Department of Operations, whose chief, Nahum Olshansky, entrusted the task to the honest, hard-working hands of Moshe Draznin.

Moshe had a reputation as a "doer." He was a quiet, soft-spoken, unambitious man who was extremely loyal to his family and to his superiors. He was clearly the best man for the job.

Moshe was the seventh of nine siblings, having grown up in a poor Jewish family in a tiny Ukrainian town called Korosten. Boys had been expected to start working at the age of ten, right after their four years of *heder*, the Jewish religious elementary school. These schools were under Rabbinical supervision, and free to young boys. Like the synagogues, *heders* were supported by local Jewish communities. Every Jewish boy in every town or *shtetl* went to the *heder* to receive this obligatory education.

Moshe did exactly what was expected of him. At the age of ten, he graduated from the *heder*, and that ended his formal education. Informally, however, he did a very smart thing—he taught himself, with help of his older sisters, who were also self-taught, to read and write Russian. This knowledge of the Russian language helped him secure his first job, one that shaped the next twenty years of his life.

Moshe became an apprentice to a local pharmacist, Mr. Shkolnik. Initially, he was set to unloading supplies from arriving wagons. Then he moved on to shelving pills and medicinal powders, and later, as he learned the Latin names of drugs, he began pulling medications off the shelves, to help Mr. Shkolnik and his son. Three years after that, when Mr. Shkolnik, Junior, left Korosten for America, the pharmacist entrusted the thirteen-year-old Moshe to dispense medications to his customers, occasionally even in his own absence.

Moshe worked for Mr. Shkolnik until 1913, when he was drafted into the Russian Army, the pride of His Majesty, the Czar of all the Russias, Nicholas II.

The Russian Army had begun conscripting Jewish men only shortly before the turn of the century. Initially, only eldest sons were drafted, but lately, all boys of eighteen and nineteen were called upon to join the ranks.

The majority of Jewish boys did not like this idea. There was no love lost between anti-Semitic Czarist Russia and its Jewish citizens, who lived predominantly in the western parts of Russia; the area known since the time of Catherine the Great as "the pale of settlement." With rare exceptions, Jews were not allowed to live in major Russian cities like Moscow and St. Petersburg. They were subject to restricted education, and, basically, had no civil rights in the mainly feudal Russian society. No wonder some Jewish boys, like Mr. Shkolnik's son, left for America to avoid conscription, and others moved to different *shtetls* or went to seek better lives in larger cities like Kiev and Odessa.

The sons of wealthy merchants simply paid bribes to recruiting officers, and thus avoided the draft. Even though several cousins of Moshe had left for America, Moshe, who lacked initiative and the spirit of adventure, had never considered leaving the country, and stayed in Korosten until he was drafted. Also, by this time, his father had died, and his older brothers had left their *shtetl*, leaving him the only supporter of their mother and two younger sisters.

His brother, Aaron, who was working at the dairy factory in Zhitomir, the largest town in the region, became involved with the Marxists. Like a hurricane, Marxism swept the pale of settlement, and grew to be a great intellectual attraction for poor young Jews. Being poor and Jewish didn't offer any hope for a decent life in Czarist Russia, and many young Jews found hope for equality and saw unprecedented opportunities in the new movement spreading through the vast Russian land.

Aaron went to their meetings, and soon became one of the leaders of the local Bolshevik cell. During his short visits back home in Korosten, Aaron told Moshe about his group. He spoke of the struggles of his comrades with police, the loud and confrontational demonstrations, his own aspirations and about the bright future for Jews in Russia.

"The first thing Jews must do," he said, passionately, "is to break their ties with religion. They should join the masses and become an integral part of the Great Russian people, affiliate with common folk and their daily problems and fight the common enemies of poor people. Peasants and workers in Russia lead miserable lives, regardless whether they are Russians, Jewish or Ukrainians. We must get rid of our chains together," he continued. " Religion separates people; breaks them apart. It defines them as distinct groups, when, in reality, people differ only by class. Poor workers and peasants are on one side, and the aristocracy, the capitalists and the landowners—our enemies—are on the other side of the struggle. Religion keeps poor people from true unity."

Aaron recruited their neighbor and his childhood friend, Nahum Olshansky, into his Bolshevik cell, and pressed Moshe to organize a small cell in their home town, as well. Moshe nearly agreed to do it, even though he was apprehensive about playing a leading role, but was drafted before he could start. Mr. Shkolnik, the pharmacist, however, knew the local chief recruiting officer, and asked him to assign Moshe to a regional military pharmacy. This was a huge favor that Moshe had not anticipated.

"He would be much more useful to His Majesty the Czar as a proficient pharmacist than as a lousy soldier," said Mr. Shkolnik to Captain Vasiliev, pointing at the five-foot-six, one-hundred-thirty-pound Moshe. Since the request was accompanied by a half-liter bottle of pure alcohol, the Captain considered it reasonable, and assigned the young recruit to the pharmacy located at the Regional Army Hospital, where Moshe spent the next five years of his life.

The Bolshevik Revolution of 1917 began in Petrograd, formerly St. Petersburg, and the cease-fire treaty with the Germans sent Moshe back home to Korosten by the end of 1918. His mother was still living in their tiny, dilapidated house with her youngest daughter, Moshe's baby sister, Hava. Another sister, Kula, had married and moved away.

Aaron, along with Nahum Olshansky, swam atop the revolutionary waves. Aaron, a big, tall, strong man, became a local commissar, Chief of the Regional "Cheka" (Extraordinary Commission for Combating Counterrevolution and Sabotage), the Communist security force *cum* secret police, all in one. Olshansky became regional secretary of the Communist Party; basically the number one person in their region.

Among the many problems they encountered as builders of a bright future for the new Soviet Russia was a colossal disaster in public health.

Almost the most imperative of all problems was the rapid spread of epidemics of louse-borne typhus. Transmitted by lice among people lacking elementary personal hygiene, the disease carried with it a sixty-percent death rate, and killed tens of thousands. Unburied corpses were left on streets, a sign of the devastation that would visit Russian and Ukrainian towns many times during the Twentieth Century.

The spread of deadly disease was so great that the founder and leader of the new Soviet Republic, Vladimir Lenin, coined the slogan, " Either Socialism will defeat the louse or the louse will defeat Socialism." The line was drawn, and the Communists were fighting one of their toughest opponents.

Regionally, the first secretary of the Communist Party, Nahum Olshansky, was in charge of this fight. Moshe Draznin was the closest person to a doctor among Olshansky's friends and acquaintances. He was also a man Olshansky could trust. And so an apprentice pharmacist and brother of a distinguished Communist was appointed Chief of the local branch of the Health Department.

All hospitals, clinics and pharmacies were now under his jurisdiction. He was given a handgun, a Mauser .45 caliber, and, like all Communist chiefs, carried it stuck in his belt, on the right side.

"In our Soviet Republic, doctors belong to the people," Olshansky taught him. "If they don't do what you tell them to do, we will arrest them, confiscate their property and exile them to Siberia. We are the people, and they work for us; for the people. Their clinics and their hospitals are now the property of the Soviets. And you, Moshe Draznin, are entrusted by the Soviets and by the Communist Party to organize health care for the workers and peasants. The Party will help you, and will demand much of you."

Moshe worked tirelessly, and never seemed to mind. He was a soft-spoken, thin man of average height, with bluish eyes and a perfectly round face. To Moshe, work was just a part of life, his daily routine since the age of ten.

In fact, he even enjoyed his new assignment. He felt he worked for the Revolution and on behalf of the Revolution. He worked for the people; for the people of Korosten, for the people of the nearby small town of Ovruch and for the people of Soviet Ukraine. He nationalized hospitals, clinics and pharmacies. He jailed people accused of stealing medications and medical supplies. He approved work-schedules for the local doctors, nurses and pharmacists. He oversaw efforts toward sanitation in his district. When it came to public health, he was it.

Eventually, the pharmacy of Mr. Shkolnik was nationalized. Moshe went to Mr. Shkolnik's house the night before it was to occur. It was around eleven p.m. when he softly knocked at his door.

"Who's there?" asked Mrs. Shkolnik.

"It's me, Moshe Draznin."

The door opened cautiously against a short chain, and Mrs. Shkolnik peeked out through the tiny opening to make sure the man was indeed Moshe. She let him in.

Mr. Shkolnik was sitting at the dining table in the middle of a large room, drinking his evening tea. The Shkolniks' house was one of the largest homes in Korosten; too big for just two people. Their three sons had left for America, and another son and their only daughter had gone to Palestine.

Mr. Shkolnik wore long, dark, buttonless pants held at the waist by an old brown belt, warm socks mended at the heels and a dark-green plaid shirt. On his head, he had a small, leather cap. The room was poorly lit by a single kerosene lamp, making his clothes darker and the color of his skin yellowish-gray. He still worked in his pharmacy, but his hours were much shorter.

The old man looked straight into Moshe's eyes. He did not know what was coming next, but he had probably guessed.

"Good evening, Moshe. Sit down. Tea?" offered Mr. Shkolnik, in Yiddish.

"No, thank you, Mr. Shkolnik. I don't have much time," answered Moshe, in Russian, preserving somewhat his official capacity. He pulled a chair from across the table, and sat next to his former employer and benefactor.

"You know, Mr. Shkolnik," he said, quietly, as soon as Mrs. Shkolnik had left the room, "we are nationalizing medical resources. Your pharmacy is the last medical establishment not yet nationalized in our region."

"So? That's what you came for? To tell me it's my turn?"

"The Soviets need your pharmacy, Mr. Shkolnik, and we need your help," said Moshe, ignoring Mr. Shkolnik's sarcasm. "We are fighting the typhus, we are fighting the dirt and we are fighting lice. The new society must win. There is no alternative. We will fight death to the very end. We have no choice, and the Government can no longer allow private pharmacies."

"When?" asked Mr. Shkolnik.

"Tomorrow."

Mr. Shkolnik didn't argue; he knew better. He kept his eyes on Moshe's face. He understood that Moshe's coming to his house was an unusual act. It was a show of appreciation and bravery that he had not expected.

"Thanks for your warning, Moshe. I'm an old man, you know. I will retire."

"Don't! Don't do that, Mr. Shkolnik." Moshe turned his eyes away from Mr. Shkolnik's gaze and looked down at his own dusty shoes. "I will have to arrest you if you do. We need pharmacies with pharmacists. You know we have no one to work in your pharmacy."

They sat silent, for a while.

"I am sorry, Mr. Shkolnik, building Socialism is not an easy thing. A new life demands sacrifices. I'd better go."

Mr. Shkolnik didn't answer. Moshe stood up and walked to the door. There, he turned back and said, in a low voice, "If you have any medications or supplies in your house, get rid of them tonight. They'll search your home. You don't want them to find a thing." Having made what would prove to be the bravest statement of his life, Moshe opened the door and stepped out into the darkness.

Next morning, around nine o'clock, Moshe and his two deputies walked into Shkolnik's Pharmacy. Moshe took out a piece of paper and read aloud.

"By executive order of the Ovruch Regional Soviet, this pharmacy is nationalized and immediately becomes the property of the people. The pharmacy will be known as Regional Pharmacy #3. Comrade Shkolnik is appointed director of Pharmacy #3, and his salary will be established by the Department of Health."

He put the paper into his pocket, and asked, "Any questions, Comrade Shkolnik?" After waiting through a minute of silence, he turned and left. That afternoon, two men from the Cheka and three health department deputies conducted a very thorough search of Mr. Shkolnik's home. They found nothing.

In 1922, Moshe married Rachel Baringoltz, an attractive, well-educated girl seven years his junior. Rachel was the daughter of a well-to-do lumber merchant from Ovruch who had died about two years before, leaving a widow and seven grown children. The eldest son, Noah, who was studying in *yeshiva,* had taken control of the family's affairs. Noah had no interest in business, and he was happy when the family lumber-trading business was nationalized. His mind was set on the Torah, and the only thing he worried about was marrying off his younger sisters, Rachel and Menya, and earning a little bit of money for himself and his mother, Haya.

Both girls had gone to private school and, by the best local standards, were extremely well educated. They had studied history, the Russian language and literature, algebra, geometry, geography, French and Latin.

No one knew why a wealthy and deeply religious Jewish merchant like Zelik Baringoltz had sent his two youngest daughters to a private Russian school. He never shared his thoughts with anyone. Even though the late Zelik Baringoltz had loved all his children, his younger daughters, notably Rachel, had occupied a very special place in his heart. Generally the autocratic master of his household, he had allowed Rachel to argue with him, had read books to her and had even discussed some of his business deals with her. She was probably the only person in the family who understood the intricacies of the lumber trade. He had died suddenly of a heart attack, the year Rachel graduated from High School, and his youngest daughter, Menya, had still had a year to go.

One evening, not too long before his untimely death, as Rachel recalled later, he said to her, "Times are going to change, and life will change for all of us, as well. You, my dear Rachel, must be prepared."

When Noah brought him to their house, Rachel liked Moshe. He wore a military-style greenish jacket with a wide, brown, leather belt, dark-green pants and well-polished black shoes. His collarless jacket was buttoned all the way to his neck, but one could still see a clean, blue shirt underneath, also completely buttoned.

She could have refused to marry him; neither her mother nor Noah had much influence on her decisions. But she knew she had to start a life on her own, and Moshe seemed an excellent partner.

Moshe adored Rachel at first sight. He couldn't believe his own luck. Such a beautiful and well-educated young Jewish woman; he could not have dreamed a better wife for himself. There was one little glitch, however, that they had to overcome. Moshe, as an aspiring Communist, did not want a religious wedding ceremony, while Rachel and her family did not believe in civil union. After a brief discussion, Rachel offered a compromise. They would have a Rabbi, and a *Huppa* in their house, and only Rachel's closest family members would attend.

The next day, she suggested, they would register at the regional Soviet hall. They wouldn't invite Moshe's relatives if he didn't want to, and, unless he himself told them, they would never know that they had had a Rabbi bless their marriage.

Moshe liked her idea and, from that day on, he would like and agree with absolutely everything Rachel had to say. The hierarchy of the Draznin family had been firmly established. At the wedding, Moshe and the Rabbi were equally afraid that uninvited neighbors would see the ceremony. But no one did.

Little Nahum was born a year later. The *bris* had been performed as clandestinely as had Moshe and Rachel's wedding ceremony under the *Huppa*.

Even though times had changed substantially, as Rachel's father had predicted, certain traditions, Rachel would not let go. Moshe worked on Saturdays, but she lit the *Shabbat* candles and, although they no longer kept kosher, she continued to prepare special festive dinners for each Jewish Holiday. The *bris* was a tradition that she would not forgo. Her brother Noah brought the Rabbi and the *mohel*, a man who performs ritual circumcision, and a few trusted friends had come to the house after dusk. Moshe had closed the shutters so the neighbors could not see the induction of little Nahum into the Jewish caste.

Meanwhile, the country had been going from bad to worse. In the midst of economic disaster, while nationalizing land and larger businesses, the leader of the Russian Revolution, Vladimir Lenin, had come up with a brilliant idea to boost their failing economy. In 1920, he suddenly began allowing private ownership of small businesses. He called it the "new economic policy" or NEP.

Tens of thousands of hard-working people in towns, cities and villages eagerly joined in this new way of doing business. Small shops, manufacturing outfits, farms, restaurants and distributorships were budding out all over the gigantic but poor country. As the concept of equality had attracted millions of poor people to the Revolution, the concept of ownership of small business attracted a huge wave of workaholics to independent small businesses.

The economy began to grow. Food appeared in the stores, harvests improved significantly and many hard-working people began to prosper. The number of industrious people taking on new opportunities and new challenges continued to grow. This economic revival lasted four years.

The end of the NEP came as abruptly as had its beginning. In 1924, a new Communist edict announced that the new economic policy had given birth to a new class of capitalists, the so-called "NEPmen," people who did nothing but exploit workers and peasants, as had the capitalists, before the Great Revolution.

The New Economic Policy ended in the old fashion. The remedy was predictable, and punishment was swift. All small businesses were nationalized, and the owners were arrested, jailed, exiled and sometimes executed. The Communists were busier than ever expropriating successful businesses from ambitious people.

But to take them away did not mean to be able to run these nationalized businesses. The Soviets desperately needed people capable of taking control of these budding enterprises.

Like most local Communist leaders, Nahum Olshansky struggled to find the right people to run the nationalized businesses. In his eyes, Moshe was such a person. In the middle of 1924, Moshe was transferred to Zhitomir, the largest town in the region, with two hospitals, many private physicians and several pharmacies, to be in charge of all hospitals and pharmacies of a large region West of Kiev. The same year, he was officially accepted into the Communist Party. He finally became a full-fledged carrier of a small red book— the official document of his membership, and the pride of every Party member in the young Soviet state.

There was another reason why Moshe and Rachel were only too glad to move away from Ovruch. Earlier that year, his brother, Aaron, and his Cheka brethren had descended upon Ovruch and surrounding smaller towns, in search of what they called "illegal grain." They had assumed that many well-to-do peasants were hiding their harvest in response to widespread nationalization, in order to sell it privately at higher prices. Aaron had been sent to the area to find hidden stores of grain, and to arrest self-employed farmers accused of hiding their harvest.

Even though the general order had only been to find and expropriate the grain and arrest those who had hidden it, Aaron and his troops went much further. Once they found the grain, they dragged their victims to the town square and publicly executed them.

"The harvest and the grain belong to people. Those who wish to hide even an ounce of grain should know what awaits enemies of the Soviet. Socialism has no mercy for those who undermine its very existence," announced Aaron through a loud speaker, before each execution. He had personally shot several people, and the town of Ovruch was terrified.

Around this time, Aaron had changed his last name to "Yavlinsky." He was now known as Aaron Yavlinsky, the commander of the local Cheka and a merciless servant of the Revolution. "Draznin" had sounded too Jewish to him, and besides, most leading Communists had been taking on Revolutionary names like "Lenin," "Stalin" and "Trotsky," so why not "Yavlinsky?"

But everyone in Ovruch knew that Aaron Yavlinsky was the brother of Moshe Draznin and, even though Moshe had had nothing to do with this horrific campaign of terror, in the minds of many, he was forever associated with his brother's bloody deeds.

"Jewish men should not be doing this. Jews should not be taking other people's lives," said Rachel, one evening after Aaron Yavlinsky and his men had publicly executed two entrepreneurial peasants in a nearby village.

"No one should be doing this," thought Moshe, agreeably, but he didn't say a word.

When Olshansky's offer came to relocate to Zhitomir, Moshe and Rachel gladly accepted. Rachel's mother and youngest daughter, Menya, went to Kiev to live with Haya's other son, Yakov, and the eldest son, Noah, moved into the Baringoltz' house. The house was big, and Noah allowed a number of *yeshiva* students to move in with him. Noah, his wife and their three children occupied two rooms, and the rest of the house was used as a study hall and dormitories for unmarried students.

In Zhitomir, Moshe continued with the re-organization of medical and health-related services. Practically everything was nationalized by that time, so he was glad he did not have to exert his Bolshevik power to consolidate the medical establishments. He simply had to assure that hospitals and clinics stayed open, that the meager supplies and medications were delivered and that the water in the town was properly treated with chlorine, and boiled in all eating establishments.

He was also in charge of sanitation in food stores and bathhouses, the small brewery and street-vendors' carts and kiosks selling sparkling water and *kvas*, a non-alcoholic beverage made in the process of fermentation of bread and yeast.

A year later, Moshe was given additional responsibilities. He was asked to supervise all Soviet-owned consumer-related small businesses with fewer than ten employees. These were small repair-shops where watchmakers, barbers, tailors, cobblers and furniture repairmen toiled for meager salaries to provide city-sponsored services.

Among these shops was one called "*Atelier* Typewriter," a typewriter-repair shop that did just that; repaired typewriters used by Soviet bureaucrats and a local newspaper. It was the only typewriter repair shop in the entire region. Two masters worked there, Gregory Gurevitch, an old Jewish man who had owned a typewriter store before the Revolution, and Anton Saroyan, an Armenian man in his mid-thirties, who had appeared in Zhitomir from nowhere about five years before, speaking broken Russian with a heavy accent. When he had arrived, he had walked straight to the "Atelier Typewriter." After a brief conversation with Gregory Gurevitch, the old master had hired him on spot as his apprentice.

In July of 1927, sixteen-year-old David Slavutsky, a son of Moshe's second cousin on his mother's side, knocked at the Draznin door. David wore a pair of long, dusty, brown pants rolled up to his knees so they would not get stuck in the chain of his rusty bicycle, a gray sports jacket that was at least two sizes larger than David and a dark gray cap. His only possession was a small briefcase containing a few shirts and underwear, which he had tied to his bike just behind the seat. He said that both his parents had died in Korosten, one shortly after the other, his younger sister had gone to live with their aunt in a *shtetl* in Shepetovka, and he had decided to come to his uncle Moshe, to look for a job in Zhitomir.

"I don't know where else I could go," he told Moshe and Rachel that evening. "I hope I can stay with you for a while."

The Draznins did not see any problem with his request, as *landsmen*, especially relatives, could stay for as long as they needed, or for as long as they wished.

Two days later Moshe took David to the typewriter repair shop.

Gregory Gurevitch needed workers. He and Anton were surrounded by broken typewriters and inundated by customers' requests for speedy repair. Besides, the old man could not turn down a request for a favor coming from Moshe Draznin, an important Soviet official in Zhitomir, in charge of all small businesses. *Today I do him a favor, tomorrow I might need his help*, thought Gurevitch. *Either way, I win*. And he accepted David as his apprentice.

David stayed with the Draznins, helping with house chores and playing with little Nahum whenever he could find time.

He didn't have much free time. The first three or four months, he spent mastering the skills of the typewriter repairman. He replaced letters, adjusted mechanical parts and repaired keyboards from early morning until late evening, six days a week.

At some point, however, he started noticing that some people frequented their shop but did not bring in any typewriters. A man would come in, sometimes with a briefcase, and spend twenty to thirty minutes in the corner, talking in lowered tones with Gregory Gurevitch. Then, David noticed, the man would exchange briefcases with Gregory, and leave. He also noticed that, almost daily, Anton would leave the shop with a briefcase and would return an hour or so later, sometimes with a different briefcase and sometimes with nothing. It was strange, but he never asked either Gregory or Anton about either the mysterious visitors or their briefcases.

One day, when Anton wasn't in the shop, Gregory Gurevitch asked David to take a briefcase to a dentist, a Dr. Malevsky. "He left it here the other day," he said. "Please, take it back to him. He works in the dental clinic on Podlesnaya Street. Make sure you give it only to him. If he is not there, bring it back. Tell him you are from me, and that I said hello."

David took the briefcase to Dr. Malevsky. This was his first assignment outside of his repair duties. The next week, Gregory Gurevitch asked him to take another briefcase to Dr. Malevsky. This time, the doctor gave David a small briefcase to take back to Gregory.

From that time on, these assignments became regular, once or twice a week.

Every time David would run such an errand, Gregory would give him a few rubles as a reward. After about five months, Gregory told him quietly, "These briefcases are full of gold, you know. Be careful."

"What do you mean, 'full of gold?'" asked David with astonishment.

"Just what you heard. There is gold in these suitcases. We buy it from different people and sell it to Dr. Malevsky. That's how we make a living, David, not from these lousy, rusty typewriters. I'll pay you more for each delivery."

"What does he do with this gold?"

Gregory Gurevitch shrugged his shoulders, "Do I care? I bet he makes gold crowns for his patients or sells it to other dentists. People love to have gold teeth. But you, you should keep your mouth closed. We could all be sent to Siberia."

"We could all be killed," added Anton, who had been listening silently from his desk. "Just be careful. Know from whom to buy and to whom to sell. That's all."

David accepted this revelation without fear or anxiety. He understood it was illegal, but had no qualms about it. It was a way of making money without stealing anything from anybody. Gregory Gurevich was simply buying and selling underground gold. What was wrong with that? And he, David, was just a courier. There was nothing wrong with that, either. They weren't stealing a thing.

But he also clearly understood the danger. Both buyers and sellers must be very trustworthy people. And no one, not even his family, should learn about the real business of their "*Atelier* Typewriter." He never said a word to either Moshe or Rachel. Instead, with his newly earned money, he began buying groceries for the family, stopping at the market once or twice a week and bringing home a couple of bags filled with food. He also bought toys for little Nahum. About once a month, he would bring something new for Nahum to play with.

"Oh, it's nothing," he'd say to Rachel, "just for my own pleasure."

The Draznins lived in Zhitomir until 1928. One day Nahum Olshansky called Moshe into his office at Communist Party Regional Headquarters and spoke to him in Yiddish. They often spoke in Yiddish when they were alone. Interestingly, it was always Olshansky who initiated conversations in Yiddish.

"I am moving to Kharkov. I have been asked to take the post of Chief of Operations of the Central Committee. It's a big honor and a position of great responsibility. Our Party wants me to do it." Moshe looked at him in admiration, and he added, with strength and honor in his voice, "Now, Moshe, I want you to come with me. I need a deputy who is honest and reliable, who is a hard-working Communist and who is loyal to me and to the Party."

Moshe was elated. He didn't hesitate for even a split second, but he couldn't make a decision without Rachel. "Nahum," he said, "I'd love to go. I'd love to work with you. I'd be honored to serve the Party. I am sure Rachel would love to do it, too, but I must talk to her before accepting your offer."

There was a bit of tension in the silence that followed. Moshe knew that strong men, especially Communist leaders, were expected to make all their decisions themselves, without consulting their wives, but he trusted that Nahum would understand. "I've made up my mind," he said, to break the silence, "but it's important to me that she agree as well."

And Rachel did. She thought that life in the capital would open up new possibilities for her growing son; a better school and greater opportunities. She had one condition, however. "We will take my mother with us, and I'm going to work," she said firmly.

"Fine," said Moshe, "she is going with us."

Moshe left Zhitomir in February of 1929. In April he received a two-room apartment on the fourth floor of the large apartment building on the corner of Chernishevskaya and Basseinaya, and moved his family to Kharkov.

CHAPTER THREE

Noah Baringoltz was a poor man who lived a simple, pious life. At thirty-two, married with two children, eight and six, he was still a *yeshiva bocher,* a perpetual student at Ovruch *yeshiva.* Inheriting the Barin-goltz house gave him roof and shelter, and basically saved his life. He spent most of his time studying the Torah under the tutelage of Rabbi Shapiro, the seventy-eight-year-old leader of the Ovruch synagogue.

Rabbi Shapiro had five sons and one daughter. All five boys became rabbis and moved away to lead their own congregations. Three of them went to America, where, apparently, there was a shortage of rabbis, one moved to the Volyn region of western Ukraine and the other settled in Mozyr, a little town on the border with Belarus. Rabbi Shapiro's daughter, Malka, married a student from her father's *yeshiva* named Menachem Sirota, who was the smartest of the students and who was preparing to take over the *shul* and the *yeshiva* when Rabbi Shapiro was laid to rest.

Reb Menachem and Malka had seven children, with their oldest daughter, Tzilya, a tall, overweight fourteen-year-old, helping her mother take care of the family.

The *yeshiva,* a five-room wing of the synagogue, had seen better times. Just ten years before, it had been home to thirty students who had rented beds from the locals and spent countless hours in the synagogue, the study rooms or on the lawn of Rabbi Shapiro's house, just across the street from the *shul.* The synagogue and *yeshiva* had been filled with their voices. Today, only five students remained. One of them was Noah himself, and he housed the remaining four students in the Baringoltz house.

Only two of his renters could afford a small payment. Two others simply helped with household chores in return for shelter. Noah was also caretaker of the synagogue and the *yeshiva*, cleaning the building, patching walls, buying and keeping candles, trimming the shrubs around the building and shoveling snow. Rabbi Shapiro paid him weekly, but not even enough to buy food for his family and his renters. Every evening except Friday night, Noah's wife, Tzipa, cleaned the bakery of Mr. Zlotnik, who gave her two loaves of bread and a little bit of money that, together with Noah's meager earnings, sustained their existence.

Even though most of the day's discussion was spent on the Torah, the Talmud and the Mishna, some current events made their way into the conversations in the Ovruch *yeshiva*.

"Equality is a wonderful thing."

"No, it's just a utopia, an unattainable hope, a futile passion. It's like a firebird that exists only in the fairy tales."

"Good for nothing. Maybe for daydreamers."

"It's against human nature."

"And what good does it do the Jews?"

"Tell me, who is going to accept Jews as equals? Unreal."

"How can Russians and Poles equate our Adonai with their Jesus?"

"But do you think the Revolution could stop pogroms? Can it bring peace?"

"What peace are you talking about? Where is it? There is no peace; not for us, anyway."

"Jews are leaving the *shtetls* ; they are abandoning traditions. People don't keep kosher homes any more."

"No one comes to *yeshivas*, either. We haven't had a new student for two years."

"We should have had all the *yeshivas* in all of Russia write letters to our new government."

"What would you write in such a letter?"

"For starters, how about asking them to protect us; to respect the learned men of Torah?"

"If the government is for equality, why not make *yeshivas* the official schools, like any other private schools? What's wrong with that?"

"Not a bad idea. I've heard there are Jewish people in the new government. If we write to them, they might support us."

"I know have a distant cousin who is a student with the Chief Rabbi of Moscow. We can write to him, he will take the letter to the Chief Rabbi, and the Chief Rabbi, blessed be he, will take it to the government."

"And we should ask students and Rabbis from other *yeshivas* to write letters, as well. This will amplify our concerns."

Rabbi Shapiro smiled, but agreed to write a letter with his students. "The best government I know is the one that leaves Jews alone. I'm not sure we are there yet. We probably won't gain a thing," he said, "but it won't hurt. We have nothing to lose."

The students sent at least a dozen letters to the *yeshivas* in Shepetovka, Kiev, Minsk, Mozyr and other places, asking the Rabbis and students to write letters of concern about Jewish life to the Chief Rabbi of Moscow, and send them through the distant cousin of Menachem, a student of the Chief Rabbi.

In four or five months, the letters began arriving at Menachem's cousin's. As requested, he took the letters to the Chief Rabbi, who read them out loud, reflected and collected the hand-written pages, mostly in Yiddish, but some in Russian, in a drawer of his bureau. A total of eight letters had arrived.

The Chief Rabbi took these letters very seriously. The concerns they expressed corroborated his own thoughts about future Jewish life in Russia, and he discussed the letters with a few of his trusted disciples.

"I don't know what the government in Moscow can do about security of Jewish *shtetls*, but I like the idea of protecting *yeshivas*," said one.

"I think exactly the opposite," said another. "Communists are atheists, and they couldn't care less about the *yeshivas*. But they claim to be the Government of the people, and the security of some of the people might interest them."

"All we want is a peaceful, traditional Jewish life. There is nothing wrong with that. Observant Jews are no danger to the Soviets. I think there's a good chance they would protect the *shtetls*."

After weeks of discussion back and forth as to what to do and where to go, the Chief Rabbi made an appointment with Leon Trotsky, the Soviet Commissar of War. Trotsky was the highest authority the Chief Rabbi and his disciples could ever dream of. Not only he was second in command of all of Russia, only Lenin being a notch above, but Leon Trotsky was Jewish, and the second-highest-ranking Communist in the world.

Leon Trotsky had been born "Lev Davidovich Bronstein," in a little Ukrainian *shtetl*, in 1879. At the age of twelve, young Lev Bronstein had been sent to school in Odessa, where he had lived in the liberal intellectual family of his mother's nephew. As early as in 1898, Lev Bronstein had first been arrested for revolutionary activity, and he had spent the next four and a half years in prison and in exile in Siberia. He had escaped from Siberia in 1902, using a false passport bearing the name "Trotsky." He had adopted this name as his revolutionary pseudonym.

In October of 1917, Lenin and Trotsky had orchestrated the overthrow of the Russian Provisional Government set in place after Czar Nicholas II had abdicated, and established the power of the Soviets in Petrograd, former St. Petersburg. Initially, Leon Trotsky had been appointed Commissar of Foreign Affairs, but, after the Brest-Litovsk peace treaty with Germany, he had become Commissar of War, entrusted with organizing the Red Army.

A brilliant speaker, a charismatic orator, an ideologue of the Bolsheviks and a man of Jewish origin, he was a perfect target for the petition of the Jewish community to defend Jewish life in post-Revolutionary Soviet Russia.

Trotsky agreed to meet the delegation, and allocated thirty minutes from his busy schedule. The delegation consisted of four Rabbis, and was led by the Chief Rabbi of Moscow.

They were shown into his office in the Kremlin, a large, bare room with a gigantic desk and bookshelves covering two walls from the floor to the ceiling. A metal wood-burning stove was in the corner, next to a freestanding, simple, four-hook coat-rack. There was only one wooden chair behind his desk. In this office, Trotsky was the only man allowed to sit.

The Rabbis, dressed in long black coats and wearing black hats, were led in and left standing, waiting for Comrade Trotsky, who was late. He ran in, literally, ten minutes later, removing his long army coat as he walked. He wore a pointed hat with a red star on the forehead and two long flaps to cover his ears. He walked to the coat rack, put his coat on the hook closest to the stove and approached his desk. He sat down, removed his hat and said, "Yes, Comrade Rabbis. What can I do for you?"

Even though "Comrade Rabbis" sounded both comical and oxymoronic, no one smiled, and certainly no one laughed. Leon Trotsky was clearly uncomfortable and visibly irritated with these four men dressed in long black coats and wearing dark hats, which they did not remove. He grew increasingly impatient as he listened to the Chief Rabbi's presentation. After about five minutes, he interrupted the Chief Rabbi, who was just in the middle of his introduction about the pogroms.

"I understand your problems, Comrade Rabbi. But why; how and why did you decide to come to me? The Commissar of War?"

"You are the Commissar of War, Comrade Trotsky. You are the leader of the Red Army. Only the Red Army can protect the Jewish *shtetls*. Only the Red Army can protect *yeshivas* in Russia and Ukraine. No one else can. You are a Jewish man; you know how important *yeshivas* are to the Jewish people. You are..." The Rabbi didn't get to finish his thought.

Leon Trotsky flew from his chair, smashing his palm against the desk, "I am a Commissar of Soviet Russia. I am responsible for the survival of the Soviet State, the first Soviet State in the world. This is not a *yeshiva* or even fifty-five *yeshivas*! Can you comprehend this awesome responsibility? This task is infinitely superior to all Jewish problems, Ukrainian problems or even Russian problems. We are talking about the Revolution that is in danger, not a *shtetl* or two. Besides, the second I joined the Revolutionary movement, I left my Jewish heritage behind. There is no room for religion in the Soviet Republic. I have nothing to do with Jewish problems, and don't you ever come to me because of 'Jewish problems.'"

Trotsky was standing, leaning forward over his desk toward the Rabbis. "I don't understand why you even thought I might be interested!" He added, pointing to the door, "I ask you to leave."

"We came to you, because we thought you might help, Lev Davidovich," said the Chief Rabbi calmly, looking straight into the eyes of the Soviet Commissar of War, "We see now that the Trotskys are making Revolutions and the Bronsteins are paying for it."

No one broke the ensuing silence, and the delegation left the office of Comrade Trotsky.

The news of this futile attempt to evoke Trotsky's help never reached Ovruch, where Noah Baringoltz continued his daily studies and his custodial work in the Synagogue and the *yeshiva*. No one talked about the letters to the Chief Rabbi of Moscow, and no one knew whether the Chief Rabbi had ever received their pleas. Four months passed uneventfully, and then, one night, Noah Baringoltz' family and their renters were wakened by a knock at the door and a child's cry.

"Reb Noah, Reb Noah, help us! Please, help us!"

At the door was the six-year-old son of Malka, a grandson of Rabbi Shapiro. "They've killed my grandpa and my father," sobbed the boy. "They've hurt Tzilya."

Noah and three other students rushed to the Rabbi's house. The Rabbi's grandson ran behind, crying loudly and smearing tears and mucus over his face. The door of Rabbi Shapiro's house was broken, barely hanging by one of the remaining hinges, and two windowpanes were shattered.

The Rabbi's body was still in his chair, leaning over the dining table. His head was turned to the right, resting in the puddle of blood that had soaked his beard and dripped to the floor. His neck was sliced, and another kitchen knife had been left between his shoulder blades, stuck all the way in, up to the handle. His face was pale-yellow in color, like the flame of the kerosene lamp burning in the middle of the dining table. His eyes were closed, but his mouth was open, as if he had died inhaling his last breath of air.

In the corner, on the floor was Malka, kneeling next to and hugging Tzilya, who was crying silently. Tzilya's dress was torn, and bloody stains could be seen on her hips and calves.

"I love you, I love you, I love you," Malka was mumbling, in Yiddish. The other children were cuddling in another corner.

"My papa's in the kitchen," said the little boy, as he entered the house behind the *yeshiva* students he had summoned.

Noah slowly moved into the kitchen. Menachem was sitting on the floor in his own blood, leaning against the stove. His eyes were still open and his lips moved slowly, as if he were trying to say something. Noah knelt next to him and held his head, turning his own head so that his right ear was at the level of Menachem's lips, almost touching his mustache and beard. Noah wanted to hear Menachem's last words.

He wasn't sure, but he thought, "Take care of my family," was the last murmur that came out with Menachem's last breath.

Malka and children spent the rest of the night at the Baringoltz house. Noah and the students cleaned the bodies, and prepared them for the funeral.

According to Jewish tradition, Rabbi Shapiro and his son-in-law, Menachem Sirota, were buried the next day. Almost all the Jews of Ovruch gathered at the Jewish cemetery. Almost everyone cried. The Secretary of the Ovruch Communist organization came as well, and spoke at the graveside. He said that they would try to apprehend the killers, and that the Rabbi was a wise man who would be missed by the community.

Seven days after the funeral, at the end of *shiva*, the students of the *yeshiva* left Ovruch. A few more days passed and Malka packed her kids and whatever else would fit into a small wagon, and moved to Mozyr, to stay with her Rabbi brother. She told Noah that she would like to go to America, and would write to her other brothers and ask for tickets.

From the day she left Ovruch, Noah couldn't sleep. One night, exhausted, he fell asleep, only to wake up in cold sweat after a short but terrible nightmare. He had dreamed that his wife and children were being slaughtered with kitchen knives by a band of drunken peasants while he was tied to the gate. The same nightmare returned the next night, and then kept coming to him nightly. Once awakened, he would lie on the bed, staring at the darkness and listening to every sound, every movement in the house. Through the remaining hours of the night, he was mortally afraid that someone would break into his house any minute. He suffered thus for two weeks.

"This life is so terrible," he said to his wife. "We must go to a better world." She had been so scared by the recent events that she did not argue. She had grown up an orphan, and Noah was her only relative and support. A few days later, Noah brought home some rope, tied four nooses and lowered them from the wooden beams of the kitchen ceiling. He dragged a bench and the kitchen table underneath. He put their two kids on the table and placed their heads in the nooses. They didn't understand what was going on.

He kissed his wife, and they both climbed onto the bench next to the table. For a few seconds, the four of them stood silent, with their heads secured in the nooses of the hanging ropes. Noah held his wife's hand as he pushed the table from under his kids' feet. Their little bodied jerked in the air and moved silently from left to right.

Noah glanced at his wife. She stood next to him, biting her lip, with her eyes tightly shut, neck resting in the noose. Without a word, Noah pushed back the bench.

Almost a week later, the neighbors discovered the bodies .

CHAPTER FOUR

N ahum loved his school. He was seven years old when he went to the first grade. City School #82 was located immediately across the street from his apartment house. It was an all-boys school and, because it was a neighborhood school, he knew a lot of the kids there. All the boys from their neighborhood, approximately ten city blocks in either direction from the school, went there. Girls went to City School #25, just four blocks away.

Nahum's first grade teacher was Maria Stepanovna, an overweight woman in her mid-forties who always wore a long, dark-brown dress with a semicircular, white collar, and ankle-tall, flat-soled, dark boots.

Maria Stepanovna adored Nahum. He was clearly the best and the brightest student in her class, for he could already read and even write many simple words. Above all, he could count, easily adding and subtracting up to twenty. There were a couple of other boys in her class who could read and count to ten, but Nahum was head-and-shoulders above everyone else in the class. Nahum was even better than her previous star student, Arkady Pilman, who had been in her class several years before.

Maria Stepanovna's experience as an elementary school teacher told her that being so well prepared for school is a reflection not only of child's ability, but also of a nurturing environment at home. What can be better for a teacher than a family with a commitment to education?

One morning, two months into the school year, Maria Stepanovna said, "Boys, I will read your names and you will tell me your nationality. I need to record it in my journal. Do you know what 'nationality' is?"

No one knew, and she explained, "Every one of us belongs to a certain group of people. We have Russians, people who belong to the great and strong nation of the Russian people. We have Ukrainians, who are like younger brothers to the Russians, and we have other smaller nationalities like Georgians and Armenians, who came from their homeland republics to live in Ukraine, and we have Jews, who don't have their own land, but live among the other people. I'll read your names now, and you will tell me your nationality."

"Kolya Aksenov."

"Russian."

She called the roster in alphabetical order.

The class was almost evenly divided between Russians and Ukrainians, until Maria Stepanovna called Felix Berenbaum. Felix was a short, chubby boy who stood up and said, in a very low voice, "Jewish."

"You don't have to be ashamed of this," said Maria Stepanovna as some kids chuckled. "It's a respected nationality of our multinational state."

There were again Russians and Ukrainians and then she called Nahum Draznin.

Nahum stood up and said loudly, "Ukrainian!" He had no idea what nationality he belonged to, but he knew they were living in Kharkov, the capital city of Ukraine, and being Ukrainian seemed only logical to him.

Maria Stepanovna put down her pencil and said, "No, Nahum. You are not Ukrainian. You are Jewish, like Felix."

Nahum was stunned. "I don't want to be Jewish!" he said. "I want to be Ukrainian. I live in Ukraine, so why can't I be Ukrainian?"

"It's not a matter of choice, Nahum," explained his teacher, patiently. Maria Stepanovna was very proud of her patience. In all her years as a teacher, she had never even once lost her temper, never raised her voice and never lost her patience with children. "Your father is Jewish and your mother is Jewish and therefore you are Jewish. You inherit the nationality of your parents and, in your case, they happened to be Jewish. You, like Felix, should not be ashamed of it. Jews are just a small group of people who do not have their own homeland, but there many true Communists among the Jewish people, too."

When Nahum sat down, tears were running from his eyes past the corners of his mouth right down to his chin, and dripping on his books. He did not want to be Jewish; he wanted to be Ukrainian. He did not comprehend why he couldn't be a Ukrainian.

Beside Felix Berenbaum, the only other Jewish kid in the class was Nahum's neighbor, Leonid Rubenstein. Leonid hadn't known it, either.

When asked by Maria Stepanovna, he said, "I don't know my nationality. I think maybe I'm maybe Russian."

Maria Stepanovna again put down her pencil and solemnly corrected him, announcing to the class that Leonid was also Jewish, just as were Felix Berenbaum and Nahum Draznin. That was how Nahum and the class learned that Leonid was Jewish, too. Maria Stepanovna finished the task of recording her pupils' nationalities, and went on with her teaching duties.

At the end of the period, the kids rushed outside to play. The fall weather was still very warm, but the schoolyard was already covered with the yellow and red leaves that fell from the maple, birch and linden trees growing around the school.

"Hey, let's play war," shouted one of the kids. "Russians against Ukrainians!"

"Let's beat up Jews!" shouted someone else and, immediately, that someone pushed Nahum from behind.

Nahum fell to the ground, stretching his arms up to protect his face. When he finally turned his head out of the fallen leaves, there was no one there but Felix Berenbaum, who stood just two or three steps behind him. All the other kids had run to the trees to play war.

Nahum slowly got up, his palms scratched and his eyes full of tears.

"Hurt?" asked Felix.

"No." Nahum shook his head. "Just a little bit," he added, as he tried to clean his bloody palms of the dirty sand.

The rest of the day was awfully slow and long. Nahum couldn't wait to get home. He refused to eat the customary after-school snack so carefully prepared by his grandmother, and fell straight onto his bed, burying his face in the pillow. He didn't cry. He just wanted to hide.

He fell asleep. When he woke up, both his parents were home. Nahum heard their voices from another room. He got up and walked to the dining room. Mama, Papa, and *bubbie* Haya were sitting around the dining table having dinner.

"I don't want to be Jewish!" shouted Nahum from the doorway, barely holding back tears. "Why do I have to be Jewish? Why?"

"Nahum, darling." Rachel stood up and stepped toward him. "What are you talking about? Tell me, what is the problem?"

"Maria Stepanovna told the class that I am Jewish. All the boys in my class are either Ukrainians or Russians. Why do I have to be different? I don't want to be Jewish. I want to be Ukrainian, like everyone else. Only Felix Berenbaum is Jewish."

"What about Leonid Rubenstein?" asked Moshe.

"Yes," Nahum agreed. "He's Jewish, too, but that's it, no one else. Only three of us in the whole class. I just want to be Ukrainian. Why can't I?"

"Tell me, Nahum? How did Maria Stepanovna tell you about being Jewish?" asked Rachel, calmly.

Nahum told her about the morning roll call and his teacher's comments.

"Maria Stepanovna is right," said Rachel firmly, hugging her shaking son. "You should not be ashamed of your Jewishness. A lot of good, smart people are Jewish. Here in Kharkov, the Jews are a minority. Back in Ovruch, where you were born, almost everyone was Jewish. Besides, being Jewish means to bring new elements of culture and tradition into our society, where all people are equal. Oh, what happened to your hands?" She had suddenly seen the abrasions on his palms.

"I fell," sobbed Nahum. "Someone pushed me in the back, screaming that he wanted to beat up the Jews."

"Oh, dear, " sighed Rachel, pressing him harder to her body. "This person will be punished very soon, Nahum. Believe me, very soon."

"My boss and your namesake, Comrade Nahum Olshansky, is Jewish," said Moshe, when they were finally sitting around the table. "And the first President of Soviet Russia was Jewish; Comrade Yakov Sverdlov. And comrades Radek, Kamenev, and Zinoviev." He added after a short pause. "They are all Jewish. Even Karl Marx, the leader of the World proletariat, was Jewish!"

Even though the list of names was impressive, these were just names; names of people with whom Nahum had nothing to do. He wanted to be like his classmates, not like distant, unknown names. When he finally went to sleep, Rachel sat next to his bed and told him, "Jews are same people as Russian or Ukrainians. We just have a little bit different traditions, but from now on we will all be the same. As you grow up, you'll see that people respect and appreciate you for your own smartness and your own deeds. They will pay no attention to your ethnicity, whether you are Jewish or not."

"But, why? Why are we Jewish?"

"Because our parents were Jewish and their parents were Jewish, and the parents of their parents. We can't change our parents, little Nahum. Do you want to have a different mama?"

No, of course not, thought Nahum, as he closed his eyes to go to sleep. He didn't want to be Jewish, but he would not trade his mama or his papa or his *bubbie* Haya. No way! Never!

Next day Nahum went to school full of apprehension. However, it seemed that no one remembered that dreadful last morning roll call, and everyone was as friendly as always. Even though he felt very comfortable again, in his classroom, he clearly sensed, now, that he was different from his classmates. Suddenly, an invisible barrier separated him from his classmates; from these Ukrainian and Russian boys. He also felt a little closer to Leonid and Felix and, although he never asked them how they felt, he sensed that they also felt more at ease with him than with other kids.

During the winter, Nahum made another important discovery. One day he was talking to his grandmother, Haya, and he realized that she spoke distinctly differently from his schoolmates, their mothers, many neighbors in their apartment house and his teachers. Her Russian was incorrect, and the way she pronounced many words was very funny. Frequently, her verbs didn't match the gender or the declination of the nouns. And he suddenly became aware that she spoke with his parents in a different language. He was certain she did it all the time, but he had always ignored it. Now he became keenly aware of it.

"It's Yiddish," explained his mother when he asked what language they were using. "The Jewish language. Jews used to speak Yiddish at home. It was their first language, '*mama loshen*,' as we call it."

"Do I have to learn Yiddish?" asked Nahum, even though he only understood about half of what his grandma would say around the house.

"No, you don't. Nowadays, our language is Russian, but if you listen carefully to *bubbie* Haya, you'll pick some Yiddish as well. It won't hurt," said Rachel.

Not only are Jews different, thought Nahum, when he was lying in his bed that night, *but they have their own language*. The language sounded funny, much harsher than Russian, with a lot of "SH" and "CH" sounds in it, and a very different "R" sound. He didn't like it. *Russian is so much better*, he thought. What else, he wondered, might be different about these Jews?

On a hot summer day in 1931, Nahum found another feature that distinguished Jews from their Ukrainian and Russian neighbors. He, Arkady, Leonid, Vasily and Lana were sitting under the farthest apple tree in their *dvor,* watching a couple of stray dogs playing in the grass. The dogs were jumping and trying to push and bite one another, falling to the ground and making screeching, roaring noises. One was a larger, yellow dog with a short tail and floppy ears, and the other was quite a bit smaller with dark, long hair, a curly tail and round ears. The yellow dog was much stronger, but the hairy one was much more aggressive, and constantly attempted to mount his larger playmate.

Suddenly, the yellow dog froze, allowing the dark one to mount. The kids watched as, for about two minutes, the hairy dog thrust his body against the rear end of the yellow dog. The minute the yellow dog moved, the hairy one fell off her back.

"What are they doing?" asked a puzzled Leonid.

"Fucking," said Vasily, plainly.

"Copulating," corrected Arkady. "It's called copulation when a male dog mounts a female. He inserts his penis into her vagina."

"Why?" Leonid was still dumbfounded.

"That's how you make children," answered Vasily, laughing. "Ask your mama and papa how they made you. They'll show it to you."

"But where? Where did he put his penis?" This time it was Nahum who had missed something.

"Female dogs, like women, don't have penises. They have a special place called a 'vagina,'" explained Arkady, "and the penis goes right in there."

Even though Nahum frequently took his bath with Rachel, he hadn't realized that she had no penis. They played in the tub together, and she washed his arms and legs and hair, and then his father usually pulled him out of the tub into a large towel and carried him to his bed. Now he remembered that, one time, his mama had come out of the tub early, and he had seen dark curly hair below her stomach, but no penis.

"How do they piss?" he asked.

"The pee comes out from there," said Lana, pointing at her crotch.

"Where is there?"

"Here," said Lana, and jumped to her feet, raised her skirt with one hand and pulled her panties away from her stomach. "See?"

Everyone rose to their feet and peeked inside.

"Wow! You have no penis," said Nahum, in amazement, staring at a little cleft at the bottom of her white belly.

"There must be a vagina that leads inside," said Arkady pointing at the cleft.

"There is one," said Lana, closing her panties and letting go her skirt. "You just can't see it from above. The pee comes straight from there, no problem. I don't need a penis."

"My pee comes out from a little hole right down the middle," said Nahum, still not quiet comprehending the difference.

"Mine too," said Vasily, "but you can't see the hole because of the skin."

"Skin? What skin?" asked Nahum.

"At the end of the penis."

"I don't have any skin at the end of my penis."

"Yes, you do," insisted Vasily.

"No, I don't," maintained Nahum.

"Let's see," said Lana, and pulled down Vasily's pants.

Vasily unbuttoned his trousers and pulled them down, along with his black boxers.

"See the skin?" said Vasily. "Let's see yours."

Nahum was stunned. He couldn't move his eyes from Vasily's penis. It was so different. It certainly had a large chunk of skin hanging down from the tip. Nahum had never seen anything like this.

"Come on, Nahum, let's see it," said Lana, and she began to pull his pants down, as well.

Nahum quickly unbuttoned his pants and pulled them down.

"Wow!" cried Vasily and Lana, in unison.

"There is no skin!" said Lana. "He has no skin!"

For a minute Vasily and Nahum stood facing one another with their drawers down, looking at each other penises. Arkady, Leonid and Lana were silently turning their heads from one boy to the other.

"I know what it is." Arkady broke the silence. "Nahum is circumcised. That's what it is. That's what Jews do."

"What do they do?" asked Vasily.

"Cut that skin off!"

"Cut it off?"

During the next wave of a complete silence, everyone was staring at Nahum's penis.

"Oh, my God!" said Lana, slowly. "Cut it off! Why?"

Her exclamation brought Nahum back to reality. With one movement, he pulled his boxers and pants up. His face was red, his palms sweaty, and he was barely holding back his tears.

"I bet Leonid has his skin cut off, too," said Vasily, as he pulled his trousers up.

"Is it cut off?" asked Lana. "Or is it like Vasily's, with skin?"

"I don't know," mumbled Leonid.

"I bet it is," said Arkady. "Let's see it."

"No, I'm not showing."

"You see, you see! That means you are circumcised. If you were not circumcised, you would have shown. Even though my father is Jewish, my mother is Russian. That's why they didn't do it to me," explained Arkady, and he unbuttoned his pants. Sure enough, he had a cone-shaped wrinkled skin hanging down from the tip of his penis.

"This looks normal," announced Lana, as Arkady buttoned his pants.

This statement was the last straw, for Nahum. Sobbing, he left his friends and ran home.

Nahum hated his parents. Why had they cut off the skin of his penis? And when had they done it? Nahum had no recollection of the act. He must have been a little baby, he thought. He truly hated his parents. Not only they were Jewish themselves, they had made him Jewish without ever asking him. He wanted to be Russian or a Ukrainian, and now he would never be.

That night, Nahum had his first nightmare, a very frightening one. He dreamed that his mother cut off his penis with a kitchen knife while his father and grandma Haya watched silently from the foot of his bed.

CHAPTER FIVE

I n the fall of 1925 Aaron Yavlinsky was summoned to Leningrad, formerly Petrograd and re-named in honor of Vladimir Lenin, who had died of
a stroke in 1924. Feliks Edmundovich Dzerzhinsky, Commissar for Internal Affairs, Commissar for Transportation and head of the Special Governmental Political Administration, or "OGPU," the initials of its Russian name,
invited local leaders of the OGPU to Leningrad for a three-day meeting to
discuss new strategies to combat counterrevolution. "OGPU" was a relatively
new name for the former Extraordinary Commission for Combating Counterrevolution and Sabotage, abbreviated "Cheka."

The Cheka had been organized by Comrade Dzerzhinsky, shortly after the
Bolshevik Revolution, as a combined secret police force, with an army of
informants and lawless brutal enforcers of Bolshevik power, and prosecutorial
branch of the Soviets that possessed the power of immediate and swift tribunal. After four years of existence, the Cheka's merciless battle against counterrevolution had instilled deep fear in the citizens of the new Republic.

The name-change from "Cheka" to "OGPU" was an attempt to soften the
image of the organization. As frequently happens in the world of governmental bureaucracy, a change of name did not result in any change in deeds. The
OGPU acquired its name in 1922, and continued its merciless fight against
real and perceived foes of the Bolshevik Revolution.

It took Aaron four and a half days to get to Leningrad from Kiev, where, by
this time, he was Deputy Head of the Kiev OGPU. He was above average in
height, a medium-built man with big brown eyes and a bushy mustache. His
eyes, brown on bluish-white, gave the impression of perpetual sadness, even
though he was almost constantly in an up-beat mood.

Aaron had to change several times, to both passenger and freight trains,
and to waste countless hours at a number of packed stations, waiting for a
train traveling in the right direction. At that time, there was no such thing as a
"ticket." Passenger trains or cars attached to long chains of freight cars were
mainly used to transport soldiers. Therefore, at each station, several low- and
mid-level officers were in charge of deciding who besides the soldiers could
be allowed to board each train.

Aaron's long military overcoat and pointed hat with its red star, the mark of the OGPU officer, made an impression on all the Red Army officers, who always found him either a seat or, in crowded cars, standing-room. A few times, he traveled on the roof of a freight car, preferring this mode of transportation to the seemingly hopeless wait for a passenger train.

Trains had no fixed schedules. Whenever an engineer and stoker had enough coal to reach the next large railroad station, they would embark on their trip. Throngs of people at the lower end of the emerging hierarchy waited for days at almost every station, until they were allowed to board a train.

Aaron was lucky. His longest wait was just shy of eighteen hours, and occurred in Orsha, a large railroad center in Byelorussia , where the station manager let him sleep for a couple of hours on a bench in his office and offered him a cup of real Georgian tea with a small cube of sugar.

When he finally reached Leningrad, he went straight to the OGPU, and proudly showed his travel documents, first to a soldier outside the massive doors and then to another soldier at the reception desk positioned in the middle of a large, cold room with white-marble columns and a slick, well-polished gray-marble floor. The room was so large and the ceiling so high that the many people crossing this enormous room seemed dwarfed by the massive columns and the vast space.

Aaron, like all other arriving attendees of the meeting, was directed to School Number 38, where the meeting was to be held. The school was about a ten-minute walk from the OGPU building. It had been selected because it was close to OGPU headquarters, and also because it had very few students in attendance. For the three days of the gathering, regular classes were held on the first floor of the left wing of the four-story building. The rest of the building was cordoned off for the OGPU.

Classrooms had been converted into dormitories for the attendees. The organizers placed between sixteen and twenty-four cots in each classroom. One room on the second floor was allocated to women delegates. It had twenty-eight cots. Every cot held a one-inch mattress covered with a wool blanket and a small pillow. Most people slept on the blankets, using their own overcoats to cover themselves at night.

Breakfast and dinner were served in the school cafeteria in two sittings, to accommodate all the attendees. For breakfast, they were given hot cream-of-wheat cereal, bread and butter and the obligatory tea. For dinner, the attendees were served cabbage soup, hamburgers made from a mixture of beef and stale bread soaked in water, held together with eggs, mashed potato, dark rye bread and compote, a glass of stewed apples, pears, and plums. Boiling water for tea was available all day long.

Aaron's cot was near a wall of a classroom on the fourth floor, the top floor of the school building. There were a total of twenty cots in this classroom, and it looked as if about half of them were already occupied.

When Aaron walked in, he found some people sleeping, taking naps after their long journeys. Two men sat on their cots reading newspapers, while one man was sending rings of cigarette-smoke through a cracked-open window.

Aaron put his travel bag on top of the pillow, took off his boots and lay on his side facing the wall, trying to catch a couple of minutes' rest. But he couldn't fall asleep. He just lay there with his eyes closed for half an hour, and got up. He left his room early, and went down to the auditorium, in order to get a seat close to the stage and podium.

But the auditorium was already more than two-thirds full. Almost all the seats up front were taken. He found a single empty seat in the third row, behind a group of women delegates. It was directly behind the smallest of the women, a young girl, not older than twenty, with a long, thick, coal-dark braid, a narrow, bony face and big, brown eyes. Her brownish-green overcoat was so long that it touched the ground when she jumped to her feet to applaud the speakers.

By five o'clock, the auditorium was full. All the seats were taken, and people filled the aisles and stood shoulder to shoulder all the way along the walls from the stage to the back of the room. Those who had come late crowded the hallway outside the doors. Armed guards kept the doors open so people could hear what was going on, but did not let the crowd in.

Comrade Feliks Edmundovich Dzerzhinsky himself called meeting to order at ten minutes after five. He was slightly over six feet tall, and slim. He wore a military jacket with khaki pants and his hallmark, a long grayish-greenish coat. He looked like a hawk, with a long pointed nose and goatee under a pair of long, thin, narrow lips. He stood up and took off his cap, but kept his coat on as he came to the podium to greet local and provincial leaders of the OGPU.

"Comrades!" he said, loudly. "We are gathered here, in Leningrad, to sharpen our vigilance and to harden our stand against the enemies of the Revolution. Our noble goals remain world-wide revolution and the complete victory of the proletariat."

He spoke with a slight but recognizable Polish accent. Grammatically, however, his Russian was impeccable.

Aaron was glued to his chair, trying to catch every word of this incorruptible and ruthless Communist. Comrade Dzerzhinsky was known as "Iron Feliks," and he lived up to his reputation.

His appeal was straightforward. "Counterrevolution must be eradicated," he announced. "We must be vigilant, for our enemy is simply waiting for the right moment to sabotage our revolutionary gains. We will accept no excuse from our enemies for being against the working people, and there will be no mercy for those who are against us. There is no need for us to engage in any discussion with counterrevolutionaries. Only bullets can persuade the enemies of the revolution. I can assure you, they will find out how persuasive our bullets can be! Bullets are our arguments, and we will not hold them back!"

He spoke for about half an hour, and bursts of standing ovation interrupted his speech every four or five sentences. Fighting spirit and the desire to defend the Revolution permeated the audience, and every emotional and militant phrase elicited spontaneous flag-waving and saber rattling.

When he finished, everyone in the room was on his or her feet, clapping hysterically. The last phrase, Felix Edmundovich had to shout over the wild applause. "And now I will yield the podium to the bravest and smartest leader of the invincible Red Army, and my fellow soldier, Iona Emmanuilovich Yakir."

The applause gained a second life. Shouts of approval filled the room: "Iona! Iona! Iona!"

Young Commander Iona Yakir was clearly the crowd favorite. The stories of his victories, though still fresh in memory of many delegates, were already legend.

"Iona Emmanuilovich," continued comrade Dzerzhinsky, "led our troops during the bloody Civil War to defeat the White Russian Army, and he is now training our soldiers to defend the Revolution of the Proletariat. I've asked him to share with you the strategies of interaction and cooperation between the Red Army and our internal security forces. Please welcome the brave Commander of the Red Army, Iona Emmanuilovich Yakir."

Iona Yakir spoke calmly and matter-of-factly about the common goals of the Army, particularly its border units, and the Security Force, the OGPU. "Our heroic soldiers protect the Revolution from the enemy attacking us from outside our Mother-land. Your task, as soldiers of the OGPU, is to root out the enemy inside our young Republic. The task is no less difficult than ours."

When he finished, some thirty minutes later, the slogans, " Death to the enemies of the Soviets!" "Death to White* power!" and "Death to the enemies of the Revolution!" filled the air of the auditorium.

The short young woman delegate who sat in front of Aaron lifted her long coat and climbed onto her seat. She threw her arms into air and shouted at the top of her lungs, "Uncle Iona! Uncle Iona!"

The Commander seemed to notice her; he smiled, and waved at her. She

---

* This refers to the "White" political faction in Russia, as opposed to the "Red" Communist fraction, and not to skin-color.

attempted to wave back, but her seat began to fold, and she lost her balance and fell back, straight on top of Aaron, and into his arms.

"Oh, my God!" she gasped.

"Wow!" responded the startled Aaron, trying to push her back onto her seat. "Can't you be a bit more careful? You could hurt yourself and people around you."

"Don't you worry about me!" she said, angrily, finally getting back to her feet. "I've fallen off a horse many times, and not broken a thing!"

"It would be a pity to break your neck falling off a chair at a meeting," replied Aaron, sarcastically.

She turned to him and looked defiantly straight into his eyes. He stared back, unblinking, directly into her own dilated pupils. The situation suddenly reminded him of a childhood game he had used to play with his brothers and sisters—who would blink first? Her eyes were wide open, staring angrily and unmoving, straight into his eyes. After about fifteen seconds, he began smiling and, finally, he blinked.

"You have big eyes and the widest pupils I've ever seen. Your eyes are beautiful."

She blinked, too, and blushed instantaneously. She turned away and waved again at Commander Yakir.

"Is he really your uncle?" asked Aaron, leaning towards her.

She answered without turning. "Yes, he is."

"And what is your name, may I ask?"

This time she turned all the way back to him. "Bronya Yakir," she said loudly, and extended her hand.

"Aaron Yavlinsky." He extended his hand. "Nice meeting you."

She shook his hand, but didn't answer, as the next speaker approached the podium and their attention shifted to the program.

With four other speakers, the program continued until eight-thirty in the evening. At he end of the session, Bronya turned to Aaron again, and said, " Come with me, Aaron, I'll introduce you to my uncle."

They moved to the stage where the speakers had gathered around the red-draped center table. Commander Yakir was talking with a short, stocky young man and another, older, one who looked like an absent-minded professor, with bushy gray hair, *pince-nez*, a gray striped suit and a dark-brown tie. The Commander saw Bronya, and beckoned her to come closer.

"Here is my niece, Bronya Yakir," he said. "I hear you are a great young security agent in Odessa. Is that right?"

"Young, yes, great—I don't know," said Bronya, offering a firm handshake to the two men.

"Sergei Mironovich Kirov," said Commander Yakir, pointing out the shorter man, "incoming Secretary of the Communist Party of Leningrad. And Comrade Zinoviev, Grigory Yevseyevich, still Secretary of the Communist Party of Leningrad, but stepping down to take a new job, as head of the Comintern."*

"We must take our successful experience to the world," said Comrade Zinoviev, as the men shook hands with Bronya.

She said, "And here's Aaron Yavlinsky from..."

"Kiev," interjected Aaron. "I am deputy Chief of the Kiev branch of the OGPU. I am honored to meet you, Comrade Yakir, Comrade Kirov and Comrade Zinoviev."

"This is so uplifting, to see young people serving our Soviet Republic," said Commander Yakir. "I am very proud of you, Bronya, and of you too, Comrade Yavlinsky."

"This is the strength of our future," added Zinoviev. "This is why the Bolshevik Revolution will never be defeated."

"How do you like our city?" asked Kirov. "Have you been here before?"

"First time for me," said Aaron.

"And for me, too," said Bronya. "I haven't had time, yet, to look around."

"You should," said Sergei Mironovich. "Leningrad is a treasure. I came in just last month from Transcaucasia. It's magnificent over there, true wonders of Nature, but Leningrad is something very special; something else. The Russian people have built a gem; even Mother Nature should be jealous. Take your time, walk the streets, meet people. What a wonderful city it is! What do you say?" He turned to Zinoviev.

"Inspiring! The cradle of the Revolution. We began building the new world right here, in the center of Leningrad, the most beautiful and the most vibrant city in the world."

"We'll have some free time tomorrow after the meeting, won't we?" said Bronya, looking at Aaron. "At least a couple of hours?"

"I'll have some time tomorrow, too. I am not leaving town until the day after. We'll walk the streets," Aaron concurred.

"I am glad Comrade Stalin asked me to take over your job," said Kirov, smiling at Zinoviev. "You've built the strongest Communist organization, here. It's going to be a lot of hard work and a great challenge to fill your shoes."

"Grigory ought to move on," said Commander Yakir. "The Comintern is a highly important task for all of us. The Proletariat must break its chains in many countries around the world, and we need a leader to make sure that happens."

---

* A contraction of "Communist International."

"Listen to him, young people, and you'll think that World Revolution is right in my hands. I do have a little bit of experience, but the task is much more than one person can do," said Zinoviev, humbly.

"Everyone knows you can lead," interjected Aaron. "You are one of the closest colleagues of Comrade Lenin. Undoubtedly, Comrade Stalin saddled the right horse."

"Thank you. You are very kind," said Zinoviev, calmly, and he touched Aaron's shoulder. "I'm off to bed. It's getting late, and I haven't been sleeping well lately."

"What? Do you feel ill?" asked Yakir.

"No, not at all. I feel fine. I guess I am overwhelmed by ordinary worries and responsibilities. Need some rest."

Yakir nodded. "Not a bad idea. I'll trot out with you."

Zinoviev, Yakir, Kirov, Bronya and Aaron were the last in the auditorium. Everyone else had left. They all shook hands. Comrade Zinoviev and Commander Yakir left the building, and Bronya went to her room, leaving Aaron with Comrade Kirov.

Kirov sat on the edge of the stage and said, "So, you are from Kiev. Deputy Chief, eh? What actually are your responsibilities?"

"I supervise intelligence gathering and special operations. My plate is full."

"I'll bet. For how long have you been on this job?"

"I started with the Cheka almost as soon as it was formed, first in Zhitomir and then in Kiev. Two years ago I was made Deputy Chief responsible for intelligence. Last year, Special Operations was transferred to my department, as well. Not that we are so smart, but we are short of people. In the end, we are all carrying a double load."

"You know, Aaron, I'd love to have a person like you on my team. Would you consider moving to Leningrad?"

"To do what?"

"You'd still be working for the OGPU, but we'd assign you to the Party Secretariat. You'll be an adviser to me on issues of security. It would be more an assessment and planning kind of job. Strategies, if you will, based on the intelligence we gather, and less of the day-to-day tasks. What do you say?"

"I would do whatever the Party wants me to do," answered Aaron, trying to hide his overwhelming excitement. "If you need me, I'll be ready to serve."

"Excellent!" exclaimed Kirov, jubilantly. He was trying to build a team loyal to him, as he moved into a new city. This young and apparently successful OGPU officer seemed to be right for his organization. "I will arrange your transfer some time in the spring. I'll just have to get my feet wet in my new pond. Would the timing be agreeable to you?"

"Absolutely." Aaron smiled at him. " I will be honored and very happy to work for you, Comrade Kirov. And for the Communist Party of Leningrad," he added, shaking Kirov's hand.

That night, Aaron couldn't fall asleep for quite some time. He was overwhelmed with excitement. This unexpected offer to move to Leningrad and work so closely with the rising star of the Communist Party, Comrade Kirov, was appealing and uplifting. The last time he looked at the green fluorescent hands of his watch, it was two-thirty in the morning.

When he woke up, most of his roommates were already downstairs, either eating breakfast or smoking, outside the school building.

Boy, I'm late! thought Aaron, as he ran to the bathroom with his shaving kit in his hand and a short blue towel hanging over his shoulder.

There were still several people shaving in the boys' bathroom. Aaron used his old straight razor and shaved quickly, using the trickle of cold water and a tiny bar of soap to make soapy foam. He washed hands, face, neck and armpits in the same rusty sink, and put his head under the faucet to let the stream of cold water run for a minute or two over his hair. He dried his hair face and torso with his small towel, and returned to his room to place the towel and the shaving tools back in his bag. He put on his undershirt, a green military shirt over his pants and a black belt with a holster on top of his shirt. He went downstairs to have breakfast.

Bronya had already finished her breakfast and was walking out of the cafeteria when they met in the doorway.

"Good morning, Bronya!"

She smiled at him. "Good morning, Aaron. I see you are not an early riser."

"I guess not," he smiled back. "Are you done with your breakfast?"

"I am. I want to go in and have a good seat while they're still available. I'll save a seat for you, if you don't mind."

"Thank you. That'd be great."

"Lovely. This way you don't need to rush your breakfast."

"I won't."

But he did. He felt he wanted to be next to her. He was attracted to her energy, her smile and her voice. He was an old bachelor who had unexpectedly found himself very much in love; in love at first sight.

Comrade Kirov opened the morning session. He spoke about the role of Party discipline for OGPU officers and soldiers. He told his audience that he was a newcomer to Leningrad, but that he brought with him the vitality and energy of the entire Transcaucasian Region. He said he wished to channel his energy and enthusiasm toward building the new structure of the Leningrad Communist Party, and to embark on the economic development of this great city.

"We still have many people right here in Leningrad, the city of our Bolshevik Revolution, who will be satisfied with nothing less than destruction of our achievements. People who cannot and will not forget pre-Revolutionary times, when the aristocracy and landowners enslaved our workers and our peasants. They are still around us, trying to sabotage our efforts to build a new society.

"The enemy is not asleep. The enemy is re-grouping. The enemy is switching to economic war. The enemy wishes to dismantle our developing infrastructure. The enemy is still here in our midst. Do not forget that, even for a split second. It is up to you, soldiers and officers of the OGPU, to bring this enemy into the light, to find him and to root him out!"

Four other speakers followed Comrade Kirov, and delivered their speeches before the one-o'clock break. Among them were the First Deputy of Comrade Dzerzhinsky and the Chief of the Leningrad OGPU. The audience was electrified no less than the night before.

After the final morning speaker had finished, someone started to sing "The Internationale ," the anthem of the worldwide Proletariat. Everyone stood up and joined in. Hundreds of strong voices sang, though not in unison, "...we will build our own new world, and those who had nothing will become masters!"

Aaron stood next to Bronya, and his coarse baritone followed her strong soprano.

"You are a fantastic singer," he said, when the applause and ovations had died out.

"My mother taught us to sing. We all sang with her almost every day."

"Would you go for a walk with me?" asked Aaron. "To see a little bit of Leningrad?"

"Surely. I'd love to take a break. I'll just tell the girls not to wait for me for lunch."

They left the school building and turned left.

"Do you know where are we going?" she asked.

Aaron confessed, "Not really. I don't know Leningrad at all. I had hard time finding my way from the train station."

Bronya pointed. "I saw a canal from the classroom window. It should be over there. Let's go there."

"Yes, let's. We can ask there someone how to get to the Nevsky."

They walked silently for about a block, then they began to talk, first about their work. He told her about several cases from his Special Operations. She told him about the cases she handled in the Department of Economic Sabotage. Then they switched to their families. He told her about his brother, Moshe, who was working in Zhitomir, organizing the health-care system of the region, and his sisters, who now lived in Kiev. He told her how he had changed his last name from Draznin to Yavlinsky. She told him about her two older brothers, who had remained very religious and decided to emigrate to Palestine. She told him about her sister who had married three years ago and gone with her husband to America, to join his side of the family. Her sister's husband's relatives had left Kishenev after the pogroms, several years before the Revolution. She told him that her father, an older brother of Commander Yakir, had been treated for tuberculosis for almost ten years. He was still alive, but was very weak and could not work. Her mother was still working in the bakery in Odessa, and the three of them were living together in one room of a six-room apartment, which they shared with five other families.

"Don't you think we live in an extraordinary time?" she asked.

"I do."

"It's not just a change in the system of government, though that's huge in its own rights. We are building a totally new life in one generation, in Russia. Look at our parents," she continued, excitedly. "They used to live in small *shtetls*, in their own Yiddish world, and they were going nowhere."

"I think it's remarkable how swiftly we have moved away into this huge world of the brotherhood of the international proletariat," agreed Aaron. "We are now a part of the world of freedom that was like forbidden fruit for our parents."

"Not even that. I don't believe they even knew that a different world could exist!"

"Yes, you're probably right. Mine, for sure, didn't know anything outside their *shtetl*."

"We are no longer tied by religion or by those silly old traditions. We are a part of the new Russia, we are joining the Great Russian People, and I hope we'll take our Revolution all over the world. I feel sorry, sometimes, that my brothers couldn't see it this way. They left for Palestine, keeping religion and tradition as the main part of their lives. Why would you take your old baggage into your new life? I'm so excited about our new life here, in the most progressive country in the world!"

Aaron was completely enchanted by her enthusiasm, spontaneity and power of conviction. He felt he simply could not go back to Kiev and lose his connection with her. He must be near her. He must do something now, immediately, otherwise she'd be gone, and he wouldn't find her, again.

"Would you…" he began, not knowing how to proceed. "I know it sounds stupid, and maybe totally inappropriate, but I feel we must stay together. I think I love you, Bronya, even though I've known you for just two days. I'm…I'm convinced I love you. Do you believe me?"

It was Bronya's turn to be stunned. She certainly liked this strong, slightly older man, but "love"? She hadn't even thought of it.

He saw her confusion and said, breaking an uncomfortable pause caused by her hesitation, "I understand it might sound terribly childish. 'What is he talking about? Love? What love? We've known each other just a day and a half.' But I'm not a child, Bronya. I know how I feel. Please don't…don't say anything. It might take you much longer to like me. I…I do understand this. All that I want to tell you is," he gasped for air, "is that I want to ask you to move to Kiev, to be near me, so we can see each other. So you can get to know me better, give it a chance, give me a chance…"

"I don't know how I can leave my parents," was all she could manage in reply.

"You just said it so eloquently, so powerfully—it's a new world we are building for working people in Russia. It's true for you and me, as well. We are building our new lives. I believe I've met my match. I want you to come to the same conclusion."

"Could you come to Odessa?"

"I would consider that, believe me, Bronya, but…" He stumbled for a moment.

"But?"

"Comrade Kirov just offered me a job here, in Leningrad, in about six months. And I agreed to take it. It's still a secret; no one knows, yet. In fact, you are the first to know, but that's where I stand. If our Party needs me here, I'll be here. You wouldn't expect me to say 'no', would you? I need to prepare for this move."

"So you want me to move twice?"

"Yes, but by that time, if you like me, we'll be married. We will move to Leningrad as husband and wife."

"And if I don't like you?"

Aaron spread his arms.

"What will I do in Kiev?" asked Bronya.

"I'll get you a temporary job in the OGPU; not in my division, of course. We'll get you a room or even an apartment. You should be able to bring your parents, if you wish, and we will just see one another in our free time. I love you, Bronya. I implore you to do it."

"I believe you, Aaron, and I seem to like you very much, but…"

"But what?"

"But, this is such a dramatic turn in my life.…"

"In *our* lives!"

"In our lives," Bronya agreed. "That's precisely why I need to think about it. To mull it over."

They were walking back slowly, holding hands and not saying a word. Bronya's small hand was completely hidden by Aaron's hairy knuckles. Without words, they both knew they were going to stay together.

CHAPTER SIX

Hershel Rips was eighteen years old, and the eldest son of Feitl and Reizl Rips. He was of average height, about five feet, eight inches tall, but very muscular and exceptionally strong. Like all the other Jewish kids of Celiba, he finished the *heder*, a local Jewish elementary school that was run by the synagogue elders and, a year later, joined his father in the logging business.

Every day after the age of eleven, he went to the forest with his father, Feitl, manager of the logging business owned by a Polish aristocrat, Count Przhewitski, and a crew of Byelorussian peasants, along with a few of their older children. In the forest, they cut and chopped trees and dragged the huge trunks to clearings, where horse-drawn wagons were waiting to haul them to the sawmill about two miles outside Celiba. Hershel loved the physical work of cutting trees, chopping wood and splitting logs. Initially, he worked with other children, mainly cutting and chopping branches from the fallen trees, but after a few years, as he became much stronger, he began working with the adults. At the same time, he also became very skillful with knives, axes and saws.

At lunchtime, all the loggers were given glasses of a sweet home-brew that was much stronger than the ordinary forty-proof Russian vodka. Anticipating this daily treat, the loggers frequently competed among themselves, just before lunch, to find who was faster at cutting down a tree, chopping off large pieces of trunk or sawing off branches. The winner's prize was both sweet and bitter—the winner would drink the loser's ration of booze at lunchtime. When Hershel turned sixteen, he became entitled to his own drink, as well. This made him a fair competitor in these games.

He loved the games, and the men and boys loved to compete with him. It was a safe bet, for them. They knew that, if he won, he wouldn't take their drinks, for he did not drink alcohol. On the other hand, if one of them won, the winner could always enjoy Hershel's ration. As he grew stronger, he stopped losing, and, when he turned eighteen, the year he was conscripted into the Russian Army, Hershel was beating every other logger every time they played.

Most of the loggers lived on the northern side of Celiba, a relatively large

Jewish *shtetl* which housed about a thousand Jewish families and about a hundred of their Byelorussian neighbors. The Byelorussians had settled there only about forty years before, right after serfdom had been abolished, when the Polish landowner started his logging business and sawmill near Celiba. They had come from surrounding villages because the pay at the logging business was much better than what they could make from the land.

A large, open field separated the Jewish area from the Byelorussian part of Celiba. On the Jewish side stood the Celiba synagogue, and many little Jewish kids used the field as their playground while their parents attended services.

Adjacent to the synagogue was the house of Feitl and Reizl Rips. One could walk directly from the big field into their backyard, where they had a vegetable garden, several apple and pear trees, a chicken coop and a barn with a cow and a horse. Next to the barn was a large water well that the Rips shared with the synagogue.

Most Byelorussians in Celiba learned to understand simple Yiddish phrases, and some could even speak it fairly fluently. That was why one of the loggers picked a Yiddish nickname for the young, strong Hershel: "*ha gheebor*," Yiddish for "strong man" or "hero." By the time the eighteen-year-old Hershel was drafted, in the summer of 1900, he was clearly the strongest man in Celiba.

Hershel felt very comfortable working with the Byelorussian loggers. They respected him for his strength and work-habits, not because he was the son of the foreman. He was always among the first to start and the last to finish the hard jobs. He was always there to help. He was certainly one of them, or "one of us," as they saw it, when it came to the hard physical work of logging.

Even though they frequently mocked Jews and made general statements that one could have considered overtly anti-Semitic, no one ever made a direct anti-Semitic remark to Hershel, or even in his presence.

Overall, Celiba was a peaceful place where Jewish and Byelorussian families lived side-by-side, an example of amicable cohabitation on the fringes of the Russian Empire. Basically, all Celibans were poor, and lived either from the land or from their meager incomes from logging. Nevertheless, besides differences in their religion, two distinct features divided the two sides.

As a rule, Jews did not drink alcohol, except for a glass of a sweet Shabbat wine, whereas the Byelorussian men were drunk almost daily, and, on Sundays, holidays and various festivals, many were inebriated to the point of unconsciousness. The Byelorussian women were jealous of their Jewish neighbors, whose husbands, fathers and brothers were never drunk and didn't beat them mercilessly in the midst of drunken spells.

The education of children was another major distinction. Jewish boys from the age of five or six were expected to go to the *heder* to study Torah, as well as reading and writing in Yiddish and Hebrew. Most, however, remained illiterate in Russian, even though they had learned varying degrees of conversational Russian. Girls did not go to school, but, when they expressed the desire to learn, were taught at home by their mothers or fathers. In contrast, the Byelorussian kids remained uniformly illiterate. There were no schools in the villages, and the Russian Orthodox Church had no interest in providing education. Peasants had been freed from serfdom about forty years before, in 1861, but had been left landless, hopeless and uneducated.

Hershel's father, Feitl, had taught himself Russian, years before and, because he was a hard worker and a literate man, he was picked by the landowner to be foreman of his logging business.

The original landowner had lived thirty miles away and, in 1885, had sold his estate to the Polish Count Przhewitski, who had visited Celiba only once since he had bought the estate. He had not been impressed with the small logging business, and had wanted to close it. But Feitl, who did not want to lose his employment at the plant, had come forward and proposed to manage the business for a couple of years.

"I can make it work and be profitable," he had said to the Count. "I am going to take a very small salary and a small percent of the profit, if the business makes money. You can close it in a couple of years, if I fail."

The Count had liked this boldness. He had also known that some of the Jews in his native Poland were great managers of Polish aristocrats' estates. The risk had been small, and he had agreed to Feitl's conditions. Fifteen years had passed, and Feitl was still manager, accountant and foreman. At the end of each year, he sent the profits to the Count, took his five percent, bought gold coins and hid them in the forest. He lived on his salary, and the hidden money was for a rainy day.

Feitl loved his children, especially his eldest son, Hershel. Even more than most, he was proud of his son's strength and love of manual work.

"With good hands," he used to say, "you will always make a living, and will never go hungry."

When Hershel was twelve, Feitl began teaching him the Russian alphabet.

"You must know how to live with *muzhicks.** You must be like them, in physical work, but smarter in your *kopf.*" He pointed to his head. "You should also know how to deal with the landlords. They have no time for business, and they need us to run things. That's why you must know Russian. Not just to speak it, but to read and write it, as well."

---

* Russian for "peasants."

Hershel, who already spoke Russian fairly fluently, found learning the language extremely enjoyable. He most cherished those short evening hours of reading together with his father. It was different from reading the Torah in the synagogue, even when he sat next to his father, there. In the synagogue, they just read, each to himself, muttering passage after passage, sometimes in unison, but most of the time Hershel was just a bit behind his father. Here at home, when they read Russian books, they read them truly together, enjoying the story line and laughing and suffering with the characters. Hershel would read out loud, and Feitl patiently corrected his mistakes and helped him with difficult words. From time to time, they would stop, and his father would explain the meaning of a paragraph or give him extra information that helped Hershel understand the book. By the time of his conscription, Hershel was as well-read as the small collection of Russian books in Celiba allowed him to be.

On August 11, 1901, Hershel Rips joined the Russian Army. The recruiting officer walked slowly along the line of conscripted youths, measuring their physiques with small eyes that were barely visible under his bushy eyebrows. Occasionally, he touched the biceps or the pectoral muscles of the silent recruits, who were afraid to move. He motioned forward several people whom he had found to be in good physical shape.

This happened to Hershel. The officer touched his muscles, walked around him, touched his neck, and gestured to him to step forward. Hershel did. The officer selected seven young men, walked through the rows of recruits one more time and added one man to the seven in the front row. He then asked his assistant to call the names of the recruits.

"Here!" answered Hershel, when the assistant called his name.

"Hershel Rips?" repeated the officer. "Are you a Jew?" His voice reflected disappointment.

"Yes, sir."

"Step back," said the officer. "Too bad you are a Jew. You would have been a good sailor." Apparently he was selecting the strongest men for the Russian Navy. Though they had been conscripted into the Russian Army for the last ten or fifteen years, Jews were not yet allowed into the Navy.

Hershel was sent first to Minsk for his basic training, and then to Smolensk, a town in Russia about 250 miles east of Minsk, on the way to Moscow. He spent the next thirteen years of his life there, until the beginning of World War I, in 1914.

As in his earlier years with the loggers, Hershel had no problems with the soldiers in his unit, even though he was the only Jew in his battalion. It was more important that he was the strongest man of his battalion. He could lift more than anyone else. He could do more push-ups and more sit-ups than anyone else. He consistently defeated all challengers in wrestling and arm-wrestling. He could pull, push and carry more than any other soldier in his battalion. He never complained, and was always in a good mood and ready to help. His strength earned him great respect; his selflessness maintained that respect for years.

After his tenth year of service, he was allowed to go home for three weeks. His family was delighted to see him. His younger brothers and sisters had grown into young lads and women, and he could hardly recognize some of them. After ten years of absence, they also had trouble adjusting to his presence. He was as strong and gentle as ever but, for the first several days, they felt he was more like a visiting uncle or a distant cousin than a brother.

His mother looked much older. Ten years of hard life had left visible marks. But the greatest change had occurred in his father. Shortly after Hershel had joined the Army, a freak accident in the forest had shattered Feitl's right arm, and it had been amputated above the elbow. He had no longer been able to work with his loggers. Even though he had continued to go to the forest with them daily, the productivity of his squad had decreased and with it, Feitl's income.

Being an invalid and unable to sustain his business had depressed Feitl profoundly. One day he had written a letter to the Count, confessing to him that he could no longer take care of the logging business, and wished to retire. The reply had come a month later, asking him to stay until the end of the year, and then to shut down the business completely. The Count had not been interested in continuing, and hadn't felt that he could find a buyer for the sluggish business.

Feitl had written to the Count again, asking him to send someone else to announce to the loggers that the business was being closed, because he, Feitl, could not bring himself to face his workers and neighbors while eliminating their only source of income, even though he had had a legitimate reason not to work any longer. This letter had received no reply. The Count had simply ignored Feitl's letter.

Feitl had worked until the Russian Orthodox Christmas, which falls on January 7, growing more depressed every day. On the Christmas Eve, he had gathered his workers, tripled everybody's weekly pay and told them that the Count was closing his logging business.

"No more work for us," he had said, sadly.

People had been shocked. Someone had asked "Why? How can he do it to us?" But others had just sat there, looking grim and dejected.

Feitl hadn't said anything. He hadn't wanted to say that his first letter about his retirement might have been the catalyst for the Count's decision. It wouldn't have helped; it would just have shifted the blame onto him. That night, almost every logger had got completely drunk.

Although Feitl was now staying at home, he didn't do any chores. The house had deteriorated, and Feitl had no interest even in the simplest upkeep. Nine years of severe depression had resulted in total neglect of the house.

Hershel didn't ask for explanations. The morning after his arrival, he began fixing the roof. He worked at least fourteen hours a day, every day of his leave. The roof, the windows, the doors and the cellar—he tried to do as much as he could. At first, his father just watched him work, silent and indifferent, but, after a week, he began helping, bringing nails, holding the paint or supporting the ladder.

Three weeks flew by in no time, and everyone was sad to see him go. Hershel didn't want to leave, either. His term of military service was twenty-five years; fifteen more than he had already served. Who knew whether he would ever see his aging parents again?

They cried, and he almost did. Swallowing his tears, he said, as he hugged his mother, "I'll try to get back. I'll try to get out. With God's help, I'll be home soon." He left Celiba for his unit in July of 1911.

To be discharged from the Russian Army was a Herculean task for a conscripted soldier. The term of service was twenty-five years, and only a crippling wound or a trauma was valid reason for an early discharge. Another way out was bribery. Hershel could manage neither. He was in ruddy health and had no money to offer. He was preoccupied, however, with the thought of early discharge, not really knowing how to approach his dilemma.

About six months later, a new battalion commander replaced their colonel. The new colonel was an older man, an Armenian who had grown up in Moscow, and spent all his adult life in the Russian army. He was a tall, broad man who loved wrestling. His arms, shoulders, chest and back were covered with dark, curly hair. With his torso naked during wrestling matches, he looked like a gigantic, hairy spider. At first, no one among the enlisted men wanted to wrestle him; he was a high ranking officer, and soldiers didn't want to offend him by being too rough or, God forbid, by pinning him. He insisted, however, on fair competition, and slowly the soldiers accepted his challenge.

Soon, the colonel realized that this stocky Jewish man, Hershel Rips, was by far the best wrestler in the battalion. He started calling Hershel to the wrestling mat almost every evening. The colonel was taller and had longer arms, but Hershel was stronger and quicker. Their daily wrestling matches elicited bets and enthusiasm among the soldiers and officers of the battalion.

One evening, after about two months of almost daily wrestling, Hershel approached Colonel Grigoryanz.

"Sir," he said calmly, "if I may, I wish to request a favor."

"What's that Rips?"

"I wish to be discharged. I want to return home, Your Excellency." He added after a short pause. "My parents are getting old. I want to help them."

"Have you forgotten that your term is twenty five years?"

"No, I haven't, Your Excellency. I know this. I've served almost fourteen, and loved every day of it. If I were not Jewish, I would've been an officer; I would've continued to serve, as you do. I've been a good soldier, Your Excellency; please, let me go."

Colonel Grigoryanz walked up to Hershel and looked straight into his bluish eyes. "I am, myself, retiring a year from now. I need a wrestling partner until then. I'll sign your discharge papers, Rips, before I retire. We'll go home together."

"God bless you, Your Excellency," said Hershel, through a lump in his throat.

Colonel Grigoryanz had every intention of discharging Hershel Rips after a year, but, a month before he intended to sign his discharge papers, Russia entered the First World War, and all conventional promises were off the table. With the unit about to be sent to the front, Colonel Grigoryanz was not allowed to retire, and he could not discharge a soldier in time of war. Reality, poor organization and the clog-mired bureaucracy of the Russian administration dictated differently.

Their unit was somehow forgotten, and never sent anywhere. For two years, they remained in their barracks in Smolensk, receiving terrible news from the front. The war was going nowhere, with neither side prevailing significantly. The Russian Army was becoming demoralized by the lack of victorious achievements on the war-fronts and by Communist propaganda calling on the soldiers to lay down their arms and go home.

And many did. By 1916, about a quarter of Hershel's battalion had deserted the base. Wrestling matches ceased to exist, and Colonel Grigoryanz was drinking daily and playing cards with subordinate officers, paying little attention to the soldiers of the battalion.

In July of 1916, a double order hit the battalion: Colonel Grigoryanz was suddenly allowed to retire, and the battalion was to be sent to the Galician front to fight Austro-Hungarian units. Colonel Grigoryanz left immediately, forgetting to sign Hershel's discharge papers.

A new colonel was assigned to the battalion, and was to supervise their departure for the front. Hershel, along with about fifty other soldiers and two officers, a middle-aged captain and a young second lieutenant, were in the same rail car. The train left Smolensk around ten o'clock in the evening. The sun was setting behind the forest west of Smolensk, and dusk settled around the slowly moving train. One of the soldiers put down his rifle and opened the door of the moving car.

"I'm going home," he announced loudly. "I'm not about to die in this stupid war. He jumped off the train without even glancing back. Everyone jumped to his feet in great excitement.

"I'm going, too!" yelled another soldier, and moved toward the open door.

Several other soldiers put down their rifles and moved to the door as well.

"Stop!" screamed the Captain, realizing what was going on, and he pulled his gun from its holster. "Stop, you, cowardly deserters! No one is going anywhere. I'll shoot anyone who comes to this door!"

The soldiers, however, continued to advance, paying little attention to the raging Captain.

"I'll shoot on 'three!'" yelled the Captain. "One! Two!"

He didn't finish. A soldier standing behind the Captain lifted his rifle and stuffed the entire length of its bayonet into the Captain's back, right between the shoulders. The Captain's eyes slowly closed, and he fell face-down onto the floor of the car, still clutching his gun in his fist.

After a moment of silence, everyone glanced at the Lieutenant. Pale as snow, the young Second Lieutenant leaned against the wall and raised his hands. "I don't..." He mumbled, "I don't... I don't mind... Please, go if you want... Please."

One after another, the soldiers dropped their rifles, stepped over the body of the dead Captain and jumped off the train. Hershel did not hesitate; he was among them.

Finally, he was going home. His military service had ended.

CHAPTER SEVEN

Although most Russian soldiers sympathized with deserters, the general order was strict and unambiguous—to shoot them when they were caught. The officers, still brimming with patriotism, were enforcing this order without a trace of hesitation. So deserters moved in small groups of two or three people, and mainly at night, hiding in the forest in the daytime. It took Hershel two weeks to reach Celiba.

He knocked at the door of his parents' house at almost four in the morning, just before dawn, with the roosters warming up. His brother Shmuel opened the door. After the initial surprise and a pair of brotherly hugs, Shmuel woke his wife, Riva, who immediately began preparing breakfast. Hershel and Shmuel sat at the large dining table in the middle of the largest room in the house, the one that served as both dining room and living room, separated from the kitchen by a big, traditional, Russian, brick-and-clay stove.

Shmuel told Hershel what had happened in their *shtetl* over the previous two years. Because Celiba was located just about a hundred miles east of the front line, it had gone from Russian hands to German ones and back, twice. Twice, the Germans had broken through Russian defenses and occupied the *shtetl*. Twice the Russian army had driven them away. In between, for about two months, Polish soldiers had briefly controlled the territory, and they were there to threaten Celiba from the northwest every time there was a power-vacuum.

When the Germans came for the first time, a middle age officer stayed in the Rips' house. He was an extremely polite and well-educated man who loved to read and to play the flute, and he spent hours asking Feitl and Reizl about the lives of Jews in Russia. He was interested in everything, from their social status in Russia to their domestic customs and religious traditions. Since the Yiddish language is based at least sixty to seventy percent on a German dialect, with the remaining words taken from Hebrew, Russian and Polish, they understood each other quite well, and, in fact, these conversations helped Feitl fight his depression, as he spent many long winter evenings in this very room, by the stove, chatting with the erudite German officer.

Feitl and Reizl, who had spent their entire lives among poor Jews and gentiles, had never seen such an educated person before. Count Przhewitski may have been an exception, but they hadn't spent enough time with him to discover his erudition.

Feitl told this German officer about his own life in the *shtetl* and about his parents, who had lived the traditional Jewish life of their own parents and the parents of their parents. He told him about the *heder*, his only school, and about the *yeshiva* in Baranovichi. He hadn't attended it, but he had known several boys from Celiba who had gone there to study, so he told the officer about them. He told him about their "*shoichet*," the ritual butcher, and the "*mohel*," the old man who performed circumcisions. He told him about Bar Mitzvahs and about the "*mikva*," a ritual bath, about marriage and Jewish holidays. He told him about his own work and life with Byelorussian peasants and with his Polish masters. He told him about the deep anti-Jewish sentiments among many Byelorussian peasants, and especially among the Poles, and also about a few of his good neighbors who were "good" with Jews. Finally, he told him that there were some Jews, now, who were leaving the *shtetls* and going to larger towns to become doctors and big-time merchants. Even though he really didn't know any of them personally, he had been told about several people from surrounding *shtetls* who had actually left.

The officer listened attentively, asked questions and took notes. Feitl enjoyed telling him whatever he knew. It was almost like summarizing his own life out loud, something he would have never done if it had not been for the curious German officer.

The officer also liked to play with children. In the spring, he took Feitl and Reizl's grandchildren for a walk, first to the open field just behind their house, and then to the nearby grove of old birch trees. He also taught them to play his flute. Feitl was even a little sad when the Germans were driven away and the officer left in a hurry, leaving some of his books behind.

The second time the Germans occupied Celiba, another officer asked Feitl for permission to stay in his house. This officer was a tall young man with *pince-nez*, long brownish hair and extremely pale skin. He loved poetry and recited many German poems by heart, to himself or to Feitl's grandchildren, who listened to those emotional recitals, but understood only occasional words. The young officer also wrote poetry, filling page after page with his small, accurate cursive.

After the Russian repelled the Germans for the second time and the Russian army pursued the Germans farther west, Polish soldiers suddenly appeared in Celiba. They were rude and almost constantly drunk. They beat up the Byelorussian peasants, whom they considered a lower class of human beings, and looted Jewish homes. They hated Jews.

One dreary autumn day, when Shmuel was digging up potatoes in the wet, muddy potato field, a group of young, drunken Polish officers passed by the Rips' house. Feitl was picking apples from his trees, not far from the water well. Riva, his daughter-in-law, was carrying two full pails of water from the well. In an instant, one of the officers jumped over the fence into their yard, and grabbed Riva from behind.

"Gotcha, Jewish girl!"

The scream of the terrified Riva filled the air, and old Feitl sprang from under the apple tree to her side in a split second. With only his left hand to fight with, he pulled the officer by the hair, away from Riva, and smashed the officer's face against his raised knee. Blood gushed from the officer's broken nose and smashed lips, as he fell to the ground.

Riva dropped both buckets of water and ran to the house, as the other officers climbed over the fence, some drawing their guns. Feitl bent his knees and clenched his only fist in front of his chest, preparing to defend himself. But it didn't come to a fistfight. Half a dozen pistol shots ended Feitl's life, right in the yard of his own home.

He fell to the ground face-up, his fist still tightly clenched. The officers left as they had come, climbing over the fence and carrying with them their moaning friend. One of them turned around and, with an expression of deep hatred on his face, kicked the lifeless body of Feitl.

"We buried him the next day," said Shmuel, tearfully. "It was the saddest day of my life."

"And Mama? Where is she?" asked Hershel, wiping the tears from his cheek.

"She's here, in the house," said Shmuel, turning and pointing to the hallway. "She was all right until about two months ago, when she was felled by a stroke. Can't move her left side, can't talk, barely swallows. Miserable, but alive. Lost a lot of weight, poor Mama."

"I want to see her."

"Sure." Shmuel stood up. "But I am not sure she understands what's going on around her. I'd be surprised if she recognizes you." He led Hershel to a small room down the hall. Hershel followed silently.

"Mama ?" Hershel knelt next to her bed. "Mama it's me, Hershel. I'm back. I'm home." He touched her hand.

After a minute of silence, Shmuel said, "We moved her here from their room. It's just easier to take care of her in this room, and it doesn't matter to her." He said it as if he thought he needed an excuse.

Hershel remained at her side for a while longer, staring into her eyes and moving his fingers back and forth over her forearm and hand. Her eyes remained wide open, but she did not seem to react either to their presence in the room or to Hershel's light touch and stroking.

They returned to the big room.

"I'm so glad you've come," said Shmuel. "Riva and I are planning to take off for America. You know her brothers have been there for several years now, and they keep nagging us to come. They've sent us tickets."

"You would have left Mama here alone?"

"Oh, no! God forbid. I just don't think she's going to last long. We would have waited. But, now that you are here, we might as well go. This country's the pits."

"Is it better in America?"

"Can't be much worse than here. There's plenty of work, they say, and I'm not afraid of work; you know that. Plus it's safe there; there's no war and no Polacks."

"You may be right."

"I know I'm right. I see no future here. The same miserable life among the people who hate us."

"This is the future our parents saw for us. They didn't go anywhere."

"There was no America for them. Besides, I feel I owe it to my children to find a better future for them. I just don't believe in what I see here."

"Where is Arkady?" asked Hershel, about his younger brother.

"Somewhere in Kiev. Smart kid; he wanted to go to school," said Shmuel. "We don't know exactly where he is, though."

Shmuel, Riva and their two little children left Celiba one month later. Hershel and his paralyzed, aphasic mother remained at home. For two years Hershel worked his rye and potato fields, and sold apples from their trees. Every day, he carried his mother to a wooden bath and then, after wrapping her in a warm wool blanket, to a recliner chair that he had built for her in the first week of his return. He fed her three times a day, giving her mashed potato, scrambled eggs and milk, all with a small teaspoon.

She never showed any emotion; not even a sign of understanding or appreciation. She showed not even a glimpse of hope for improvement. Because of her inability to move, the skin on her buttocks and on her right shoulder eventually cracked and broke with infection. Three months later, the infection spread until it covered a third of her back. She also caught a cold that rapidly involved her lungs, and then, after a week of high fever and unconsciousness, she died. Hershel buried her next to his father in the Jewish cemetery, a mile east of Celiba.

By this time, the war had ended, and the Bolshevik Revolution was sweeping the land around Celiba. "The new government is giving land to the people," said people in Celiba. "It's our land now—let's work it!"

Hershel was among those who accepted the new government, if not with open arms, at least with open minds. He liked the new slogans that appeared everywhere, promising to transfer power to the working people, to end exploitation and religious intolerance and to establish equality among people. *We must give it a chance,*he thought. *The new government offers us hope. It should work.*

Hershel had the idea of transforming their old, abandoned sawmill into a grain mill. He was still single, and physically as strong as ever, and he had all the time in the world. It was a big job, but he bravely started alone. He dug out some of his father's gold coins (unfortunately, he knew about only a couple of the sites his father had used to bury his coins) and bought some used equipment. Later, a couple of Jewish neighbors and a couple of Byelorussian peasants joined him. The work went faster and, by the harvest of 1921, the new mill was ready to accept rye from the surrounding fields.

Hershel ran his mill very efficiently, and paid the peasants fairly for their rye. Both his reputation and his business began to grow. The New Economic Policy of the Soviets seemed to be on his side, encouraging small businesses to flourish. He sincerely believed in his newfound fortune.

One evening, a local matchmaker, a skillful *yenta*, Madame Rosen, came to see him.

"Hershel," she said, aggressively, as soon as she had sat at the table, "is there anything wrong with you? Or not?"

"Nothing. Nothing that I know of. But what do you mean, wrong with me?"

"What I mean, Hershel, is, if there is nothing wrong with you, then it's time for you to get married, isn't it, Hershel?"

"Oh, that's what you are talking about," smiled Hershel. "There's nothing wrong with me, nothing indeed, and I agree, Madame Rosen, it's time to marry."

"Hershel," said Madame Rosen, "do I have a bride for you! Ah! I do! I surely do! I have a bride just for you!" Her round face, framed by a black-and-red shawl, displayed a wide smile and supreme confidence. She became overly friendly, once she discovered that she had a receptive client.

"She is a beauty," she continued. "Long, dark hair. Black like coal, like the wing of a crow. Big eyes, thin hands. She is only nineteen, a doll. I'm telling you, Hershel, she's made for you. And," she paused and looked straight into Hershel's eyes, "she comes from a wonderful family."

The next Thursday, Hershel and Madame Rosen left Celiba for another *shtetl*, Dukora, some forty miles southwest, to see the bride and meet her family. They arrived a couple of hours before the Sabbath.

"The family is very observant," remarked Madame Rosen. "I'd recommend we go to the *shul* with them." She used the Yiddish word "*shul*" for "synagogue."

Hershel was indifferent to religion. While in the army, he had eaten "*treif,*" or non-kosher food, and hadn't kept the Sabbath. Since his return to Celiba, he had been going to the *shul* on high Holidays and, because his house was next door to the synagogue, whenever the congregation needed a tenth Jew for prayer, a "minyan, " as it's called. Nevertheless, he knew all the traditions and all the prayers. When he was called to the "*bimah*" (the raised part of the synagogue where the Holy Book lies open) to read the Torah, he led the congregation as if it were a routine and ordinary matter for him.

His prospective father-in-law, Reb Berl Kogan, was dully impressed. Reb Berl Kogan was from a family of famous Rabbis and, even though he had not become a Rabbi himself, he was a deeply religious and observant man. He was so much respected by his fellow Dukorans that they called him "Reb Berl," meaning "Teacher Berl."

He introduced his daughter, Fanya, to Hershel at the Sabbath dinner in their home. Madam Rosen had not exaggerated—Fanya was a very attractive girl. She was about five feet four inches tall and very thin, with long, black hair arranged in a single braid. She had beautiful, sun-tanned skin with a bit of natural red in her cheeks, and a pair of smiling, dark eyes, that revealed her gregarious, gay personality, even when she was silent and somewhat scared.

Hershel liked her very much. He nodded approvingly to her father, who grinned widely, as if he had never doubted the reaction of a suitor.

No one asked nineteen-year-old Fanya about her interest in this older man, who was closer in age to her father than to her, or in the marriage. She was the youngest of eight children, four boys and four girls, and the only remaining unmarried girl in the family. She knew it was time to get married, as her older sisters had. It was time to enter the real life; true adulthood. She would have preferred someone younger, maybe someone she knew, but her parents had made this selection for her, and she did not know she could have had a say in the matter.

Two months later, after a wedding in Dukora, Fanya moved into Hershel's house in Celiba. She didn't particularly like her husband, and, truth be told, she was a little bit afraid of him, but he was very gentle, and worked long hours, leaving their big house in her domain. In 1923, she gave birth to their first son, Feitl, and, in 1925, to their daughter, Reizl. Finally, Hershel had his parents back. Another child came in 1927, a boy whom they named "Yakov."

The same year, a letter arrived from America, from his brother Shmuel. He wrote that he and Riva had four children, now, and that he ran a small bakery in Brooklyn that he had been able to buy with money he had saved when he had worked for Riva's brothers, who had also lent him an additional sum. America was safe, he wrote, as they had thought it would be. Plenty of work for everyone who didn't shy away from hard work, and the Jews were happy there. He ended his letter by saying that he'd be happy to send Hershel a ticket, if Hershel wished to come.

Hershel wrote back that he had a family now; a wife, Fanya, and three little ones, and a good business in Celiba: a mill and a grain elevator that served many peasants in the area. There was less anti-Semitism after the Revolution, he wrote to his brother, and there were a lot of Jews in the local and central governments. And the new regime was supporting a New Economic Policy, or NEP, allowing small businesses to grow. He thanked Shmuel for his offer to send him a ticket, but, "Thanks, but no, thanks." He'd stay in Celiba, at least for now. That was the last time they ever heard from each other.

The New Economic Policy came to an abrupt end a matter of months after he mailed his reply to Shmuel. In 1928, the local authorities, on orders from the Central government, began arresting self-employed peasants and small-business owners. They called them "*kulaks*" or "fists." No one knew how this term had come about or what it really meant. Someone said that these self-employed people had grabbed the money in their fists and held it away from the proletariat and from their poor brother-peasants, and that was why they were called "*kulaks*."

When the arrests began, Hershel came up with his own definition of "*kulak*." He thought they were called "*kulaks*" because they slept on their hard fists instead of soft pillows, so they could wake up early and start their hard work.

Whatever the origin of the term was, the simple fact remained that a person called a "*kulak*" was subject to arrest and confiscation of all his property.

When the arrests commenced in their area, Hershel realized that his turn was very near, but he didn't know what to do. He wished he had asked his brother for a ticket to America, but now it was too late; he could be arrested any day, now. He thought of giving his mill to the government voluntarily, but could not quite bring himself to take the first step and besides, there wasn't really anyone to give it to. He waited, knowing the sword of Damocles was hanging dangerously over his head.

It struck a week later, on a gray, drizzly day. There was a small Russian Orthodox church in Celiba, a tiny wooden building made of large logs and capped with two onion domes. It stood kitty-corner from the Rips' house, at the opposite side of the field from the houses of the Byelorussian peasants. Why the Church had been built next to the synagogue and on the Jewish side of Celiba, no one knew; it had stood there for many years before Hershel was even born.

The Russian Orthodox priest, Father Konstantine, walked to the Church through the grass- and clover-covered field and, as a short cut, he liked to traverse the Rips' backyard.

The late Feitl had liked Father Konstantine and, on many occasions they had used to have a drink or two, right there in the yard. On some cold winter nights, the priest would stop at Feitl's on his way home. They would eat hot boiled potatoes with sour cream that Reizl put on the table, and drink home brew. Feitl had even built a special gate in his back fence to allow Father Konstantine to cross the yard any time he wanted.

Hershel didn't drink alcohol, but he allowed the priest to cross his property. "A friend of my father," he said to the priest, "is my friend as well." Father Konstantine still visited the Rips' house and Hershel, on his way home from the church, and on many occasions, Hershel offered a small glass of vodka to the aging clergyman.

That evening, the priest stopped by as usual. He swallowed his vodka and said, bending forward toward Hershel's ear, as he bit off a large piece of dill pickle, "I've heard they're going to take you in, tomorrow."

"Where did you hear that?" asked Hershel, without much surprise in his voice.

"People say," replied the priest. "You know, when people say something, it usually turns out to be true."

"I guess so. Thanks for the warning."

"Let me have another one. It might be my last one, here."

Hershel poured the priest another glass of vodka and, this time, took one for himself, as well.

"To you, Hershel. Your father and you have been good neighbors," said Father Konstantine, raising his glass. "And...don't you ever trust the Communists," he whispered.

"And to you, Father," said Hershel and touched the priest's glass with his own. "I feel the same way about you. To your health."

After Father Konstantine had left and darkness had settled over Celiba, Hershel saddled his horse. "I'll send for you and the kids, " he said to Fanya. "Probably by the end of the winter, if we are lucky. Here's money; hide it well, and use it as needed. Take care of the kids and don't worry about me. I'll be all right, and I'll be back."

He kissed the sleeping children, and left immediately. Next morning, when the local authorities, led by Comrade Gorelik, came to arrest Hershel Rips, *kulak* and mill owner, he was miles away.

"He didn't come back from work last night," said Fanya, sobbing. "I don't know what to think. Don't have a clue where he might be. This has never happened before. He's always come home." She said this in Yiddish, and Comrade Gorelik translated her mumbling to the rest of the group.

Hershel was heartbroken. He had not felt so badly since the awful morning when he had learned about his father's death. He also felt deceived by the new government. He had wanted to believe the Soviets. He had wanted to work hard to help the new power become even stronger. He couldn't understand why he had been targeted, just because he owned a mill. What kind of crime was that? He and his mill would only have been helpful, he thought. He could find no logic in the government's approach, and he felt totally lonely and utterly helpless. The only way he could imagine being safe was on the run.

Hershel had walked away from his mill and from his home. He had walked away from Celiba. Walked away thinking that he would never return. He went all the way south, crossing southern Byelorussia and the entire Ukraine, to the eastern side of the Crimean peninsula, at the junction of the Sea of Azov and the Black Sea. He stopped in a town called Kerch, on the shores of the Sea of Azov, adjacent to the short, narrow waterway connecting the two seas.

The Crimean peninsula was home to almost one and a half million Crimean Tartars, a Turkish tribe who shared the rocky peninsula with a Russian minority. In Kerch, however, over seventy percent of population were Russians. It seemed like a good place to hide and a great place to start a new life.

He found a job working for the town of Kerch as a groundsman and gardener, pruning trees and maintaining lawns and shrubs in public areas. He had no communication with Celiba or Dukora for almost a year.

Back in Celiba, Fanya took care of their home and their three little children. People talked about Hershel, but no one, including Fanya, really knew where he had gone or where he was now.

Officially, the mill and grain elevator had been nationalized, but no one worked there. Without an owner or even a manager, they stopped functioning, exactly as Hershel had predicted while pondering whether or not to give up his mill voluntarily. Even though there were a few people who could have operated the business, they were frightened to step forward. Now it officially belonged to the people and to the State, as the leaders of the local Soviets liked to say, but no one wanted to step forward and take responsibility for it.

Father Konstantine heard mutterings in his church.

"His father dropped out of the logging business and we lost our livelihoods; now he's dropped out of the mill business and we lose our income again."

"It's all the Jews' fault," added another voice.

"I'll bet his family is doing well. Just look at his wife; she isn't begging for food."

"He must've stolen all our money."

That Sunday night, around two in the morning, the Rips' house was set on fire. Someone poured kerosene at three corners of the house and lit it. Luckily, the day before, a heavy, wet snow had covered Celiba. The house was simply too wet to catch fire quickly. The roof was completely covered in snow, preventing the flames from jumping from one side to the other.

Fanya was awakened by the heat and the crackling of the burning logs. Before she even realized what was happening, one of her Jewish neighbors had broken through the door and run inside, waving his ax.

"Fire! Fire!" he yelled. "Grab your kids and get the hell out!"

Fanya grabbed Feitl and Reizl and ran outside, all in their sleeping garb.

"One more! One more is inside!" she screamed to a group of neighbors who had come to fight the fire.

No one seemed to pay any attention to her screams, but, after about five minutes that seemed like an eternity, someone ran out of the house carrying little Yakov, still wrapped in his blanket.

"Thank God I found him," he said, panting, as he transferred the little boy to Fanya's hands. It was one of the Byelorussian men who had come across the fields to help fight the flames.

The neighbors saved very little. They dragged out the big commode containing some of the family's clothes, a couple of chairs and a bench that had stood by their dining table. Someone opened the barn and let the cow out. Everything else, including the chicken coop and the apple trees, went up in flames.

Neighbors led the crying Fanny and her frightened children away. Next morning, they put them on a wagon, tied the cow behind and moved them to Dukora, to her parents.

After eleven months in Kerch, Hershel went to his supervisor and asked for leave without pay. "I like Kerch," he said, quietly, "I wish to settle here and move my family here. I need about three weeks to go back to Minsk and bring my wife and children here." He lied about Minsk, because he was afraid of naming his real home town. "One never knows," he thought, "how things get connected and who knows whom. Better not to mention anything from my real life." It was late fall, and there wasn't much work to be done, so his supervisor let him go.

Within a week, Hershel arrived in Dukora, at his in-laws'. He thought he would stay there, and send his father-in-law to Celiba to fetch his family. He had no idea that their house in Celiba had burnt down, and that Fanya and kids had actually been living in Dukora for almost ten months. He cried when he heard the story, hugging his children and listening to their scary accounts of the fire.

Hershel hid in his in-laws' house for three days. He wouldn't trust the neighbors, anymore; there were many Communists and sympathizers in the *shtetl*. Three days later, under cover of darkness, the family left Dukora, traveling first in a wagon, then by train and finally by horse, to Kerch.

He rented two rooms in a large house in the Russian part of town. When he had been living there alone, he had rented a room from a Tartar family, the family of one of his co-workers, on the outskirts of Kerch. Even though Hershel got along with the Tartars very well, he wanted his children to grow up in the environment of the Russian language. Thus far, the children spoke mainly Yiddish, the only language their grandparents knew, and Hershel felt they must learn Russian, go to Russian schools and play with Russian neighbors. So much did he want them immersed in the Russian language that he spoke only Russian at home, even though Fanya spoke Yiddish to him on many occasions.

They also changed children's names. Feitl became "Pavel" and Reizl became "Rosa." Yakov remained "Yakov," but they called him by his diminutive name, "Yashenka."

Life treated them fairly well in Kerch. Hershel enjoyed his work as a gardener and groundsman, and spent his free time helping his neighbors fix up their homes, playing with the children on the sandy beaches of the Sea of Azov and reading books to his beloved daughter, who loved to cuddle in his lap and listen to the fairy tales he read to her, imitating different characters with his voice.

Fanya ran the household, and the children played and attended the local schools. Two years passed, and Hershel started thinking of buying his own place. He was, indeed, ready to settle.

One Sunday afternoon, when Hershel was helping his neighbor put on a new roof, a couple of kids came running and screaming, "Hey, Hershel! Big kids are torturing Pavel in the plum orchard!"

Hershel and several neighbors dropped their hammers and ran to the orchard, about half a mile south of their neighborhood. As they approached the orchard, they were met by loud cries from Pavel and by the roaring laughter of other kids, both boys and girls. Pavel was hanging among the branches of a plum tree, his wrists tied to a branch with a clothesline. His shoes, pants and underpants were lying on the ground a foot or so beneath his dangling bare feet. His face was red and swollen from crying, from fear and from desperation. A circle of older kids, some as old as their twenties, stood around, laughing and watching, as a tall blond lad pointed at Pavel's genitals with a twig. "You see," he was saying to the others, poking at Pavel's penis, "Jews have it the same as Moslems and Tartars."

Hershel charged like a wounded bull. The blond boy hadn't anticipated such a ferocious attack. Or maybe he just hadn't thought this middle-aged, not very tall, balding Jew would be so strong. The very first punch completely knocked the wind out of the young fellow. The second punch in the face flattened and bloodied his nose, and knocked out a few teeth.

As the first fell to the ground, another of the oldest kids jumped Hershel. Hershel caught him by his arm, swung him into the air and threw him up and against the tree. Others began to run away.

Hershel, in a rage that clouded his mind, returned to the blond fellow lying on the ground. He lifted the man's body with his left hand and struck his face with his right fist, time after time after time, until his neighbors pulled him away. The blond fellow's face was a mess, and it wasn't clear whether or not he was still alive.

Hershel cut the rope holding Pavel's wrists to the branch, put him down and helped him get dressed. He hugged his son, who pressed his swollen face against his papa's chest. He walked away, carrying little Pavel in his hands.

Within an hour of the incident, Hershel felt terrible for beating the blond man so badly. He knew his rage had gone beyond the point of reasonable punishment, even for such a terrible humiliation of his son. He was sorry. He should have stopped, he thought. But the deed was done, and remorse wouldn't help.

He didn't wait, either, for the revenge that he knew would be swiftly planned, or for the criminal charges that might be brought by the relatives of the blond young man. He gathered his family and two suitcases of household things, and left Kerch at dusk.

Hershel took his family to the home of his Tartar friend, who led them out of town to a Tartar village, where they spent the night and the next day. The following night, the Tartars smuggled them out of the Crimean peninsula to Ukraine, where they caught a train to Dnepropetrovsk, a Southern Ukrainian city, where Hershel's younger brother, Arkady, worked at the metallurgical plant.

In 1932, Hershel and his family opened another chapter in their lives, this time in a suburb of Dnepropetrovsk.

CHAPTER EIGHT

I n March of 1934, the Kharkov school district announced a day of celebration of the life of Pavlik Morozov. It was the second anniversary of Pavlik's death, and the country had decided to mark it with a show of commitment and unity.

Pavlik Morozov had become a legend in Communist Russia literally overnight. He had been born and lived his short life in a village called Gerasimovka, on the Western edge of Siberia. His father had been a hard-working man who, at the time of the New Economic Policy, had been able to develop a relatively productive farm. Over the next couple of years, he had become wealthier than most of his neighbors and, when the New Economic Policy was abruptly stopped by the Communists, he had been labeled a *kulak*. He had been ordered to turn over to the Government his little farm and the entire harvest his farm had generated. The elder Morozov had decided to hide his crop .

Pavlik Morozov would not have that. Being a Young Pioneer, a member of the Communist-sponsored organization established in 1922 for children from nine to fourteen years old, Pavlik had gone straight to the OGPU (the internal police force fighting counterrevolution) and told them where and how his father had hidden tons of grain from the Soviets. An open meeting had been called right in the Morozov family home, where the fearless Pavlik had exposed his father. The grain had been found, and his father had been arrested immediately and publicly executed as an enemy of the Soviet Republic.

Initially, the story had not received much attention, but when, about a year later, some of his father's relatives had killed Pavlik in an act of gruesome revenge, Pavlik had become a national hero, a martyr and a role model for millions of children in the Soviet Union. Every Pioneer knew that Pavlik had put his Communist country above and ahead of his own father, and that, by doing so, he had paid the ultimate price. He had been killed by enemies of the State, but he had inspired a generation of Young Pioneers and Communists.

To commemorate the second anniversary of Pavlik's death, the Pioneers were given a special task. On Thursday morning, the headmaster of School #82 addressed the Pioneers. They stood in rows in their school uniforms: tightly-buttoned, long-sleeved, light-blue shirts, long, gray pants and gray jackets. Under the collars of their jackets, they wore red Pioneer neckerchiefs.

Nahum stood with his class, proudly displaying his red neckerchief, the front ends of which covered the lapels of his jacket, and the back of which lay between his shoulder blades as a large red triangle. He was eleven years old, and had been admitted to the Pioneer organization just the year before.

The Pioneers lined up along the walls of the school gym, and the teachers stood silent, next to their pupils. The headmaster walked down the middle, turning from one side to the other as he spoke.

"Pavlik Morozov sacrificed his life for you, for the country, for our beloved Soviet Union, for all of us." The headmaster spoke very loudly, as if the strength of his voice would add importance to his message. "He recognized that his father was an enemy of the Soviet Republic. He knew his father was hiding grain from the Soviet citizens. He was hiding it from you and me!

"Pavlik knew good from bad. Some children might not have turned their fathers in. They would have thought that family ties were more important. But Pavlik was a real young Communist; a true Pioneer. The Soviet motherland was much more important to him. If his father was an enemy of the people, he knew he must stand with the people.

"He was killed by enemies like his father. But his spirit is alive and well. It is in all of us. If we see an enemy of the Soviet people, we'll bring him to light, even if he is our father! It is an obligation of the Young Pioneers to watch for these enemies in their own homes, in their own families, among their own classmates."

Nahum listened attentively, catching the headmaster's every word. How lucky he was, he thought, that his father was a true Communist. He loved his father; he certainly wouldn't want to have him killed. He had no enemies in his family; at least, he couldn't think of anyone, right at the moment.

"Today," the headmaster continued, "we have decided to announce a healthy competition among the Pioneers of the Kharkov schools. This coming Saturday, every Pioneer is required to find and bring to school some scrap metal. Scrap metal is very important for our economy. Therefore we will gather every piece of scrap metal we can find.

"The school that collects the most scrap metal will win the city-wide competition. Within each school, we will identify the best class and the best Pioneer; the one who brings the most scrap metal to the schoolyard.

"The teachers and I are counting on you. Our school #82 will be one of the best in the city. Our Pioneers are the best Pioneers in Kharkov!"

"Hooray!" The gym erupted. Hands went up and Pioneers jumped up and down in their rows. "Hooray!"

Enthusiasm permeated Nahum all day. All day, he could think of nothing but Pavlik Morozov and scrap metal. *I wonder*, he thought, *how much scrap metal Pavlik would have found.* He was certain that Pavlik would have found a lot. *His father must have been an awful monster*, thought Nahum. He couldn't have been as good and gentle as his papa. The thought of turning in his papa was incomprehensible to him. He had an image of Pavlik's father as a big, fat, abusive man with a long mustache, bushy eyebrows and large teeth. He was scary and terrible.

On the way home, he spoke with Leonid.

"Do you want to go and search for scrap metal together?" he asked.

"Nope," said Leonid, with great self-confidence. "I know a place where I can find some scrap metal. I'll go alone. I want to win this competition. Do you know any places?"

"No, I don't, but I'll ask my papa. He might know," said Nahum, with disappointment in his voice, because his friend had just turned him down.

"Ask my papa!" Leonid mocked him. "Pavlik Morozov didn't ask his papa. He turned him in."

"But my papa is not an enemy of the people!" shouted Nahum.

"How do you know? Do you watch what he is doing? Do you listen to his conversations with your mama and with his friends? If you did, you might learn something."

"What have you learned?" asked Nahum, in awe.

"Nothing, yet, but I am always on guard, keeping my eyes and ears open. Don't you? You should."

"Uh...uh..." Nahum stumbled for a moment. " Yes, of course. I do. I do keep my eyes open."

Nahum got home at two in the afternoon. His Grandma Haya, gave him a plate of fried potatoes that she had kept in the frying pan, wrapped in a large kitchen towel in order to keep them warm. He ate his potatoes with a glass of milk, and set out to do his homework.

He usually finished his homework quickly and went outside to play with other kids in the back yard, but today he couldn't concentrate on his work. He had to read every paragraph twice, sometimes even three times, to decipher the meaning. Math problems also seemed more difficult today. When he finally finished his home assignments, it was almost four o'clock, and he decided to stay home and wait for his mama, who would return from work around five.

Rachel worked as a bookkeeper in a large engineering firm. She excelled in math, and understood the ever-changing governmental regulations better than most in her firm. Also, both at work and at home, she had superb organizational skills. Her books were always in perfect order, her calculations were timely and her household ran without a hitch. Every morning, Rachel prepared a list of tasks for her mother (she wrote them in Yiddish) and a shopping list for Moshe. She knew exactly what should be ready by the time she got home from work, and what she would do then.

Moshe had a busy job, but a perfect one for these difficult times. His best friend, boss and mentor, Nahum Olshansky, was in charge of the General Affairs of the Central Committee of the Ukrainian Communist Party. It was a very high position in the hierarchy of the Party. Moshe was Olshansky's official Deputy, and responsible for the wellbeing of the families of Party bosses.

His responsibilities were precisely defined. He had to ensure that the families of the members of the Central Committee and the families of a few other top Party and Soviet officials had food on the table, clothes to wear, entertainment to enjoy and anything else they might desire.

No one ever asked him where he was able to get meat, bread, salt and vegetables in the famine-stricken Ukraine; everyone knew that Moshe would make daily deliveries of groceries six days a week, month after month. Wives of Party bosses called him for special items or asked him to send them a car to take them to the tailor's or the clothing stores. Moshe was equally responsive to their needs and whims.

As far as his own family was concerned, Moshe was both too modest and too scared even to create the impression that he might have taken for himself or for his family more than he deemed absolutely necessary. Nonetheless, what little he took was much more than ninety-nine percent of the population could even have dreamed about. The Draznin family always had bread, butter, milk, meat and potatoes.

As soon as Rachel opened the door of the apartment, Nahum ran to meet her.

"Mama ! Mama!" He was overwhelmed with excitement. "We will have a special competition in honor of Pavlik Morozov!"

"How nice," answered Rachel, smiling.

"Do you know Pavlik Morozov? Do you know him?"

"I know of him. I believe he is a real hero."

"I want to be just like him."

Rachel took a long look into Nahum's eyes. He stared back at her, as if to provoke a response. Finally, she said, "I'm very proud that you want to be a hero like Pavlik Morozov. Just remember, his father was a really bad man, a *kulak*. Pavlik had no choice but to report him to the authorities. Our papa is a true Communist; you don't have to worry about him."

"I know that," said Nahum, with a sigh of relief, "but Leonid said he was listening carefully at home to what his parents talk about between the two of them and with their house guests."

"Everyone should be on guard," replied Rachel, cautiously. "This is true, but spying at home? I'm not sure how good that is. I want to tell you, Nahum," she said bending over to her son and hugging him, "if you ever hear anything you find suspicious or unusual, please tell me first. We love our papa very much, don't we? We don't want any harm to come to him or to any one of us. We'll discuss it first, won't we, Nahum?"

"Yes, Mama. We will."

That evening, his parents spoke Yiddish between themselves much more than usual. Nahum understood only that they were talking about him and Pavlik Morozov, but couldn't get the details. Also that evening, Cousin David Slavutsky stopped by.

David had moved to Kharkov a year after the Draznins. He had convinced the regional Soviet officials to establish a typewriter-repair shop. "Someone has to repair the typewriters of government institutions," he had said, and they had agreed. Now the city of Kharkov was paying him a small salary, and, quickly and diligently, he would repair broken typewriters at all governmental establishments.

It hadn't taken him too long to set up new contacts with local dentists and watchmakers, who were now buying and selling gold through his typewriter-repair store. He had simply transplanted to Kharkov the only business he knew, and now lived in a small room in the back of his shop. He frequently stopped at the Draznins for dinner and, whenever he did so, he would bring candies or cheese or fruit or a toy for Nahum. He would never come empty-handed.

"David," said Nahum, at the dinner table, "this Saturday we will have an important competition. We'll compete to see who can find the most scrap metal. This is the second anniversary of Pavlik Morozov's death, and the Pioneers will compete in his honor."

"Good for you Pioneers!" David laughed. "Where are you going to get scrap metal?"

"I'm gonna search around our apartment and down the street."

"And so will all other Pioneers from your school. And maybe from other schools as well. Didn't you say it's a city-wide competition?"

"Yep, I'm sure they will." Nahum began to realize that he had no idea how to find scrap metal.

"How much do think you'll find?" David persisted.

"I don't know. Some must be scattered around." Suddenly, Nahum's confidence had disappeared.

"Hm. I don't know how much is scattered around, but I think I've seen one pile of scrap metal," said David, shaking his index finger at Nahum.

"Where? Where did you see it?" gasped a re-energized Nahum.

"If I'm not mistaken, it's not too far from my work," answered David. "Do you know what, Nahum?"

"What?"

"Come to my office on Saturday, say around ten in the morning, and I'll take you there. In fact, you'll see it; it's right behind our shop. By the way, bring your teacher with you."

"Why?"

"Because if I'm remembering correctly, there's a lot of scrap metal there. You won't be able to carry it away alone."

"You think I may be able to win the competition?"

"Oh, I don't know about that, but you'll do well."

Rachel broke into the conversation. "David, are you serious?"

"Why not? Someone has to find scrap metal. The someone might as well be Nahum." David grinned. "Don't tell anybody." He shook his finger again. "Come and collect it."

Nahum could barely wait until Saturday morning. It was especially difficult to keep secret what David had told him. More than once, he was about to tell Leonid that he knew where to find scrap metal but, every time, he was able to overcome his desire to share the news. He remembered well that Leonid hadn't wanted his company in the search.

Saturday morning was cold and rainy. It was more like a fall rain than a springtime one; small, frequent drops, sharp as needles, pushed by an east wind, fell at a sharp angle and seemed to penetrate even winter coats, gloves and hats. The drops were so cold that they didn't melt the banks of dirty snow at the sides of the streets, but covered them, instead, with a thickening film of ice.

The Pioneers and teachers gathered in the schoolyard at eight in the morning, with their backs to the rain and the collars of their coats raised. The headmaster made a short speech and, fighting the pelting rain, gestured to them to go and find scrap metal. Most of the children left the schoolyard and roamed through the streets and back yards of the neighborhood, searching. They carried back metal rods, small metal sheets, pieces of pipe and old and broken household items.

Nahum walked through his own back yard and found only a small tin can, which he brought back to the schoolyard. The headmaster stood there in the rain, next to a large commercial scale brought to the school by regional officials. He kept a log of who had brought what and how much it weighed, and he entered Nahum's name into his roster. "I'm sure you can find more, Draznin," he said, "just go and search better."

"I found some," answered Nahum, hesitation in his voice, "but there's too much there. I can't carry it alone."

"Where's 'there?'" asked the headmaster.

"About ten blocks up the street. That way. Would you go with me?" And Nahum pointed along Chernyshevskaya Street.

"Ten blocks, you said. Are you sure?" The headmaster was intrigued, but didn't really want to walk that far in the rain.

"I'm sure." Nahum wasn't sure at all, but he decided to trust David. "I can take you there."

Luckily, the wind and the rain subsided a bit, and it was easier for them to walk. Nahum was very anxious, and the closer they got, the more he felt his heart beating rapidly and blood pulsing in his temples. It took fifteen minutes to reach David's typewriter-repair shop. Along the way, the headmaster asked twice whether Nahum was sure he had seen scrap metal. Nahum, relying totally on David's promise, twice answered affirmatively, even though his heart was racing in his chest.

The shop was a small, one-story building wedged between a large apartment house on the right and a welding shop on the left. There was an open space immediately behind two of shops, the typewriter-repair shop and the welding one. On top of the dirty, icy snow that still covered this open space was a huge heap of scrap metal; all sorts of twisted metal sheets, long sticks, links of wrought iron fencing, broken car parts and even a couple of railroad rails.

"That's it! That's it!" screamed Nahum, jumping up and down and pointing at the heap of metal. "Do you see it? I found it! I knew it was here!"

The headmaster couldn't believe his eyes. "It must belong to somebody," he said, finally. "Probably to this welding shop. I'm going to ask." He went straight through the snow into the shop.

"No, it's not ours," said a man in the shop. "We don't need it. There's nothing we can do with this junk. You can have it. As a matter of fact," he added, "if it's not too far, I can drive you guys and this crap to your school."

It took them an hour and a half to pile the heap of metal into the man's old pickup truck. Nahum and the headmaster climbed into the cabin, and the man drove them to the school. Unloading went much faster, as the other teachers helped to place the metal on the scale.

It weighed one and a half tons.

"It's clearly a new school record," said the headmaster, entering the numbers into his book. "Nahum, you are a hero," he added with a smile. "Unless someone finds a huge amount of scrap metal, you will undoubtedly be the winner of today's competition."

Nahum was completely wet, tired and extremely happy. He had found the scrap metal where David had said it would be, and he had helped carry it to school. He felt like a hero, and he had cleanly won the school competition.

The rain stopped in the afternoon, and freezing temperatures turned the film of water into slick ice. Nahum came home wet and dirty, but exuberantly happy. "Mama! Papa!" he shouted from the doorway. "I won! I won the competition! I found the scrap metal that David told us about, and I won! Let's go and tell David. Can we go? Can we?"

"First wash your hands and face, and change," said Rachel. "Eat something and we'll go."

An hour later, the three of them went to see David, who was at home in the tiny apartment behind his store. The "apartment" was really just one room, no larger than 180 square feet or so. David's small bed stood along one wall, with a long dining table with space for six right in front of it, so that the bed could be used as a bench when he wanted to sit at the table. A cupboard stood along the opposite wall, and by the room's single window stood another table with a kerosene primus, a couple of pots and a kettle.

To Nahum's surprise, David was not alone. He was eating dinner, hot dogs and boiled potatoes with the man who had helped Nahum and the headmaster transfer the scrap to the school that morning.

"Come in, come in," David invited them. "Meet my friend and neighbor, Max Zusman. He runs the welding shop next door."

"I met you this morning," said Nahum, in a low voice. He was stunned to see this man with David. "You helped us with a pile of scrap metal."

"That's right, young man. How could I forget? Carrying all that stuff in the cold, nasty rain. To your health, champion!" Max raised a shot glass filled with vodka, and downed it without delay.

"Did you win the competition?" asked David. His wide smile revealed large, tobacco-stained teeth.

"I'll be damned if he didn't!" barked Max. "There was a lot of the crap! One and a half tons!"

"I did," answered Nahum, softly. He was intimidated by Max.

"Nahum was ecstatic, and we came to thank you for recommending the spot," said Rachel, noticing Nahum's hesitation. "He was so happy when he came home."

"He should have been. It's a big deal for a Pioneer to win an important competition and to help his country at the same time," said David. "Are you going to join us at the table?"

"No, thanks," said Moshe. "We have just eaten. We simply came to share Nahum's success. We thought you might want to know, since you directed him to the heap of scrap."

"Yes, indeed. And I am very proud of you, Nahum," said David. "You are a great Pioneer. Stay the course, my friend, stay the course!"

When they had left, David poured more vodka into Max's glass. "You see," he said, raising his own shot glass, "paying you for this scrap metal was worth it, every ruble of it, just to see him happy."

Monday morning, before classes resumed, all the Pioneers of School #82 lined up for the morning salute to the Party. "Young followers of Lenin are always ready!" they shouted in unison, and they raised their right arms in front of their faces in the traditional Pioneer salute. Nahum shouted it as loudly as he could. He was happy and ready to follow Lenin and Lenin's ideas for many years to come.

After the salute, the headmaster said, "I want to congratulate every one of you who participated in the Saturday scrap-metal hunt. It was a very successful endeavor. We gathered one-point-six tons of scrap metal. Pioneer Nahum Draznin, from the fifth grade, beat the school record alone, when he found and brought in one and a half tons! Come forward, Nahum. Stand next to me."

Nahum hadn't expected this turn of events. His heart beat loudly in his chest and his face flushed with sweat as he crossed the gym to stand next to the headmaster.

"Pavlik Morozov would have been proud of you," said the headmaster, "and thanks to Nahum Draznin's contribution, our school, Kharkov school #82, was the best in town, and won this year's city-wide contest."

Nahum stood next to the headmaster in front of the four lines of applauding Pioneers, blushing with humility and smiling with confidence and pride. He saw his neighbor, Leonid, applauding reluctantly and looking fairly grim.

Nahum's pride grew even larger the next week, when, at the Monday morning Pioneer salute, the headmaster said, "Today is a special day for our school. We have received a telegram from Moscow that I wish to read out loud to all of you. I want to ask Nahum Draznin to stand next to me."

Red-faced, Nahum came out of his line and walked to the middle of the gym to stand next to the headmaster in front of the Pioneers and teachers lining the rectangular perimeter of the gym.

"Congratulations, Nahum," said the headmaster pompously, and offered Nahum his firm handshake.

"Thank you," answered Nahum so softly that even he could only barely hear his own voice. He had no idea as to what was going on or what was about to happen.

The headmaster pulled a telegram from the inner pocket of his jacket, opened it, looked over his glasses around the gym, and started reading.

"Congratulations to Pioneer Nahum Draznin, Kharkov School 82.
Pioneer Draznin collected one and a half tons of scrap metal.
Record set entire Ukraine.
The country proud Nahum Draznin, true young Leninist.
I offer my handshake Nahum Draznin.
Be ready, Young Pioneer."

The headmaster posed for just a few seconds and added, "Signed—Comrade Stalin."

The entire school froze in silence. All eyes converged on Nahum, who had tears in his eyes.

"Comrade Stalin himself sent you a telegram, Nahum," said the headmaster. "This is the highest reward a Pioneer can dream about. We are proud of you. We salute you. Be ready, Soviet Pioneer!" And he raised his right arm in a proud salute.

"Always ready!" Nahum shouted back, and raised his own arm.

"Hooray!" responded the four lines of Pioneers, and their cheers filled the gym.

CHAPTER NINE

In the first week of April, Aaron Yavlinsky came to Kharkov on a business trip, to see the First Secretary of the Ukrainian Communist Party, Comrade Postyshev. Aaron was still working for Comrade Kirov, heading his personal security team and serving as his confidant and adviser. Officially, he was employed by the NKVD (the new name for the OGPU), but unofficially, he was directly attached to Kirov, to do whatever the First Secretary of the Leningrad Communist Party asked him to do.

Sergei Mironovich Kirov's political career continued to rise and shine. People loved him and considered him a true defender of the workers' rights and needs. Respect for him was incredibly high, not only in Leningrad, where he was the undisputed leader of the Communist Party and the City government, but all over the young Soviet Republic. His name was almost on a par with the name of Stalin. He had been elected to the Politburo, the highest governing body of the Communist Party, where he passionately defended his point of view and argued openly, even with Comrade Stalin. Twice in the previous year, Kirov had convinced other members of the Politburo to vote with him against Comrade Stalin's opinion.

Naively, he had underestimated the importance of his disagreements with Comrade Stalin. He had not taken these debates personally, and he had never thought that others, particularly Comrade Stalin, might. To Kirov, the debates were strictly part of the business of running the country. The best ideas must prevail, he thought.

One issue that put him and Comrade Stalin on opposite sides was the question of punishment for past mistakes. Only seventeen years had passed since the Communist Revolution, and many people were slow to accept the new rules, even those who would eventually accept them simply because they saw no alternative. Many were still skeptical, and some had just recently become Communist converts.

Comrade Stalin was adamant that no one, regardless of current status, who had not accepted the new rules at the beginning must ever be forgiven, even though the person might later have embraced the Soviet and Communist ideology and approach. In his unwavering cruelty, Stalin felt that these people must be punished without mercy or leniency. Kirov, being a much softer person, and more pragmatic in considering the needs of the country, argued that many of these people could be extremely helpful to the new Republic, and, once they understood and acknowledged their previous mistakes, and switched allegiance, they should be allowed to join the ranks of Soviet citizens without punishment.

"People are our best resource," he argued during a protracted debate in the Central Committee. Since he was a better debater than Stalin, and incomparably more eloquent in expressing his thoughts, Kirov had prevailed in this particular debate, and his version had been adopted by a simple majority. For a brief moment, Comrade Stalin, who never liked to argue publicly, appeared visibly disappointed, but he quickly regained his composure, and the issue seemed closed.

One of the Party leaders who shared Kirov's opinion on this subject was Pavel Petrovich Postyshev, personal emissary of Comrade Stalin to Ukraine. In 1934, officially, Postyshev was First Secretary of the Ukrainian Communist Party, second in command to the General Secretary of the Party, Stanislav Vikentievich Kossior. *De facto*, however, Postyshev was the number-one man. He had been sent to Ukraine by Stalin himself for the very specific task of squashing and completely eradicating Ukrainian nationalism from every level of governance and every aspect of life.

"Ukrainians must fully and unconditionally accept the Russian people as their older brothers," Stalin said to Postyshev, "and you are responsible for this."

Why Kirov sent his most trusted man, Aaron Yavlinsky, to see Postyshev remains unclear, but be that as it may, Aaron arrived in Kharkov in the very first week of April. He stayed with the Draznins.

The next morning, Moshe took him to the building of the Ukrainian Communist Party Central Committee, never asking his brother why he had come to see Postyshev. Aaron, being in the secret service, never volunteered the information.

Nahum had heard a lot about his Uncle Aaron, but didn't remember him at all. His Papa, who also hadn't seen his brother for a number of years, had told him that Uncle Aaron lived in Leningrad with his wife, Bronya, and their two little sons, Vilen and Kim.

Both names were actually acronyms: "Vilen" stood for "Vladimir Ilyich Lenin," and "Kim" for "Communist (spelled with a "K," in Russian) International of Youth" (spelled with an "M," in Russian). Nahum also knew that Uncle Aaron worked shoulder-to-shoulder with a great Communist leader, Comrade Kirov. This alone was more than enough reason to be extremely proud of his uncle.

Aaron arrived just before dinner. He wore his gray civil-war army overcoat that buttoned all the way up to his neck and was held tight around his waist by a black-leather belt with a big handgun in a black-leather holster. He also wore a military cap and tall, black boots. Nahum was greatly impressed.

When his uncle shook his hand, Nahum was planning to put all his power into squeezing back. He thought he needed to do that to overcome his shame and embarrassment at not having his red Pioneer neckerchief around his neck when his uncle walked in.

Uncle Aaron walked in, removed his overcoat, offered a firm handshake to Rachel and Haya, and hugged his brother, Moshe. Then he extended his hand to Nahum.

"Hello, young man. Pioneer, I presume?"

"Oh, yes. Certainly!" said Moshe, before Nahum could even blink an eye. "A great Pioneer. He just received a personal telegram from Comrade Stalin congratulating him on an outstanding scrap metal hunt. How do you like that?" The proud father beamed with joy.

"Incredible! I can only imagine how proud your parents are of you." Again, Uncle Aaron shook Nahum's hand, which he was still holding in his large palm, strongly and vigorously.

Uncle Aaron was big and strong, but he was also a surprisingly quiet man. He ate silently, didn't initiate conversation and answered mainly either "Yes" or "No," or in short phrases.

"How is Bronya?" Asked Rachel.

"She's fine. Going back to work."

"Who is with the kids? How are they, by the way? They must be big boys, now."

"Going to daycare. Vilen is six and Kim is three."

"How long are you going to stay in Kharkov?"

"Only two nights."

"This year, Passover is very early. Is there a chance you can stay with us an extra day to have a *seder* with us?" asked Rachel.

Aaron looked straight into her eyes, put down his knife and fork and said firmly, "Rachel, I am as far away from this Jewish religious rubbish as Kharkov is from China. Don't forget, I am a Communist. I don't want to hear about this religious rubbish."

"This is not religious rubbish. It's our tradition," she fired back.

Moshe wanted her to stop this sudden heated discussion, and kicked her foot, under the table. But Rachel continued, "When our Russian neighbors paint eggs and bake rum cake for their Russian Orthodox *pasca*, it's a good old Russian tradition, but for us to have a Passover dinner is 'religious rubbish,' is it?"

"Yes, it is. And let me tell you, Russian Communists do not paint eggs and do not celebrate their Pasca either. Those are hangovers from the old days. Besides, you know very well, Rachel, *Hagadah* is filled with prayers to God. We Communists can't read it. We must not pray. Isn't that right, Moshe?" He turned to his brother.

"We don't do that, Aaron," interjected Moshe, who seemed embarrassed. "Rachel just wants to have dinner, that's all." He kicked Rachel's foot a second time.

This time she complied.

"Good," said Aaron. "I'd be very disappointed."

Discussion had ended, and the rest of the dinner was silent.

Uncle Aaron slept in Nahum's bed, and Nahum was relegated to a two-inch mattress on the floor. He didn't mind it at all. He was only glad to yield his bed to his famous uncle.

The next day Aaron spent at the Central Committee building, and came back only around seven in the evening. He hung his coat in the tiny coat closet, and put his belt with its holstered gun over the back of his chair.

"Uncle Aaron, may I see your gun?" asked Nahum, at dinner.

"Sure," said Aaron, and he pulled his gun from the holster. He removed the bullets before handing his heavy gun to Nahum.

Nahum lifted the gun with both hands and pointed it at his grandma.

"Nahum, never point a gun at people!" exclaimed Moshe. "Put it down!" Moshe hated guns and, truth be told, was somewhat afraid of them. He hadn't liked guns since the time of his military service in the Czarist army. He had a gun and, as a high Party official, had to carry it, but he did it reluctantly, frequently hiding it from view, and always without bullets.

"Why do you carry a gun, Uncle Aaron?"

"A Communist must be ready to defend the Revolution at every step, every minute of his life."

"Are there so many enemies?" asked Nahum, curiously.

"Plenty of them around. Not as many as before, but they are still around."

"Have you killed enemies, Uncle Aaron?"

"Nahum, Aaron, let's change the subject," said Rachel, firmly. She remembered very well how Aaron had executed people in Ovruch. "I don't want to talk about this. Please."

"Yes, Rachel, we will change the subject. Let me just tell you one thing, Nahum. A real Communist must be strong and unyielding. Once you yield to your enemy, he will always have the upper hand. Remember what Comrade Lenin said—'He who is not with us is against us.'"

Rachel and Moshe did not react, but looked down at their plates.

Uncle Aaron spent that night, too, in his nephew's bed, and left the next morning. Again, he shook hands with everyone, but this time he hugged his little nephew and said, "I know you'll be a real Communist. I can see it in your eyes. The telegram from Comrade Stalin is very telling."

Nahum was the happiest child in the world. He knew he would be a real Communist like his father and his Uncle Aaron.

The next Friday, the Olshanskys came for dinner. Rachel had reminded Moshe several times to invite them. "Don't forget to ask them, and make sure they are coming," she had said repeatedly. She put a new tablecloth on the dining table, a white one with a peach hem, and a set of her Holiday dishes.

There were seven of them at the table. Moshe sat at the head of the table with Nahum Olshansky to his right. Next to him sat Nahum's wife, Maria, a tall, overweight woman in a long blue dress with a white-lace collar. Then came Luba Olshansky, a thirteen-year-old, tall, like her mother, but skinny, with a couple of pimples on her face and a long brown braid. Next to her, at the foot of the table, were Nahum, wearing a long-sleeved bluish shirt and gray knickers, then Grandma Haya and Rachel, next to Moshe on his left, completing the circle. Rachel also wore a long dress, with small, purple polka dots.

First, Rachel served *gefilte* fish with spicy red horseradish, and chopped herring with apples, followed by stewed potatoes with carrots and small cubes of beef. The men drank a couple of shots of vodka, and the entire company talked about the early and unusually warm spring, about children and about relatives in Zhitomir and Kiev.

As it had turned out, it was the first night of Passover, but there was no mention of this until Rachel put an apple pie on the table and said, semi-sarcastically, " It would have been nice to have a slice of *matzo* for Passover, but I guess an apple pie will do, in a Communist family."

"Oh, boy!" exclaimed Nahum Olshansky. "Is it Passover, tonight? We have completely lost track of the Jewish Holidays."

"When we lived in Zhitomir, we knew the dates of holidays from my mother, but here, without her, I no longer have a clue," Maria Olshansky added.

"Thanks to Rachel for reminding us," said Nahum Olshansky, with a smile. "To Rachel's sharp memory !" He raised his shot glass.

"It's my mother," said Rachel. "She is the keeper of Jewish traditions in our household. Or whatever is left of those traditions," she added, with a sigh.

"Rachel, can you light candles?" asked Maria Olshansky. "I'd love to have the feeling of *seder*."

"Oh, sure." Rachel was only glad to oblige. She pulled two candles and two silver candlesticks from a drawer of her cupboard, and put them on the table. She lit them silently, and then said something strange that Nahum couldn't understand. All the adults said, "*Amen.*"

"I'd love to have *matzo*. Too bad we don't have any," said Maria Olshansky. "I still remember the *seders* in my parents' home."

"How can you eat *matzo*?" Luba Olshansky cried, suddenly. "Some girls in our school say there is Russian children's' blood in it. Yech!"

Nahum didn't like *matzo* at all. He had tried it the year before, when his Grandma Haya had given him a slice one afternoon when he came home from school, and he had found it had no taste. But blood? He had never known about the blood. He was petrified. It sounded terrible.

"There is no blood in it!" Nahum Olshansky raised his voice. "It's traditional Jewish food. It has no blood whatsoever. How can my daughter believe these terrible lies?"

Luba's mother was clearly taken aback by her daughter's remark. After the initial shock, she said, "Luba, darling, how can you even imagine that we, your daddy and I, can eat anything with human blood in it?"

"But the girls said…"

"No, no, no. Don't believe these terrible things. There's no blood in *matzo*."

"You know, " said Moshe, who had suddenly noticed the grim look on his son's face, "let's talk about something much more pleasant than that. Did you hear that Nahum won first place in gathering scrap metal and received a telegram from Comrade Stalin himself? By the way," he turned to Rachel, "Let's blow out these silly candles. There's plenty of light in the room." And he waved his hands rapidly in front of the candles, to put out the small flames.

The telegram from Comrade Stalin made a great impression on the Olshanskys. Both Nahum and Maria congratulated him loudly, and Nahum even raised his shot glass in a toast to the Young Pioneer. But the praise sounded very hollow to Nahum, who was preoccupied with Passover, *matzo* and the candles.

The rest of the meal was boring and uneventful. Moshe spoke with Nahum about their work, Maria and Rachel talked about health of their mothers and Luba and Nahum bragged to one another about their achievements in school.

It wasn't the first time Nahum had argued with Luba about whose school was better, who had the better teachers or who was the best student in the class. In the past, he had never yielded to her on any of these topics. Tonight, however, he was so deeply immersed in his other thoughts that he easily conceded almost all the arguments.

When the Olshanskys had left and his parents and grandma were clearing the table, Nahum said, with strength and conviction, "Tomorrow I will have to tell my headmaster that my parents celebrated a Jewish religious holiday."

The phrase struck like lightening. Everyone stopped as if frozen in place.

"I remember Uncle Aaron said that real Communists do not celebrate Jewish holidays," continued Nahum, but this time much more softly. The first reaction of his parents startled him.

Moshe was first to react. "Do you want us to be arrested? Are you a total fool or just pretending to be one?"

"I'm not a fool. I saw what you were doing. I saw the candles! I heard about *matzo*!"

"Yeh? Didn't you see that I blew out those candles? Did you hear us pray or read a religious book? What else did you see and hear, little spy?"

"*Mein Gott! Mein Gott!*" mumbled Haya.

By this time, Rachel had regained her composure. She put down the two plates she was still holding, sat at the table and said, "Nahum, sit here for a minute, my son, and let's reason together." She pulled him by his sleeve and patted his hair as he sat down next to her.

"First of all, it was I who mentioned the Holidays and lit the candles. No one else did. So, if anyone to be arrested, it should be me. If this is to happen, you won't have your mama. They will not let me out. They may actually arrest Papa, too, you know, and you will be an orphan. Grandma will probably die from the sorrow, and they will take you away to an orphanage. I know, I know," she gestured to Nahum who wanted to say something, "some orphanages are not that bad, but nevertheless, that's where you'll end up and, since you are not of legal age, yet, you'll have no choice in the matter.

"Second, there's no religion in what I did tonight. I simply mentioned a tradition, like the traditions of our neighbors who paint eggs for their Pasca. You've seen them do it every year, and they will certainly do it this year again. I'm sure that even your headmaster eats those eggs and rum cake. He is as good a Communist as one can be."

"But Uncle Aaron said the Communists don't do it. He knows; he is a real Communist!"

"Third, " continued Rachel without reacting to Nahum's tirade, "I wanted to please my mother, who loves her traditions. She is an old woman, and she has only her memories, her traditions and us. By mentioning Passover, I wanted to make my mother happy. I hope you'll consider making me happy when I am old.

"Finally, as your papa just said, there was no religion in what we did. We didn't pray, we didn't have *matzo*, we didn't keep kosher and we didn't read any religious books. We don't even have any, here.

"Let's go and sleep now. Mornings are wiser than evenings. We'll see tomorrow what you think. Just remember that we love you, and we'll support you no matter what you decide. But we would never, never, never do anything that might take you away from us." She leaned forward and kissed him on his forehead. "Go to sleep, Nahum. We'll clean up a bit and then go to sleep, too."

That night, Nahum couldn't fall asleep for a long time. He admitted that it was his mother who had started this whole commotion with Passover, and that his father had actually tried to put an end to it.

What would Pavlik Morozov do? he thought. *His father was a monster and beat him up, and he hid grain from the Soviet people. My mother loves me, and she didn't do anything wrong to anyone else. But she did light the candles and she did prepare what appeared to be a Passover dinner. That's religion; that's wrong. Real Communists shouldn't do it. And my papa didn't even stop her right away. Comrade Olshansky also didn't have anything against it. He is a real Communist, too.*

He went back and forth for quite a while. Finally, after he closed his eyes but before he dozed off, he saw an image of his grandmother lying dead in a simple coffin that stood on their dining table in the middle of their large room. She was in her white nightgown, and pale, her eyes closed, and no one else was in the room. Only his mother's voice sounded repeatedly, from all four corners of the room, "Why did you kill your grandmother? Why did you kill your grandmother? Why did you kill your grandmother?"

With that, he fell asleep.

There had been another conversation at the dinner table, one that Nahum had completely missed, because of his worries. Nahum Olshansky had told Moshe that they had received an order to move the seat of the Ukrainian Government back to Kiev, which was about to be restored as the capital of Ukraine. That meant that, in a matter of months, the Central Committee of the Ukrainian Communist Party would also be leaving Kharkov and going to Kiev.

"This means, Moshe," he said, nodding approvingly, "that we are all moving to Kiev. An official announcement is scheduled for Monday."

Rumors about the move had been circulating for quite a while. Kiev was the traditional capital of Ukraine and the site of a strong Nationalist movement. Nationalists, some of them Communists as well, wanted to see Ukraine independent from Russia or at least an equal partner to Soviet Russia. The position of Moscow was exactly the opposite—to maintain Ukraine in the fold of the Soviet Union as a totally dependent Republic.

In order to break the will of the Ukrainian Nationalists, Stalin and the Politburo had prohibited deliveries of food to famine-stricken Ukraine. The forced collectivization of farms had been destroying Ukrainian agriculture, and no help had come from its big brother. People had been dying of hunger in tens and hundreds of thousands, if not millions. Corpses had been left in the streets and back yards, but still, no help from Russia.

The capital had been moved away from Kiev, the bastion of nationalists, to Kharkov, a city with much stronger pro-Russian sentiment. Three non-Ukrainians had been placed in charge of the Russification and taming of Ukraine. These men were on a mission to eradicate opposition: Stanislav Vikentievich Kossior, of Polish origin, Pavel Petrovich Postyshev, a Russian, and Lazar Moiseevich Kaganovich, a Jew.

Now, finally, when the last of the Nationalists had been driven away from the power of Kiev and the will of Ukraine had been broken and drowned in blood, the capital was going back to Kiev.

The Ukrainians were now subdued younger brothers and sisters of the great Russian people.

Moshe told Rachel the news after Nahum went to sleep. Rachel was shocked. She felt very comfortable in Kharkov, she liked her job, she liked their apartment, she knew their neighbors and she liked Nahum's school.

"When do you need to make your decision?" she asked.

"What do you mean?" This time Moshe was surprised by her question. "Whenever the Central Committee moves, we will move." To him, the situation was crystal clear—whatever the Party told him to do, he would do.

Rachel didn't answer. When they woke up in the morning, however, she said firmly, "We are not moving to Kiev. You'll work with them until they move, and then you'll find yourself a different job here in Kharkov."

"I can't quit my job with the Party! What am I going to tell Olshansky? My wife won't let me go? What kind of Communist response is that?"

"We are not moving to Kiev. That's the end of it. You can tell Olshansky whatever you wish in whatever form you find appropriate, but we are staying."

Moshe raised the question once again after about three weeks, only to receive the same answer. "We are not moving."

To his surprise, Nahum Olshansky easily accepted his decision to stay. "Whatever is best for your family, Moshe," he said. "We'll miss you, but I understand."

Moving the Government to Kiev was a logistical nightmare but, by the time the last department of the Central Committee had left Kharkov, Moshe had found another job as Director of Purchasing at a small poultry factory. He used his old connections to get food and other household items, but his official position and status had declined substantially. He wasn't upset, however. His wife was happy, and that was good enough for him.

Moshe started his new job on September 1 of 1934, and on December 1 of the same year, Sergei Mironovich Kirov was assassinated in the hallway near his office in the Smolny Palace, in Leningrad. The news shocked the entire country. It was the first political assassination since the killing of Uritzky and wounding of Lenin, in 1918.

The day before Kirov's assassination, Aaron Yavlinsky received a phone call from Ivan Zaporozhets, the second-in-command of the Leningrad NKVD. Zaporozhets asked Aaron to come to a special training session on December 1, at noon.

"By the way," said Zaporozhets, at the end of their conversation, "bring with you Comrade Kirov's bodyguard. What's his name; 'Borisov,' isn't? Or you want me to call him directly?"

"Yes, 'Borisov,'" answered Aaron. "Why do you need us both?"

"It's not a subject for a phone conversation, Yavlinsky. Come in tomorrow, and you'll see."

When Aaron and Borisov arrived at the NKVD the next day, they were told that Ivan Zaporozhets had left unexpectedly, and that his deputy would conduct the training. "However, his deputy is busy until two o'clock and the session will only start then."

"Why in the world did he ask us to come at noon?" asked Borisov, with visible displeasure. He didn't like to leave Comrade Kirov alone for that long. "We are going to lose a whole day, with you guys."

At two o'clock they joined about a dozen security men and six bodyguards for a two-hour session on how to coordinate the functions of bodyguards and NKVD officers.

"What a colossal waste of time!" exclaimed the outspoken Borisov, as they left the building to walk back to the Smolny Palace, headquarters of the Leningrad Communist Party.

They left the NKVD building at quarter past four and were just a few blocks away from the Smolny Palace when, at four-thirty, Kirov was shot.

Leonid Nikolaev had entered the Smolny at three in the afternoon. It was a cold, dark afternoon; the short period of daylight in this Northern city was over. Nikolaev was a young man in his late twenties, of about medium height, and slim. He wore a long winter coat with its fur collar raised to warm his ears, as he did not have any headgear. An outside security guard checked his pass and his papers and allowed him in. Surprisingly, there were no security guards inside the building, and Nikolaev slowly made his way to the third floor, to the hallway just outside Kirov's office, where he waited patiently.

That day, Sergei Mironovich Kirov had worked at home, finishing a report on an important meeting he had attended a couple of days before. He only arrived at the Smolny at four in the afternoon. He went straight to the office of his trusted aide, Mikhail Chudov, where he, Chudov and a couple of other aides discussed a few points in his report. At four-thirty, Kirov stepped into the hallway leading to his office.

Comrade Kirov was a short man, with a round, smiling face, barrel chest and wide shoulders. He was a perfectly round target. As he passed the dark corner immediately outside the door of his office, Nikolaev moved in from behind the corner and shot him in the back, right between the shoulder blades.

The sound of the shot rattled the Smolny Palace. People ran toward Kirov's office from every direction. Sergei Mironovich Kirov had been killed instantly, and his assassin arrested at the scene of the crime.

Seven minutes later, Aaron Yavlinsky and Borisov entered the Smolny in the midst of incredible commotion.

"Kirov has been shot!" shouted a man at the doorway. "They've killed Comrade Kirov!"

Aaron and Borisov raced to the third floor. Kirov's body was still on the floor, face down, arms and legs spread to the sides. Nikolaev had been taken into someone else's office to await orders. Mikhail Chudov called Moscow. He was told that Comrade Stalin, with his entourage, was leaving for Leningrad immediately, to conduct the inquiry personally.

The same night, Stalin issued a decree that was adopted by the State as a set of new laws on December 2. The new law legalized the accelerated, simplified, conclusive examination of political cases, and mandated the execution of death sentences in such cases immediately after the passage of the sentences.

At the crack of dawn on December 2, Kirov's bodyguard, Borisov, was arrested and accused of conspiring to kill his boss. Soon, it was reported that the car that was transporting the despondent Borisov from the Smolny Palace to the NKVD had been involved in a traffic accident, and that Borisov had been killed. He was the only victim of this accident.

Aaron Yavlinsky was arrested on December 5. They came to his home at night. It was about two in the morning when a loud, impatient knock at the door woke not only Aaron and his family, but many neighbors, as well. At the door were six people in NKVD uniforms. Aaron recognized two of them.

"Aaron Yavlinsky," announced one of the men, "you are under arrest for conspiracy to kill Comrade Kirov. Give up your weapon."

Aaron, who was still barefoot and wearing only his undershirt and military pants, reached for his gun and handed it to the man nearest him.

"Put on your shirt and boots," ordered the first man.

Bronya was petrified. What were they doing? What were they talking about? What conspiracy? He couldn't have been conspiring to kill Kirov. Kirov was his idol, his boss and his friend. But she couldn't get the words out of her mouth. It was dry, and her sandy tongue was literally glued to her palate. She held little Kim in her arms, pressing his body to her chest, while Vilen stood next to her, clinging to her left leg.

Within five minutes, it was all over. The men were gone and Aaron was gone with them. He hadn't even said good-bye. He hadn't even looked at her. He had just put on his shirt, donned his boots and left.

As the last man out slammed the door, tears came to Bronya's eyes. She cried loudly, clinging to her two frightened sons.

On December 12, Bronya Yavlinsky, with her sons Vilen and Kim in tow, dragged her heavy suitcase to the fourth floor of the Draznins' apartment building in Kharkov. It was six o'clock in evening when she knocked at their door. All three of them looked terrible. They were tired and disheveled, and the children had dirty hands and faces. The younger, Kim, was crying silently, and the older, Vilen, was breathing loudly through his nose. Every time he exhaled, a large bubble appeared in his right nostril. They wore winter coats, warm hats and knitted mittens.

Rachel led them in and helped undress the boys while Moshe brought in their heavy suitcase. Nahum sat at the dining table, observing his relatives. Bronya and Rachel took Bronya's children to the bathroom. Haya happened to have a pail of still-warm water that she had boiled for her own bath, so they were able to bathe the children.

After the bath, Haya and Rachel put food on the table. Vilen ate well, still making loud noises as he breathed through his nose. Kim just picked at a few things and held onto his mother, unwilling to let go of her skirt even for a brief moment.

Because the adults didn't want the children to understand what they were saying, they spoke in Yiddish. This was somewhat difficult for Bronya, who understood Yiddish quite well, but, since she hadn't spoken the language for many years, had a very hard time answering. So the conversation didn't flow easily, and they waited until children went to sleep.

Moshe placed a mattress on the floor of their bedroom, and Bronya lay down with her children until they were asleep. Then she returned to the larger room.

Nahum was asked to go to sleep, as well, but he just lay in his bed, facing the wall, with his eyes closed, pretending to be sleeping and trying to catch every word Bronya uttered as she told Moshe, Rachel and Haya what had happened to them in Leningrad.

She described what she knew about Kirov's murder and Aaron's arrest, and her fears for her own life. For about a week after they had taken Aaron away, she hadn't been able to get any information about him, even though she was an NKVD officer herself, and had been back on duty for almost a year. People had seemed to avoid her, and her colleagues hadn't wanted to talk to her at all.

Finally, she had read in the newspaper that seventeen of Kirov's former bodyguards, all NKVD officers, had been implicated in the plot to kill Comrade Kirov, and all had been sentenced to death. The article indicated that they had conspired with Zinoviev and his followers to allow Leonid Nikolaev, the man who had fired the fatal shot, to get inside the Smolny and kill Kirov.

With this article in hand, Bronya had gone to see Ivan Zaporozhets, the second-highest-ranking officer of the NKVD.

"Do you know what is happening with Aaron?" she had asked. "Is he one these people?" And she had extended a newspaper to Zaporozhets.

Zaporozhets had got out of his chair, walked around his desk to her, helped her to her feet and hugged her, tightly but briefly. Not a word had come out of his mouth until he stepped away from Bronya and said, loudly, so that his secretaries in the antechamber could hear, "Your husband was an enemy of the people, and he deserved his punishment. These people were executed yesterday. I don't want to talk to you any longer. Leave this office immediately!" And he had turned away.

"Enemy. He said he was an enemy," she repeated to the Draznins. "Aaron is an enemy. What can be more ridiculous than that?"

Uncle Aaron was an enemy! resounded in Nahum's head. *It can't be true. He was a real Communist!*

"I don't even know where his body is," sobbed Bronya.

They sat in complete silence.

Uncle Aaron has been killed, thought Nahum, in awe. *Executed. For what?* He was afraid to move and reveal that he wasn't asleep.

"The next day," continued Bronya, "I went to work and found out that Zaporozhets had been arrested that night. I was so scared, I had no idea what to do. I went back home at lunchtime, packed up the kids and caught a night train to Kharkov. I still don't know what I'm going to do."

Bronya and her children stayed only one day with the Draznins. The next evening, Moshe took them to the train station, and they went to Kiev. In Kiev, Bronya stayed with her mother, her father having died a few years before. After a week, she went to see her uncle, General Iona Yakir, who was Supreme Commander of the Soviet Army in Ukraine. She didn't dare to go to his office, and instead went to see him at his home.

General Yakir was supportive. He offered her a cup of tea, and listened carefully, with tight lips twitching occasionally. He didn't interrupt her at all.

When she had finished, he stood up, walked back and forth across the room for about a minute and then said, "If I were you, Bronya, I'd trust the Party. I am not saying that Aaron was an enemy of the people or that he wanted to kill Comrade Kirov. I believe you; he certainly didn't. But...he was probably deceived by his friends or people around him. I'd go back to Leningrad. Nothing is going to happen to you. The Party and the NKVD know that you are innocent. They will take care of you. You are a Communist, Bronya, and an NKVD officer. You can't run away from problems. You must face them, and put your faith in our Party."

Bronya didn't argue. She listen quietly, wiping away the tears as they dropped from her watery eyes to the corners of her mouth. She thanked her uncle, when he had finished, and went back to her mother's. The very next morning, she and her sons left Kiev for Orienburg, a town in Siberia.

Why Orienburg? She didn't know. Several years before, she had heard from someone at work that Orienburg was a place that was very difficult to get to. It sounded perfect to her, right then.

She wrote to the Draznins:

Dear Rachel and Moshe,
We are leaving for Orienburg. Please keep it secret. I'll get in touch when we settle. If something happens to me, please take care of Vilen and Kim. Kiss you, yours, Bronya.

A week later Rachel read the letter at dinner.

"Where's Orienburg?" asked Nahum.

"In Siberia," answered Moshe. "Remember, this is a secret." And he pointed his index finger at Nahum. Moshe wasn't happy with Rachel reading this letter out loud.

"I know." Nahum looked at his parents and asked, "Was Uncle Aaron really an enemy of the people?"

"I don't think so." Rachel shook her head.

"We'll never know," said Moshe, sadly.

"All I know," added Rachel, "is that he lived by the sword and he died by the sword."

CHAPTER TEN

T he town of Dnepropetrovsk was created on the left bank of the mighty river Dnieper in 1783 by Prince Potemkin, who named it "Ekaterinoslav," in honor of his Empress and lover, Catherine the Great. The town, located some four hundred miles south of Kiev, grew slowly until the railroad connected it with Kiev, Odessa and the Donets coal basin, initiating its industrialization. Its name was changed to Dnepropetrovsk (the city of Peter on the Dnieper) in 1926, nine years after the Communist Revolution. With iron ore from Krivoy Rog, manganese from Nicopol, coal from the Donets and electricity generated by the power of the river, Dnepropetrovsk was an ideal site for the metallurgy and machine industries.

With the industrialization of the Soviet Union, the destiny of the small town changed forever. By the 1930s, several large plants had already been built, and a few more were in the process of construction. Arkady Rips, younger brother of Hershel, was Director of Production in one of the industrial plants in Dnepropetrovsk.

Arkady had left Celiba in early 1916 and gone to Kiev in search of a better future. He had clearly been the most ambitious of the Rips children, and had had no desire to stay in the *shtetl*. A friend in Celiba had had cousins in Kiev, and had arranged a place for Arkady to stay.

Arkady's host in Kiev was a math teacher at the evening engineering school, and he introduced Arkady to the idea of studying. Arkady found a construction job that occupied him from early morning until five in the afternoon, and enrolled in engineering classes at night. Five years later, he received his engineering certificate, and was sent to Dnepropetrovsk as a young engineer at a metallurgic plant that was in the final stages of construction.

Arkady was a very bright man, and grateful to the new government for his education and employment. He joined the Komsomol, an organization of young Communists, and moved to Dnepropetrovsk with pride, energy and enthusiasm. By the time Hershel knocked at his brother's door, Arkady was married, had a two-year-old daughter, had been promoted to Director of Production at his metallurgical plant and was a candidate for membership in the Communist Party.

Hershel hugged his younger brother, who was shorter and not as broad, but who otherwise looked very much like him. Both brothers had large, almond-shaped, hazel eyes, and high foreheads that extended into round, balding heads. They both had prominent jaws and small, meaty ears.

The two families stayed together for ten days, until Hershel rented a large room in a dilapidated house on the West side of the city park. The house was made of logs, boards and plywood, with small windows and a metal roof. It had four rooms and one kitchen, and each room was occupied by a different family.

The owner of the house was a plumber who, with his wife and two adolescent sons, lived in the largest room and rented out the remaining three. The plumber was a big, strong Ukrainian with a bushy, blond mustache. He always wore the same washed-out, blue muscle shirt, regardless of weather, and dark-brown, soiled, greasy pants. In the winter, he simply put on his padded winter jacket over the muscle shirt. His wife was a quiet woman with long, brown hair in two thick braids that coiled in circles on the top of her head. Both of them worked at the turbine factory.

The smallest room was rented to a bookkeeper, a tall skinny, disheveled person, and his wife, a loud, foul-mouthed woman, who screamed constantly at her husband and argued endlessly with everyone else. The third room was occupied by a schoolteacher and her eleven-year-old daughter. The teacher was a slightly-overweight woman who had taught elementary school in a small Ukrainian town, and come to Dnepropetrovsk after the accidental death of her husband. The tall, loud wife of the bookkeeper thought the teacher flirted with her ill-looking husband, and barraged her with verbal abuse almost every time they met.

The Rips family rented the final room. It had two double beds, one for Hershel and Fanny and the other for the two boys, and a wooden twin bed for Rosa. A large dining table stood in the middle of the room and a cupboard along one of the walls. Like every family in the house except for the owners, who used the kitchen, the Rips family used a kerosene primus to cook their meals and boil water right there in their own room.

The house was situated at the top of a large, undeveloped plot of land, most of which belonged to the city. It should actually have been an extension of the park, but the steep slope was constantly washed by rain, which dumped mud from the top of the little hill into the park, and so it had been left undeveloped.

A single-stall outhouse was located immediately behind the house. To avoid the morning rush and the cold, winter-night excursions to the outhouse, each family had a tin pail that was used for urine, and was emptied into the outhouse late in the morning.

Arkady helped Hershel with his job-hunt, as well. They built their search around Hershel's strength in agriculture, and, in a matter of days, found him a job as an agriculturist on a nearby collective farm. It was only about seven miles west of their rented home, on the outskirts of Dnepropetrovsk.

Every morning, Hershel rode an old, rusty bike to the farm and returned at dusk. He quickly got into the groove of his work, and loved it. He organized a sowing campaign, fostered crop-health and led the way at harvest-time. He was living off the land and toiling along with simple, hard-working people.

During the snowy days of winter, it was impossible for him to return home, and he frequently stayed on the farm for days or even weeks at a time. Fanya took care of the home, and the children went to the neighborhood school.

After about year and a half, Hershel approached the plumber, his landlord and neighbor.

"What do you think, Fedor? What if we approach the city and ask for a permit to build a new house for maybe five or six families on the vacant land?"

"What would I get out of it? There's no chance they'd let us own it. What's the point?"

"The point is we'd build a better home. Each of us would have our own new three- or four-room apartment. We'd also build outdoor storage space and indoor bathrooms."

"But I'm gonna lose my renters."

"No, you won't. You can still rent the rooms in your apartment. That's not going to change."

"Maybe you're right."

"I know I'm right. All we need is a permit. We can build it with our own hands. And the city will go for it, since they'll get three or four apartments."

It took seven months and numerous conversations with Fedor before he finally agreed to talk to the city. As Hershel had predicted, the city was receptive, and within two months they had an agreement. The agreement was actually better than Hershel had expected. The city paid Fedor a small sum of money for his old house, and then rented it to two other families.

Hershel and Fedor were obliged to build a retaining wall and proper drainage to prevent mudslides into the city park, and the city sent their own workers, two unskilled alcoholics, to help Fedor and Hershel build a new two-story apartment house.

Fedor and Hershel also built six single-room outdoor storage units, one for each apartment. Clearly, the most important and useful feature of their new digs was an indoor toilet connected with the city sewer system. This alone made the entire endeavor worthy of a huge effort. Fedor, the plumber, beamed with pride when he showed his indoor flush-toilet to his buddies from work.

All the parties kept their sides of the agreement, and, a year and a half later, the Rips family received a three-room apartment with a large balcony, on the second floor. A wide, wooden staircase led straight up from the front yard all the way to the small entry hall of their new apartment. A door to the left of the entry hall opened into a large room that served as dining room, living, room, family room and a play and study room for the kids. The balcony was off this room. From this room, one could enter the two bedrooms, straight ahead, and the kitchen, to the right. From the kitchen one could walk into the toilet-room. They finally had a real home.

Hershel continued working on the collective farm and, even though the pay was below what he could have received at an industrial plant, he was happy. Frequently, the farm had no money to pay its workers. Instead, the farm administration allowed the peasants to take home eggs, a chicken, a sack of potatoes or a cabbage. Hershel was paid in a similar way. He built a little coop in his storage shed and kept several chickens there. On Friday evenings, he would go to his shed, lock himself in and kill one of the birds for Fanya to cook the following week.

One Friday evening, as he walked into his shed, Rosa quietly tiptoed in behind him. He opened the shed and realized that he had left something at home. He left the door of the shed ajar and returned home for a brief moment. Rosa, who had always wanted to see what her father did in the shed, squeezed in and hid herself behind some sacks of potatoes.

Hershel returned with a big pot, put it on the ground, took an ax in his right hand and caught one of the birds with his left. He held the chicken by its head in his large fist, swung it around his own head and, with a quick, jerky motion, twisted its neck and dropped the chicken onto the stump in the middle of the shed. He chopped its head off with an equally quick swing of his axe. His left hand still held the chicken's head, and the headless body of the bird fell off the stump and ran around in circles, splashing blood from its neck all over the floor of the shed. Frightened, Rosa began to cry, from her dark corner behind the potatoes, "Papa! Papa! Help me! Help me!"

Poor Hershel didn't know whether he should catch the headless chicken or pull his daughter from behind the sacks of potatoes. He went for the chicken. Then the chicken's body fell to the ground, its movements reduced to a few sporadic convulsions.

"Rosa! What are you doing here, my girl?" he shouted, stuffing the chicken into the large pot he had brought.

"I. . . I came to watch you work in the shed," she answered, through her tears. She came out to Hershel, who knelt on the bloody ground and hugged her with both arms.

"Oh, that's so sweet of you, baby. Everything's fine. I just didn't feel like going to the store tonight, so I..." he couldn't find the right words, "so I...you saw what I did? I prepared a chicken for Mama to cook."

"Why did it run without its head?"

"My fault. It dropped out of my hands. It didn't run without its head. Solely my fault. Please, don't tell anyone about it. I don't want anyone else to be scared. It was just my fault."

"I won't."

And she didn't, until about three years later, almost at the end of the school year, when her older brother, Pavel, announced at the dinner table that he was going to his class party that Sunday night.

"We're going to have a dance at school," he said, proudly.

"I hope it's going to be a well-supervised event," Hershel responded.

Fanya chimed in. "Oh, these schools never supervise their students. Every time they have a party, something bad happens."

"Not every time," retorted Pavel. "Last time we held a dance, nothing happened."

"Thank God," sighed Fanya.

"Can I go with you? Please?" asked Rosa. She was a very slim, short, quick girl, no taller than five-foot-two, with a beautiful brown braid. She was aware of the attention she attracted from boys, and enjoyed it greatly. She constantly flirted with Pavel's friends, despite his stern reaction.

"Papa, can I go with him? Can I?"

Pavel looked down at his plate, avoiding eye contact with Rosa and his father. He didn't want to take her, but also didn't want to voice a contradiction or to get into a confrontation. He just hoped that his father wouldn't let her go to the dance.

Hershel was firm. "No, Rosa. You can't go. This is a party for big kids. Wait until your class has a dance, in a year or two."

"I know everyone in Pavel's class!" Rosa argued. "They are all Pavel's friends. They come to our house. I know them; you know them. Why can't I go?"

"Because I said so." Hershel was extremely firm. "You are not going to the dance with the older boys. End of story."

Rosa jumped from her chair and ran to the children's bedroom. At the door, she stopped, turned back and screamed, through her tears, "If you don't let me go to the dance, I'll tell everybody, I'll tell everybody..." she swallowed her tears.

"What are you going to tell everybody?" asked Hershel, in surprise.

Pavel, Yakov and Fanya lifted their eyes from the table and stared at Rosa. After a few seconds of complete silence, Rosa fired back, "I'll tell everybody that you kill chickens in the shed!" She dived into her room and slammed the door.

Pavel choked on his food and Fanya looked fearfully at her husband who remained stern for a moment, then smiled widely and silently shook his head, remembering a headless chicken and his frightened daughter in the dark shed,

The next Sunday, Pavel and Rosa went to the dance at his school. It was Rosa's first dance, but she felt as if it was nothing new. She loved to dance, and she didn't skip a beat at the party.

One after another, Pavel's friends invited his younger sister to dance. She was the shortest girl at the party, and the young teenage boys felt tall and strong next to her, as they did not with the much taller girls of their own class.

"I never knew you had such a cute sister," said one of Pavel's friends to him, as they watched her dance.

"What do you mean you never knew? You've seen her in my house a million times!"

"She looked different in your house."

"How different?"

"Just different. Not as cute."

The dance ended at nine o'clock. Pavel, Rosa and several of their friends walked home in a large group, taking a shortcut through the park. As they approached the little hill that separated the park from their yard, they saw Yakov sitting on top of the retaining wall, crying and smearing blood from his nose and lips all over his dirty face. He held two of his baby teeth in his right hand.

"Who did it?" shouted Pavel. "Who beat you up?"

Yakov didn't answer, but, sobbing, pointed at a group of older boys smoking next to the drinking fountain. Pavel ran to them.

"Who hit my brother?" he screamed at them. "Who did it?"

The oldest boy, who was probably eighteen at the time, exhaled rings of smoke and said, "I did. I drew blood from his Jewish nose. So what?"

"Why did you beat him up? What did he do to you? "

The boy shrugged his shoulders. "I can beat you up, too, Jew boy, if you don't get lost." He exhaled another ring, this time straight into Pavel's face, while his friends giggled.

Pavel measured the kid with his eyes. The boy was obviously older, taller and stronger than he, so he certainly couldn't beat him with his fists. That was clear to both groups of kids, Pavel's friends and the older smokers. Pavel's hand went into his pants pocket, and he pulled out a small penknife that he had bought just a couple of days before, and carried with him to show to his friends. In a split second, he opened the knife and stabbed it into the big boy's chest, very close to his left shoulder. The blade was short, no more than an inch and a half long, and it was somewhat dull, so it inflicted pain as it penetrated the skin and muscles.

Pavel drew the knife back and raised his hand for a second strike. The other boy moaned with pain, dropped his cigarette and grabbed his chest. When he took his hand from the wound, there was blood on his palm. Overcome by the ferocity of Pavel's attack and by his own fear of blood, he fainted.

Everyone stood frozen until the big boy regained consciousness. He sat up on the ground, holding his shoulder, and began to cry. Pavel turned and ran home, his friends behind him. They climbed over the retaining wall, dirtying their pants and dresses in the soil, picked up Yakov, who was still sobbing there, and ran across the yard and up the stairs to Pavel's apartment.

The children piled into Pavel's apartment, talking and shouting all at once, pouring out the story of the night. "They're big boys! They beat up Yakov! Knocked his teeth out! He hit him with a penknife!"

Hershel waved his hand, "Wow! Stop it. Only one of you." He suddenly saw his daughter among the kids. "Rosa, tell me what happened."

"Here," answered Rosa, and she pulled Yakov from the back of the group, "look at him, Papa."

Dirt and blood smeared all over his frightened face, Yakov began crying again, not so much from the pain as from humiliation. Then he extended his hand and opened his fist. On his palm there were two yellowish baby teeth, tinted with blood.

"We found him crying at the edge of the park," said Rosa, and Fanya grabbed the sobbing Yakov and pulled him to the kitchen to wash his face and hands. "A group of big boys was nearby, and one of them said that he had beaten up Yakov. He called him a 'little Jew boy.' This boy was tall and much older than us."

Hershel's teeth clenched, tightening the muscles over his temples. He remained silent.

"This kid challenged Pavel to defend Yakov," continued Rosa.

Only now did Hershel's eyes turn to Pavel. Pavel stood by the dining table, listening to Rosa, but kept his gaze firmly on his father's face.

"Pavel couldn't really beat him. He pulled his small penknife and stabbed the boy in the shoulder." She stopped her tirade.

"Is that it?" asked Hershel, after a short pause.

"That's it," said Rosa.

Hershel rose from his chair, went to Pavel, and hugged him. "You did the right thing, son, defending your brother. But you should use your fists, not a knife. A knife can only bring you trouble. I want you to be strong and fight for your family. This is good. Just don't use knives; instead, use your hands and your brain.

"What happened then?" he asked, when the tension had subsided.

Yakov came from the kitchen with a smile that revealed a toothless mouth surrounded by swollen lips.

"Nothing happened," said Pavel. "We left while he was crying. Can't be anything serious; the knife is very small." He pulled his penknife from the pocket and showed it to his father.

"I hope you're right," said Hershel, shaking his head. "Well, children, it's time to go home," he added, gesturing to Pavel's friends to leave.

When they had left, Hershel locked the door and checked all the windows. "Do you think any of those kids know you?"

"I don't think so," said Pavel. "I didn't recognize any of them."

He was probably right. No one came to their apartment, and there was no sign of reprisal, either that night or during the next week. Pavel stopped thinking about the incident, but Hershel was still on guard until, one evening, while he was locking the front door, he said aloud, "Sometimes, one is just lucky."

In the fall of 1939, Pavel's school announced a competition for the best-built model ship. The winner, the school said, would be sent to the sailing class at the Dnepropetrovsk boat station. For a couple of years Pavel had been infatuated with the boats and steamers sailing up and down the Dnieper River. He knew all the local merchant ships and could spend hours watching riverboats and their crews from the riverbank.

The Sunday after the competition was announced, he went to the library and found a picture of a Russian battleship. As carefully as he possibly could, he copied the picture onto a blank sheet of paper. He took his drawing home and put it on the dining-table in front of Hershel.

"We have a competition in school for the best model boat," he explained, "and I want to try my hand at it. I want to build this battleship."

"It's not going to be too easy," Hershel warned him. "It's a sophisticated boat you have here."

"May I try?"

Hershel encouraged him. "You certainly may. However it comes out, it's worth trying."

The next day, Hershel brought home a large chunk of a pine tree trunk and a couple of smaller chunks of branches. "I brought you some wood so you can start on your model," he told Pavel. "I left it in the shed, where my tools are.

You're welcome to use whatever we have. Just be careful not to hurt yourself."

His workbench didn't offer a great variety of tools—a hammer, a chisel, some sandpaper and a short, sharp saw with a wooden handle. Pavel worked slowly, planning and measuring before every cut. He remembered well an old Russian saying his father had told him on many occasions, "Measure seven times, and cut only once," and he adhered to its wisdom.

Every day, after classes, Pavel worked in the shed with the door open wide to let daylight into the dark room. He sat on a low step-stool in front of a large block of oak that was stained with chicken blood and covered with sawdust, which Hershel used to split wood for their stove and to cut off chicken heads.

Children who played in the yard and who, from time to time, crowded at the open door of the shed, were the only ones to witness his slow progress. Soon the shape of a battleship began emerging from his large log. When the hull of the battleship was finished, he carried it, carefully and proudly, to the apartment. He held it under his right arm, supporting it from below with his left hand. The body of the vessel was two feet long, about ten inches wide and ten inches tall. The hull widened gently from keel to deck, as it should, and from the pointed bow to the broad stern.

At home, he placed his ship at the foot of his bed, and returned to the shed to cut and build masts, additional decks, funnels, turrets, a rudder, radio antennas, a compass and a captain's bridge that would eventually be glued to the main deck. Cutting out small pieces proved even more difficult than shaping the hull from the log. Slowly, he carved out and stacked three decks, one on top of the other, four masts, two funnels, two radio antennas and ten turrets, five on each side of the hull . He painted each individual part navy gray, added black, green and several red lines, and his model looked like a true battleship.

About ten weeks before he had to turn it in to the competition committee, Rosa broke the mainmast and the compass bridge. She didn't do it on purpose; it was an accident. It happened during a routine pillow fight with her brother, Yakov.

All three kids slept in one room, with two beds along the left-hand wall of the bedroom and the third along the opposite wall. A small desk in front of the window separated the two beds that were away from the bedroom door, and a large, pine wardrobe stood along the right-hand wall, between the door and the single bed. This single bed behind the wardrobe belonged to Yakov, the youngest of the three children. Pavel slept in the bed immediately across from Yakov, and Rosa slept in the bed closest to the door. The model of the battleship now stood on a chair located between the wooden foot of Pavel's bed and the bronze-colored headrest of Rosa's.

By now, Rosa was fourteen years old, but she didn't have the privacy of a bedroom of her own. The boys would undress and jump under the blankets in their boxers, paying no attention to their sister's presence, but Rosa began feeling uncomfortable changing into her nightgown when they were watching. She asked them to face the wall, and Pavel always did this obediently. Yakov, in contrast, did everything he could to peek at her. Usually, he pretended to be asleep, flat on his back with his eyelids trembling above the narrow slits through which he followed every move of his sister. When she discovered his strategy, she began beating him with a pillow until he turned toward the wall, and they repeated this routine every night.

Lately, he had devised a new trick in order to watch her change. He would turn toward the wall for a couple of minutes, and then suddenly jump to his feet and run past her out of the room, screaming that he was going to get a drink because he was awfully thirsty, or that he wanted to go to the bathroom, because he "just couldn't hold it." She would hit him with a pillow as he passed, but that didn't seem to be a deterrent.

The evening the battleship was broken, he pulled his usual trick. "I'm so thirsty!" he shouted, running past Rosa. She was standing at the head of her bed, as she had just slipped into her nightgown. She grabbed her pillow and swung it at her brother. He extended his arm to protect his face, and the pillow bounced off his elbow and sprang back toward Rosa, its corner hitting her in the eye.

Screaming, "Ouch!" she let pillow go and covered her face with both palms. Momentum took the pillow straight into the battleship, breaking the mast and the compass bridge.

The snap of the mast froze Yakov in his tracks and overcame Rosa's pain. Pavel, who was lying in his bed facing the wall, rose slowly toward the foot of his bed. They all looked at the chair where the battleship lay. Even though the model was completely covered by the pillow, they knew something was broken. Pavel leaned over the foot of his bed and lifted the pillow.

"Ah!" came out of Rosa's mouth.

The mainmast, broken in its lower third, fell onto the floor. The compass bridge was broken in several places, but was still attached to the upper deck.

"You, bastards!" yelled Pavel, and he tossed the pillow in Rosa's direction. "Look what you did!"

His scream propelled Yakov out of the room, announcing to the entire house, "Rosa broke Pavel's battleship! Papa, come and see it! She broke Pavel's ship!"

Rosa caught the pillow and fell on her bed, face in the pillow, crying, " I didn't mean to! I didn't want to!"

When Hershel and Fanya entered the room, Pavel was sitting on the floor next to his broken model, his face in his palms, ready to cry from frustration and despair.

"Look, look what your favorite daughter did to my model," he said. "A week before the competition."

Hershel looked at the model and said, "Things happen. I'm sure she didn't mean to break it. I'll help you fix it. We have time."

"I don't want your help. I wanted to build it by myself. It's my model."

"You did. You built it all by yourself. No one helped you. I'm saying the part Rosa broke, she and I will rebuild. Isn't that right, Rosa?" He put his large hand on the head of his crying daughter.

Rosa mumbled something unintelligible through the tears, not really knowing how she could help.

"You boys go back to sleep while Rosa and I get to work," said Hershel, in the same soft, quiet voice. "Get dressed, Rosa. Let's go and do it."

It was ten-thirty at night when Hershel and Rosa left the house.

"Where are we going?"

"To work. We have to rebuild the mast, you know."

"But you are walking to the park!" said Rosa, with surprise in her voice.

"Oh, we'll just take a little turn, to vent our feelings, and be back." He took her hand in his and they walked in silence through the park. He led her to the ice cream stand that, surprisingly, was still open on this cool autumn night. "Ice cream?" he asked, with a smile.

"Yes!" she answered happily, and she squeezed his large hand.

"What about you?" she asked a minute later, when she was holding a cup full of vanilla ice cream.

"No, thank you. I have a sore throat," he said. "I don't want anything cold."

"Papa, I wanted to tell you what happened."

"No, no, don't tell me anything. I know you didn't mean to break it. How could you wish to ruin your brother's work? I know you didn't."

"It was Yakov who kept peeking at me while I was changing. I hit him with my pillow as he ran by me, and the pillow flew into the battleship. I'm so angry with him!"

"I am sure he won't do it after tonight. It's a good lesson for him. But you, you shouldn't be angry with him. After all, he is your brother, and you can't be angry with your family. We are together, no matter what happens. You see, Rosa, you can choose your friends, you can choose your husband, but you can't choose your parents and your brothers. You can only lose them, if you become too angry, and that would be a tragedy. Never be angry with your family."

Rosa finished her ice cream as they approached the house.

"You go right into your bed," said Hershel, and he kissed her forehead. "I'll stop at the shed to pick up some wood for the mast."

"I thought I would be helping you," said Rosa with, hesitantly.

"You already have. You got rid of your frustration and anger. It's a great help for me to know you are no longer angry with your brother."

When the children woke up the next morning, they found the new mast and captain's bridge on the dining table in the main room. Hershel had already left for work, leaving a short note under the mast.

"Pavel, I hope the replacement parts are to your liking. You might paint them, when you return from school. I can help you glue them in tomorrow, if you need my help. By the way, Rosa was of great help last night. I want you to thank her. Love you all, Papa."

Pavel read the note aloud, looked critically at his sister and younger brother and carefully carried the new parts to their room. He painted them that afternoon, and glued them to the battleship the next day. The battle ship looked perfect, as if nothing had happened.

The next Monday, Pavel covered his model very carefully with newspapers and carried it to school, straight to the office of the principal. Four other kids brought in their models, as well. All the models were placed on the principal's desk.

"Oh, my!" gasped the principal when Pavel slowly unwrapped his model. "This is a beauty!"

Pavel's model was indeed a distinct one. Two of others were single-sail boats made from cardboard and *papier-maché*, and the other two were simple rowboats, each with a single pair of oars glued to their sides.

"I will take these models to competition headquarters, later today," said the principal. "I want you to help me carry them. It's in the Palace of Pioneers, about ten block away."

Early that afternoon, the principal, several teachers and the five participants marched to the Palace of Pioneers. Each boy carried his own model, and a crowd of supporters and friends swarmed around them. In the palace, a large room was devoted to the display, with each model standing on its individual table, covered with a red cloth. A card bearing the name of each maker was prepared by the secretary of the judging committee and placed next to the model.

"The decision will be made in two weeks," said the principal, as they walked back to school, "and the winner will be announced one week before the winter break."

The judging committee was a large one, made up of the principals of all the schools in Dnepropetrovsk schools and members of the local Communist Party. The head of the city school district was the chairman. He and his entourage walked slowly from one display to another, truly enjoying the show. Even the least successful models had been made with great care and above average skill. Perhaps half a dozen models stood out from the rest, and the members of the judging committee took written notes.

Then they came to Pavel's battleship. The Committee chairman stopped in front of it and gasped. There was total silence as the members at the back tried to peer at the model over the shoulders of those in front. Two of them picked up the small table upon which the model lay, and pulled it into the open space in the middle of the room. The committee assembled around it, forming a tight circle. A good five minutes passed before the chairman said, "This might be the winner." He read out the name of the student who had made it. "Pavel Rips. Whose school is he from?"

"He is from mine," answered Pavel's principal, with a broad smile on his elongated face, and he proudly raised his hand.

"Congratulations!" said the chairman. "Let's see what else is here." And he led the procession toward the remaining models.

The group stopped briefly in front of several other models and, at the end of the tour, each of the committee members selected and ranked the five best. Four members of the counting subcommittee went with the chairman to a small office to count the votes.

"We have a clear winner," announced the chairman to the small group of vote-counters. "Pavel Rips has received all the first-place votes. Stepan Fomichenko has come second, Ivan Gulko third, Vladimir Konev fourth and Vitaly Voronov fifth." He looked around, slowly moving his gaze from one face to another.

The members sat silent, uneasy under the gaze of the chairman.

"Funny sounding name, 'Rips,'" said one of them, quietly.

"Jewish?" asked someone else.

"He is Jewish," said the principal of Pavel's school, who was a member of the committee.

The members looked at one another, trying to guess whether any of them might be Jewish.

"It shouldn't matter," said Pavel's principal. "His model's clearly better than anyone else's."

Now everyone was looking at the chairman.

"It is much better," he said, with a sigh. "No doubt about it. But how come we don't have a Ukrainian kid who can win a competition in the Ukrainian city of Dnepropetrovsk?"

"I believe it would be an important boost for Ukrainian children's morale if a Ukrainian kid won," said another member.

"We can't take it away from him. Just look at his workmanship! Look at this beauty!" exclaimed the principal of Pavel's school.

"If it were only a question of workmanship, I would agree with you. But it is a much greater issue that we have at hand. And beauty, after all, is not a proletarian value," said the chairman. "We should see this competition as beyond parochial boundaries."

"I think it's the prerogative of this committee to adjust the vote as needed for the greater success of the competition. I propose to change the winning vote administratively in favor of Stepan Fomichenko," said another member, forcefully.

"I agree," said the chairman. "Who is in favor of this administrative adjustment?"

Everyone raised his or her hand, and all eyes turned to Pavel's principal. He blushed and timidly raised his hand halfway.

"It's unanimous," announced the Chairman. "The Committee recommends accepting the model by Stepan Fomichenko as winner of the competition."

"I think Rips will be very happy with second place," the chairman summed up, after the counting committee had unanimously supported the change. "He did a good job, after all."

When they announced the names of the winners to the full Committee, one of the principals said to another, "Wow! I was sure the battleship model would win. With the secret ballot, you never know what can happen."

The next day, the results of the competition were announced at all Dnepropetrovsk schools. It was also announced that the models would be displayed for the public for the entire next week. Pavel was ecstatic. He was thrilled to win second place. It was the happiest day of his life. He could hardly wait to tell his father, and take him to the Palace of Pioneers to see the models.

They went the next Saturday. All the way to the Palace, Pavel was the happiest boy alive. His entire family marched with him to the drumbeat of his exaltation and jubilation. Only when they stood in front of the winning model, elevated a little over the second-prize winner, Pavel's battleship, did they understand that he had been robbed.

"I can't believe I didn't win first prize," mumbled Pavel. "I can't believe his model is better than mine."

"It isn't," said Rosa. "Yours is much better."

"Hey, hey, children," said Hershel, putting his arm around Pavel's shoulders. "You should be proud of winning second prize; this is an incredible achievement. Doesn't matter who won first."

"But..." There was a lump in Pavel's throat.

"I know, I know, yours looks so much better. You never know with these committees. Let's be happy with what you have."

Pavel could hardly keep back his tears, as they walked out of the building. At the door, they bumped into the school principal.

"How come, how come I didn't win?" asked Pavel, trembling.

"I can't see how his model could lose," added Hershel.

"His model didn't," answered the principal, after a short pause. "His name did."

CHAPTER ELEVEN

On June 12, 1937, Moshe came home from work in a somber mood. He pulled a newspaper from the pocket of his jacket and laid it on the dining table in front of Rachel.

"Who could have thought it?" He shook his head. "Our best generals have turned out to be capitalist spies."

Rachel opened the paper. Immediately under the paper's name, "*Pravda*" ("The Truth"), the main headline announced, in large black letters, "Marshal Tukhachevsky and seven Commanders have confessed to spying for Capitalist governments."

"Oh, my!" she gasped, looking at the headline, and began reading.

Nahum jumped from his chair and bent over his mother's shoulder, so he could read the article, as well.

"Look! Look!" he shouted. "Bronya's uncle, Commander Yakir, is one of them!"

"What terrible news! I can't believe it," said Rachel, as she finished reading the list of names of the confessed spies. "Tukhachevsky, Yakir, Uborevich, Eideman, Kork, Putna, Feldman and Primakov."

"You'd better believe it; they confessed," said Moshe, and he looked at his son suspiciously.

"They were arrested on May 26," said Nahum, continuing to read. "All of them confessed except Yakir, who denied his involvement even under the heavy weight of indisputable evidence obtained from other conspirators. The traitors were sentenced to death, and the execution was carried out on June 11, 1937."

Nahum returned to his chair. No one spoke until Moshe repeated, "Who could have thought?"

Nahum looked at his parents. They turned their eyes away. "How can this be?" he asked. "Why would these men become traitors? It makes no sense. It's like what happened with Uncle Aaron. He couldn't have been a spy!"

"They've confessed!" said Moshe, slamming his palm against the table. "Don't ask stupid questions! Innocent people are not executed!"

They stared into each other's eyes.

"Wait a minute! Wait a minute!" interjected Rachel. "You both might be right. We don't know what these people did. Sounds awfully strange that they were spies, but there are so many enemies of the Soviet Union. We just don't know, and we just have to trust our government, Nahum."

"And I don't want any discussion on this subject, anywhere and with anyone. It's dangerous even to think about it," said Moshe.

"Papa is right, Nahum. One day we will find out who are our friends and who our enemies, but we shouldn't talk about this," said Rachel, ending the discussion.

Nahum was now fourteen years old. He sensed a tremendous disconnect between the demagoguery of official, Party-controlled life, and the lives of ordinary people like his Uncle Aaron, and even folk like his parents. People seemed to be frightened, closed to one another and in a constant state of anxiety. He thought of this often and, on more than one occasion, wished he could discuss his observations with his parents. But he didn't. He understood that his father would not deviate from the Party line, and his mother would use every means in her power to avoid substantive discussion, switching instead to family, health and a successful future.

On the afternoon of August 21 of the same year, Luba Olshansky arrived from Kiev. She was almost seventeen years old and tall, like her mother, with dark hair and a large forehead exactly like the one that distinguished the face of her father, Nahum. She arrived with two bulging, and probably very heavy, suitcases.

She called Moshe the day before her arrival and asked him to meet her at the railway station. Moshe was so surprised and even frightened by her sudden call to his work that he didn't ask her why she was coming. She said that she would explain everything upon arrival.

Moshe sensed that something was wrong, as he had already heard that his former bosses, the first and the second men in the Ukrainian hierarchy had been arrested for presumed treason. Both, of them, Comrades Kossior and Postyshev, were old Communists and leaders of the Ukrainian Communist Party, and their arrests had been an incredible shock to everyone in Ukraine. Moshe guessed that something might have happened to his friend, Nahum Olshansky, as well, but he didn't ask a single question over the phone.

That evening, he was very nervous at the dinner table and, when Nahum left the room to return to his homework at the desk in their bedroom, Moshe told Rachel, in lowered tones, "Luba Olshansky called me today at work and said she'd be here tomorrow. I guess the Olshanskys are in trouble."

"I'm not surprised," said Rachel, solemnly. "After they took Kossior and

Postyshev, one can expect anything." Softly, she added, lifting her eyes to the ceiling, "God knows how happy I am we didn't move with them to Kiev."

Moshe met Luba at the station, and helped her with her heavy suitcases. They took a tram to the corner of Chernishevskaya and Basseinaya streets, and walked the quarter-block to the Draznin's apartment house. Moshe dragged the suitcases, one by one, to the fourth floor. Even with Luba pushing the suitcases from behind, he had to stop at every floor for a breather.

Rachel put their meal on the table, and sat across from Luba. Moshe was at the head of the table, looking suspiciously at his son, who had pulled his chair over to sit next to Luba. Grandma Haya sat in a corner of the room.

"I don't want to eat, Aunt Rachel," said Luba. "I'm not hungry at all."

"I know, I know. Try just a few bites. You look so exhausted. I'm sure you haven't eaten for a quite a while."

"You're right, I haven't, but I'm still not hungry. Can't even think of food."

"Please..."

Luba took a few spoonfuls of chicken noodle soup, slurping in the long white noodles.

Two minutes later, she said, "Thank you," and put her spoon next to her plate.

"Nahum, don't you need to do your homework?" asked Moshe, anxiously.

"No, I don't. It's all done."

"What happened?" asked Moshe, ignoring his son's predictable answer. "Tell us what's going on."

Luba put her both elbows on the table and crossed her arms in front of her plate. She looked calmly at Moshe and then at Rachel, and said, "A week ago yesterday, they came at one o'clock in the morning, knocking loudly at the door. We woke up scared. Papa went to open the door. They were screaming, 'Olshansky! Olshansky! Open the door!' There were probably a dozen of them. All in civilian clothes.

"One of them, a tall, balding man with red eyes and a bulging belly, pulled out his documents, showed them to Papa and told him to dress and go with them. He said, 'Citizen Olshansky, you are under arrest.' Papa didn't say a word, but Mama kept whispering to me that everything would be fine, that this was just a mistake and that they'd let Papa go in no time, probably the very next morning. 'He's such a devoted Communist,' she kept telling me.

"It was the first time I ever saw Papa cry. When he hugged us to say goodbye, tears were all over his cheeks, pouring into the corners of his mouth and dripping off his chin. I felt his tears on my face the whole night.

"Within fifteen minutes, they were gone, and Papa was gone with them. He didn't come home the next morning, as Mama had said he would, even though we waited all day.

"We had just gone to bed at midnight, when they knocked at the door again. This time there were just six of them. The tall man with red eyes walked in first.

"'Citizen Olshansky,' he said, and my heart sank. I was so afraid they would take Mama away. She was also scared speechless, and she hugged me tight. 'We have an order,' he said, 'to confiscate your furniture. It will be taken in for extensive search. We will inform you when you can claim it back.'

"And he waved to his men, who began carrying out our furniture, piece by piece, and loading it onto a truck parked in the alley. They left us my metal bed and our kitchen table. It was so bizarre, I couldn't understand what they could possibly be looking for in our furniture. They threw our clothes on the floor, put all our dishes in the corner of the main room, breaking half of them, and left. The whole episode took about two hours.

"Mama and I cried together in my bed. We didn't sleep all night. Just cuddled in my bed and cried.

"Next morning, Mama seemed to regain some energy. She said, 'I can't believe they needed our furniture. I'll go to the NKVD and find out. It simply cannot be true. I know a couple of people there; I'm certain they will help. You stay home and wait for me. I'll be right back.'

"I didn't want to stay alone in an empty, cold-looking apartment. I begged her to take me with her. 'What if it takes longer?' I said. 'I don't want to be here alone. I'm scared, Mama. Please, can I go with you?'

"She looked at me with such determination and force in her eyes, and said, 'Fine, we'll go together.'

"We walked in silence for about thirty minutes. The outside guard let us into the building. In the vestibule, she said to a soldier with a long rifle, 'I'm Maria Olshansky, here's my passport, and we are here to see Comrade Gavrilov.'

"He seemed to know Comrade Gavrilov, as he asked her to sign her name in the book and said, 'Second floor, to your left.'

"We found his office right away. He was there alone, working at his desk. He got up, greeted Mama with a handshake, and asked us to sit down.

"'What can I do for you, Maria?' he asked, when he returned to his chair.

"Suddenly Mama began crying. He remained silent, waiting for her to start. She calmed down a bit, dried her tears with her handkerchief, and said, 'Nahum was arrested two nights ago. But last night they came again, and removed all our furniture. I think it's a mistake. I can't believe the NKVD needs our furniture. There was a tall man, bald and with protruding belly; he seemed to be in charge.'

"'Do you know his name? Did you see his identification?' asked Comrade

Gavrilov.

"'No. He showed his documents to Nahum, the night they took him. I don't know his name.'

"'How did you know he was from the NKVD?'

"'He told us that the first night. I remember it well.'

"For a minute, we all remained silent; only Mama occasionally sniffing and drying the tears off her nose.

"Comrade Gavrilov rose from his chair and said, 'You know, Maria, I don't know what to say. Why don't you walk around the building, wander about the hallways and, if you see him, just come back and tell me. Your daughter can wait here. I simply don't recognize anyone from your description. Tall and bald and a bulging belly... Don't know.'

"Mama nodded agreeably, stood up, patted my shoulder and left the room. Comrade Gavrilov returned to his desk, waved to me and got back to his papers. I don't know how much time passed. It seemed to be a good half-hour. I was already bored and tired of waiting when Mama's scream filled the room.

"'Here he is! Here he is! I recognize him! It's him!' Her voice was coming from somewhere very close to Gavrilov's office, almost next door. I wanted to get up and run to her, but Gavrilov gestured to me to stay, and ran out of the room. I heard voices and Mama's cry, and then silence, complete silence, until Comrade Gavrilov returned.

"'Quickly,' he said, and he grabbed my arm, 'Let's go. Let's get out of here.' He pulled me out of his office, down the stairs and out of the NKVD building.

"I ran next to him, mumbling, 'Where's my mama? Where's my mama?'

"In the street, bent over, putting his face almost to next mine, he whispered, 'Your mama's been arrested, like your father. Both of them are English agents. Your mama was spying for your papa. She just confessed. She will not be going home any time soon. If you are smart, go away and stay with relatives.'

"He didn't wait for my answer; just gave me a light push on my shoulder, and went back inside the building.

"That was it, Aunt Rachel, that was it. I don't know where my mama is. I don't know what to do. We have no family in Kiev. I was afraid to go to anyone else. I came to you. Do you think they'll let my parents out? Uncle Misha? What do you think?" She called Moshe by his Russified name, Misha, and reached out to touch his hand.

He was very pale, and he sat staring at his fingers, which he had squeezed into fists. Rachel was crying. She pulled a handkerchief from the left sleeve of her dress and buried her face in it. Nahum was afraid to move.

"What am I going to do, Uncle Misha?" repeated Luba.

"Do you still have to go to school?" asked Moshe.

"No, I have just graduated. I wanted to become a teacher," she answered softly. Suddenly, as if realizing that her dreams had just been shattered, she burst into tears.

Rachel ran around the table to her. She knelt next to Luba and hugged her. "Don't. Don't; don't cry, Luba. We'll come up with a reasonable plan."

"I want my mama. I want my papa back with me. Why? Why did they take them away? What did they do?" cried Luba, loudly.

"Luba, Luba, my love, don't cry. Don't ask these questions. They might come back. They are wonderful people, your parents. We'll figure out what to do."

Rachel kissed Luba's tearful face and wet hand, trying hopelessly to calm her down.

Luba stayed with the Draznins for two weeks. At first, they put a small mattress on the floor next to Nahum's bed, and she slept there for two nights, until David Slavutsky brought a narrow, rollaway bed. David also found a job for her as a receptionist at a dental clinic.

Moshe introduced her to the dean of the teaching college, whom he knew from his days in the Party Central Committee, and she signed up for evening classes there. The college had dormitory, and she moved in, sharing a room with seven other girls.

While she stayed with the Draznins, she helped with household chores and spent some time with Nahum in the park named after the famous Ukrainian poet, Taras Shevchenko, and at the zoo. At night, now that they shared a room, they talked.

"Luba," Nahum asked one night, as they lay in the dark in their beds, "do you think your parents were arrested because they were Jewish?"

"I don't think so," said Luba. "Look, Comrade Kossior and Comrade Postyshev were not Jewish."

"I know," interrupted Nahum. "And Marshal Tukhachevsky was not, and many others, but I still wonder."

"We are a little bit different," agreed Luba, "but I don't believe they singled us out."

"Yep, you're right. But tell me, how come so many leading Communists turned out to be enemies and spies?"

"Who told you they are spies?"

"They were arrested for spying. Do you think they are all innocent?" Nahum sat up in his bed, and added his father's strongest argument. "And they all confessed."

"I don't know about all of them, but my parents are no spies," said Luba, forcefully. "I don't believed they confessed to something they didn't do."

"That's why it's so weird. How can this be? And you know what else is strange?"

"What?"

"You can't ask anyone. It's as if everyone is afraid. Like my papa. He won't talk to me about these arrests, at all. He thinks if I were to talk to anyone about it, he would get arrested."

"He might be right. Look what happened to my mama."

"I also sense that he is. That's why I don't talk to anyone; just you. You see, his brother, Aaron, was arrested and executed as an enemy of people, and I don't believe he was one. Then Commander Yakir, an uncle of Aaron's wife, Bronya. He couldn't have been a spy; no way! Then Comrades Kossior and Postyshev, and now your parents."

"My parents have not been executed!" Luba hushed him.

"Yes, yes, I know, but they were arrested as spies! It just doesn't fit."

"I hope the situation will soon clear up, and my parents will return home. Someone must be making a lot of mistakes."

"That's what my mother says," said Nahum. "I hope she's right."

On September 1, Nahum went back to school and Luba moved into the college dormitory.

For Nahum, the school year began uneventfully. There were two new students in his class, and everyone from the previous year had returned to school. It was their seventh year in school, the last year of mandatory education. Nahum knew that the next year would be different. Many of his classmates would go to trade schools or join the workforce, and some of the young workers might switch to evening school; for others, education would end.

Of all his subjects, Nahum particularly liked Algebra. He loved solving problems and equations; "X equals this" and "Y equals that." His math teacher, Maxim Petrovich Perikatipolye, noticed his interest in math almost instantly, and began giving him extra homework, additional problems and more equations.

Nahum accepted the challenge eagerly. Some nights, he would sit at his desk at home until one or two in the morning and, with rare exceptions, solve all his math assignments.

Maxim Petrovich was a large, imposing man with a huge tuft of untidy gray hair and an equally gray, long, bushy mustache. He was exceptionally strict with his students, and very stingy with good grades.

"God knows everything there is to know in math," he used to repeat, in his rich deep voice, after every test, "and only He can get an 'A' on a test. I know

math very well, and only I can get a 'B.' The best of you can only have 'Cs.'"
And he graded accordingly.

Nahum received "C+" consistently, as the best student in the class. Some
time in November, however, he was stunned to see a "B" on a test he had got
back. A short note under the large "B" said, "It's only fair that you get a 'B.'
You haven't made a single mistake on your tests from the beginning of the
year." Nahum was elated.

One day, a week later, Maxim Petrovich didn't come to school. The school
principal, who had been a math teacher in the past, came in to substitute.

"Where is Maxim Petrovich?" asked one of the students.

"He is no longer working here. That's all you need to know," was the brief
answer. "Your new math teacher will be here next Monday."

The boy with whom Nahum shared a desk leaned toward him and whispered, "He has probably been arrested."

Nahum felt sick. He didn't know what to think. He had heard from boys at
school that people were being arrested overnight, but, except for his Uncle
Aaron and Nahum Olshansky, he did not know of anyone, personally. Besides, Aaron had been arrested in Leningrad and Nahum Olshansky in Kiev; it
was happening elsewhere, and not just in his class.

"My algebra teacher, Maxim Petrovich, didn't come in today," he said to
his parents. "The principal said he is no longer with the school, and the boys
said he had been arrested."

"Nahum, dear, don't ask any questions at school!" pleaded Rachel.

"I don't; I'm just asking you."

"It's possible he was arrested," said Moshe. "Some people are being arrested overnight. Just mind your own business, and you know what that is—to
study. That's all. There's nothing we can do about this."

The same night, the Draznins were awakened by a knock at the door. They
all piled into the little hallway, and a pale Moshe opened the door.

There stood the janitor of their apartment complex. Over his pajamas, he
wore dirty trousers and a jacket. The smell of alcohol filled the hallway when
he spoke.

"Comrade Draznin, we need you as a citizen witness, down on the third
floor."

"Yep, certainly; I'm coming," said Moshe, with a sigh of relief. He almost
ran back into his room to change.

"Pilmans'," whispered the janitor to Rachel, and waved his arms.

Moshe went downstairs with the janitor, only one floor down, and Nahum
heard a loud knocking and a man's voice, shouting, "Citizen Pilman! Open
the door!"

Moshe returned in about twenty minutes. He went straight to bed. Until he fell asleep, Nahum could hear the baritone sobbing of his father and the soft crying of his mother.

From that night on, before going to bed, Moshe would prepare a little package, a toothbrush and a pair of underwear, and leave it on the chair in the hallway, just in case they came to take him away.

Three days later, Nahum ran into Arkady Pilman as they were walking home from school. Arkady, who was one of the most popular boys in school, never walked alone. He was always in the middle of a group, laughing, screaming, joking and clowning. This time, he was walking alone. Nahum walked just a few steps behind, silently but keeping pace. He thought Arkady noticed him, but he didn't turn back and didn't say a word.

On the stairway, as they began negotiating the stairs, Arkady to the third and Nahum to the fourth floor, Nahum said, "Arkady, not everyone who is arrested is an enemy."

Arkady stopped suddenly and barked back, "How do you know? Who told you he was arrested? Oh, yeah! I remember, your papa came to watch it. It's not your damn business to know what's going on in our house! Do you understand? Not your business!"

"I'm sorry. I thought I was still your friend."

"There are no friends here. None! And I don't want to have friends. I'm all alone!"

Nahum shrugged his shoulders, "As you wish."

They continued climbing the stairs. On the third floor, Arkady pulled out his key, opened the door, walked inside and slammed the door behind him.

Nahum climbed the two more flights, upset with himself for initiating the conversation. His parents had told him repeatedly not to speak about these arrests with anyone; literally no one. And he had just broken his promise. Besides, what good had it done? None. Arkady had just got mad, and rightly so. *I shouldn't have started it*, thought Nahum. *I'll never do it again.*

In May of 1938, another loud knock at the door woke Nahum and his family at two in the morning. Three people in civilian clothes, plus the janitor and a neighbor from the first floor, were at the door.

"Citizen Draznin," said one of the men, "you are under arrest."

Rachel cried silently as Moshe dressed equally silently, but with tears in his eyes. He picked up his little package of toothbrush and underwear, kissed her on the forehead, hugged and kissed Nahum and Grandma and left. Nahum stood frozen at the doorway of his room, his head jerking violently every time a loud hiccup full of alcohol-vapor escaped the mouth of the janitor.

"Mama, what are we going to do now?" He leaned on his mother, after the door had closed and the sound of heavy steps had dissipated in the silence of night.

"Live," said Rachel, swallowing a tear. "I don't know how, not yet, but we will live. We have no choice." A moment later, she leaned to him across the dining table and said, "I beg you, Nahum, don't ever talk to anyone about this, not even your closest friends. I beg you."

A week later, it was Arkady who spoke first. He came to Nahum in the hallway of the school after the third period and said, "Let's go outside."

"Sorry I jumped on you," he said, quietly, as they walked through the schoolyard. "You know the feeling."

"I do."

"You were right; not everyone arrested is a spy."

"We shouldn't talk about this."

"They keep arresting people every day. So many of our neighbors."

They kept walking toward the schoolyard fence. Nahum closed his eyes for a second, and saw his mother leaning toward him over the dining table, saying, "I beg you, Nahum, don't ever talk to any one about this, not even your closest friends. I beg you."

"Arkady..." Nahum stopped, turned to his friend and whispered in his ear, "I'm afraid for my mama. I'm afraid for your mama and for both of us. I don't want to talk about this."

He stepped back two steps, away from Arkady, and added, this time at full voice, "You told me you were alone. Now I am alone. Every one of us is now alone. Let's keep it that way."

Nahum turned around and started walking quickly back to school across the dusty schoolyard. He entered the building just as the school bell rang to announce the beginning of the next lesson.

It was Geography class. The homework assignment was to study Spain. Because of the Civil War there, in which Soviet Russia was firmly behind the revolutionary force and against the Fascists and their leader, General Franco, Spain was constantly in the news and in the school curriculum.

The teacher, Malvina Alexandrovna, was a tall, skinny woman with a long, dark braid set in three circles on her head and held down by numerous bright-red hairpins. She also wore large, heavy, rust-colored glasses that were wider than her face, and covered half her cheeks. She always started her class with the same phrase: "Will anyone volunteer to present our homework?" No one ever volunteered.

Today, as she strolled between the rows of desks, she said, "I believe Kurochkin is volunteering today."

The heavy breathing of Nikolai Kurochkin was the only answer.

"Would you please come to the map and tell us about the physical characteristics of Spain?" added Malvina Alexandrovna.

Kurochkin, an overweight boy who was an average student and the class clown, made his way to the blackboard, the middle part of which was covered with a world map. He stood behind the teacher's desk, to the right of the map, and looked at the map, trying to find Spain quickly.

"The class is ready to listen," announced Malvina Alexandrovna. "What do we know about Spain?"

Kurochkin wiped sweat from his forehead with the back of his hand and said, "Spain, like Italy, is a peninsula. Italy, like Spain, borders on France. Italy has the shape of a boot, its area is about 300,000 square kilometers and its population is about forty five million people."

"Spain?" asked Malvina Alexandrovna.

"No, I'm talking about Italy, now," answered Kurochkin.

"What mountain range is in the north of Spain?" asked the teacher.

"Interestingly, Spain, like Italy, indeed has mountains in its northern part. In Italy, these mountains are a part of the Alps."

Malvina Alexandrovna's mouth was wide open as she listened to Kurochkin's answers. "What are the names of some Spanish rivers?" she asked, in a barely audible voice.

"Both countries," replied Kurochkin, bravely, "have important waterways. In Italy," he paused, and the entire class gasped loudly for air, "the main river is the Tiber." And he pointed at the map.

"Are you making a fool of yourself?" screamed the teacher, "or you are mocking me?"

She approached Kurochkin, who was sweating profusely, large drops on his forehead reflecting the sunlight and making various parts of his face yellowish, reddish or purplish.

The students froze in their seats, not knowing what to anticipate.

"Why are you telling me about Italy when I clearly ask you about Spain?" demanded Malvina Alexandrovna.

"I thought the homework was about Italy," mumbled Kurochkin, and the class burst into laughter. "I've studied Italy."

"Ah, you have?" The teacher seemed to gain the upper hand. "And may I look into your notes to see what you wrote when I told you that Spain would be your homework?"

As Kurochkin walked to his desk to produce his notebook, Nahum looked into his own and noticed that he hadn't written anything about his homework assignment. Without any real reason, Nahum pulled out his pencil and scribbled in, "Italy."

Meanwhile, Kurochkin had given his notebook to Malvina Alexandrovna, and she read to the whole class, "Italy." She raised her eyes to Kurochkin, "So you made a mistake, Kurochkin. I remember vividly that I asked the class to study Spain. Is this right, class?"

The class was silent.

"Class, who studied Spain?" asked Malvina Alexandrovna, pacing between the two rows of desks. She added, "Those who studied Spain, please, raise your hands." She looked around and saw no hands. "Nobody? Very curious." She turned to her best student. "Draznin, what did you study?"

Nahum leaned forward and bent over his books, as if he wanted to hide.

"Draznin, stand up when I am talking to you." The teacher was visibly irritated.

Nahum slowly rose to his feet. Everyone in the class was watching him. He knew that, but he only threw a quick gaze at Kurochkin, whose drops of sweat now looked like soap-bubbles.

"I studied Italy," said Nahum, softly. His face was burning red.

"What?" It was the teacher's turn to gasp. After a few seconds, she said, "Can I see your homework journal?"

Calmly and silently, Nahum lowered his head and extended his journal to her. The class was mesmerized. Kurochkin was about to die.

"I-TA-LY," read Malvina Alexandrovna loudly, with wide-open eyes that almost filled the lenses of her gigantic glasses, and then she lowered the journal. She dropped it onto Nahum's desk, returned to her chair and asked once more, "Did anyone study Spain? I take it you didn't." After ten seconds of silence, she said, "Fine. Spain and Portugal is your homework for tomorrow, and we will have a short test on Spain, Portugal, and," she paused, and added, sarcastically, "Italy, since you've already studied it."

When Geography class was over, Kurochkin approached Nahum. Laughing and yelling, the entire class formed a circle around them.

"I wrote 'Italy' instead of 'Spain' in my journal just for fun, yesterday, thinking she might ask me and I'd play this little joke," said Kurochkin, gaily. "I hadn't been called upon for about a month. It was time. Why did you write 'Italy' yesterday?"

"I didn't. I just scribbled it in when she asked to see your homework journal," Nahum confessed. "I didn't have anything written down, and somehow I wrote 'Italy' the minute she asked to see your journal."

"Lucky me!" yelled Kurochkin. "It was great!"

Suddenly, from a nerdish "A" student, Nahum had turned into a popular one. For the first time in years, he felt he was part of the group.

Over the next several days, the people in his class became his friends, sharing games, laughter, pranks and trouble. He found out that the fathers of several of his classmates had been arrested. The mothers of one boy and one girl in the class had been arrested and sent to prison. All along, he had thought that women were not being arrested, and that the arrest of their family friend, Maria Olshansky, had been an aberration, but apparently it hadn't.

Life at school was much more vibrant than life at home. Since Moshe's arrest, Rachel seemed to work longer hours, and was much less talkative. Dinners were spent in silence, and she filled her evenings either working with the accounting papers she began bringing home from work, or reading. Once Nahum asked to go to see a movie, but she refused.

"The movies are upbeat comedies," she said softly, "and my life is just too sad for that." Nahum went with his school friends.

The summer of 1938 was long and hot. School ended at the end of June and, in July, Nahum began working part-time for David Slavutsky, delivering packages of typewriter-parts and messages either from the Post Office or from in-town suppliers to and from David's business associates.

"He will be my *legal* messenger," David told Rachel, trying to calm her fears that Nahum might be carrying something illegal. And, to his credit, he never asked Nahum to carry either gold or money.

The rest of his free time, Nahum spent either reading classical literature or playing dominoes with the adults in his back yard. Nahum loved to read. Ever since he had become spellbound by the story-telling skills of Arkady Pilman, he had swallowed one book after another. Dominoes was just another way to relax and occupy his mind. He was also flattered at being accepted by the adults as a good player whom they invited to play every time they needed a fourth person at the table.

Occasionally, he talked in the *dvor* with some of his former buddies, but mostly, the kids would sit silent for hours in the shade of the apple trees, just eating sunflower seeds, splitting the shells with their front teeth and spitting the remains on the ground.

Arkady Pilman rarely came down to join them. He had just graduated, and was preparing to go on to engineering school in Kiev. Even though he was an excellent student, as the son of an arrested colonel, he was worried about his future. He wanted to get out of town, and he was studying seriously for the school-entrance exams that were scheduled for the second half of July.

Yurka Gremko dropped out of school at the end of the seventh grade, and worked in construction, with a street-paving company. His skin was always covered with particles of black asphalt, which penetrated so deeply into the creases and under his nails that he looked ten years older than his real age. He was also drinking heavily almost daily, with other workers, immediately after their shift. His breath always smelled of alcohol and his clothes of diesel fuel. Whenever he did show up in the *dvor*, he only waved at his former friends, and joined the adults at the dominoes table.

Leonid Rubenstein was not allowed outside. His father forbade him to be with the other boys.

"Only to the school and back!" he told him, firmly. "No social contacts!"

Once, Nahum invited him to do their homework together at Nahum's apartment, but Leonid refused.

"My papa won't let me. He's afraid of being arrested. Doesn't want us to be with anyone," he replied.

Vasily, the "Red," was the most frequent person in the *dvor*. He, like Arkady, graduated that year, and he had decided to join the Army. He had a month left before his eighteenth birthday, the age of the draft, and was spending it doing nothing except taking care of his father, Ivan Nikolaevich, who had become a terrible alcoholic.

Vasily's mother, Maria Tikhonovna, a nurse at the hospital, had been arrested about year before. NKVD agents had taken her away straight from work, on the night shift, and Vasily and his father had found out about it when they went to the hospital to look for her because she hadn't come home the next morning.

Ivan Nikolaevich had been devastated, and turned to alcohol. The first time he was found drunk to unconsciousness was about three days after her arrest. He was lying next to the fence of the neighboring apartment house. From that time on, he drank almost daily, frequently to unconsciousness, falling down helpless in the streets, in the park and in the hallways of the apartment buildings. Somehow, he still kept his job as a draftsman, but his entire salary was going into his new lifestyle. Then, in February, he had died in the street, about a block away from their apartment building. Drunk, he had been making his way home when he had fallen into a snow bank, where he had been found, frozen to death, in the morning.

From that time on, Vasily and Lana had lived alone. Vasily had continued with his school, but his sister, Lana, had dropped out, saying that she had to work to feed herself and her brother. No one knew what she was doing, but neighbors noticed that she was bringing strange men to her apartment. Rumors spread very fast.

By the end of the summer, Nahum felt completely bored and awfully lonely. He was ready to go back to school. Arkady left for Kiev, where he had been accepted at the Polytechnic Institute. Vasily joined the Army. The domino games were no longer of interest or excitement to Nahum.

Every morning, he would go to the bakery to buy a loaf of fresh-baked bread, and, around noon, he would go the corner grocery to buy milk. At that time, milk was fetched in a large cistern, once a day, and was dispensed into tin containers that people would bring with them, one liter per person. Nahum liked to arrive at eleven-thirty, to beat the crowd. He hated standing in line.

In the afternoon, he either sat with a book under the tree in the *dvor* or played the occasional game of dominoes with the retired neighbors. He was bored, and could hardly wait until September first, when school would resume.

Even though school wasn't too challenging, he felt better, there. Over the summer, he had grown to almost six feet in height, and he began playing basketball with other kids both in the schoolyard and in the gym. He continued his interest in math.

Although the new math teacher didn't challenge him at all, Nahum and his classmate, Felix Berenbaum, found another way to test their mathematical abilities. Felix' father had some old math texts and brainteasers that both boys enjoyed solving.

Somewhat unexpectedly, Nahum also took a liking to Biology class, his new subject, that year. The year before, they had studied Botany, and it had been boring, with a lot of memorization. All the names of flowers and plants; who could remember them? This year, it was Zoology and Entomology, the fascinating study of animals and bugs. The students still had to memorize a ton of Latin names of the families, subfamilies and other details, but the overall subject was of great interest to Nahum.

Felix also liked Biology, so Nahum had himself a good, new friend who shared a lot of his interests. Once a week, usually on Sundays, Nahum and Felix would go to the Zoo in Shevchenko Park, a thirty-five- or forty-minute walk from Nahum's apartment.

"Bears belong to the Family *Ursidae*, which is closely related to the dog family, the *Canidae*," said Felix, when they stopped in front of the bear-cages.

"This one is *Ursus thibetanus*, an Asian black bear." Nahum pointed. "And that one, in the next cage, is *Ursus arctos*, the brown bear."

"And the one across there is *Ursus maritimus*," said Felix, pointing at a polar bear on the other side of a wide alley.

It was a fun game. They walked from one cage to another, firing the common and Latin names of the Zoo animals at one another. Soon they knew every animal in the Kharkov zoo by its common and scientific names.

At home, however, the situation was still miserably gloomy. Rachel worked hard, and tried desperately to be there for Nahum's every desire. But there was no spark in her words and no interest in her behavior, as if she were simply going through the motions of living.

Change came unexpectedly. In the middle of October, to every one's surprise, an article in *Pravda* suddenly suggested that there might have been a number of arrests that had not been just. "We bent the stick too much," said the article. "Some of the arrested people are innocent, and are victims of overzealous prosecutors."

It was no secret that everything that appeared in *Pravda* was sanctioned by the Communist Party Central Committee. Nothing was left to chance. But not many people understood the meaning of this small article.

"Does it mean the arrests are over?" some wondered.

No matter what people thought, no one imagined that some of the arrested would actually be freed. But that is exactly what happened. In each city, a small number of people who had been hauled away as "spies and enemies of the people," just a few months before, were suddenly released.

There was no apparent reason behind the choosing of the lucky ones, but it was thought likely that a majority of freed individuals had been sentenced to relatively short terms, and so had not yet been shipped to the labor camps.

About a week after the article appeared in the press, in the dusk of an October Ukrainian evening, a light knock on the door surprised both Rachel and Nahum.

"Who's there?" asked Rachel, approaching the door as Nahum was coming out of his room.

"It's me. Moshe," answered a weak voice, and Rachel swung the door open.

Unshaved and crying, Moshe almost fell into her arms. Nahum rushed to them and hugged them both. Grandma Haya came from the kitchen to the hallway, crying and praying in either Hebrew or Yiddish—Nahum couldn't understand either one. Rachel pulled the whole group inside as Moshe continued to cry and kiss his wife, his son and his mother-in-law.

"I can't tell you what happened," he said, as they sat around the table. "I don't understand a thing. They took me in and read a statement to me that I was confessing to being a French-Anglo-American spy. They told me that if I didn't sign this confession, they would arrest you, Rachel, and execute me. I signed.

"Two weeks later, they brought me in front of three judges, who read my confession, found me guilty and sentenced me to ten years in a labor camp. Since then, I've been waiting to be sent to the camp.

"Nothing happened until yesterday. They brought me again in front of a single man, who told me that there had been a mistake; I was not a spy, and I was being released and reinstated in the Party.

"I could hardly believe my ears. I bet someone finally complained to Comrade Stalin, and he reversed this terrible injustice. I always knew Comrade Stalin was unaware of these arrests of innocent people."

"There was an article in *Pravda*, said Rachel, "saying that some innocent people had been arrested and that this should stop."

"That strengthens what I say," said Moshe. "Thanks to Comrade Stalin, we are together again!"

Moshe, Rachel, and Nahum Draznin in Zhitomir, 1925

Nahum Draznin as student of the Kuibyshev Medical Military Acedemy, 1941

Moshe, Rachel, and Nahum Draznin in Kharkov, 1933

Nahum and Rosa Draznin shorty after their wedding in Chelyabinsk, 1943

Left: Nahum Draznin and David Slavutsky, 1933

Nahum Draznin in Minsk, 1956

Herschel and Fanya Rips with their children, Pavel, Rosa, and Yakov in Dnepropetrovsk, 1935

Pavel and Rosa Rips, 1945

Pavel (seated), Rosa, and Yakov Rips in Dnepropetrovsk, 1940

Left: Jehuda Lerman as medical student in Munich, 1913

Maria Lerman (Kirchik)
in Zhitomir, 1960

Victor Lerman and his father, Dr.
Yehuda Lerman in Zhitomir, 1940

Maria Elkin (Kaploon)
in the early 1950s

Judith (Dina) Lerman (Elkin)
in 1949

Left: Abraham Elkin in the
early 1950s

Victor and Judith Lerman in Minsk, 1955

Victor Lerman, an Army doctor, 1944

Victor Lerman (center) with his parents, Jehuda and Miriam Lerman, his wife Judith (left), sister Elena (right), and daughter in Zhitomir, 1947

Judith Lerman, an Army doctor, 1944

Boris and Elena Draznin (Lerman) on their wedding day, 1965

CHAPTER TWELVE

O n Sunday, June 22, 1941, at three-fifteen in the morning, a year and ten months after the signing of the infamous German-Soviet Non-Aggression Pact, the German Army invaded the Soviet Union. The operation, code-named "Barbarossa," in honor of the medieval German emperor who had won great victories in the East, was designed to move rapidly deep into Russian territory, and cut the Red Army into small pockets that could be defeated decisively. The goal was to wipe out Russian power before the snowy Russian winter set in.

By this time, Germany had occupied almost all of Europe. Austria and Czechoslovakia had been annexed, Poland, Denmark, Norway, the Low Countries and France had been conquered and the Balkans and Greece had been taken, with the help of Mussolini's Italy. Lonely England was desperately resisting the new order in Europe. To the east of the new German Empire lay gigantic Russia, which had felt protected by the Non-Aggression Pact signed in 1939.

Comrade Stalin and his mighty Soviet Russia were completely unprepared for the attack. Because they had ignored numerous warnings about Hitler's real intentions, the onslaught came as a terrible surprise.

At six o'clock in the morning, after some bombing, more than two hundred fifty German divisions crossed into Russia, travelling in three directions. Field Marshal Wilhelm von Leeb led his troops toward Leningrad, Field Marshal Fedor von Bock aimed at Moscow and Field Marshal Gerd von Rundstedt marched across Ukraine.

As the Red Army crumbled, pulling back eastward, northward and southward, away from the advancing German tanks and infantry, and abandoning one town after another, panic and rumors of German atrocities spread eastward with incredible speed. In these initial months of the war, the response of the Soviet Government had three main objectives: to slow the retreat as much as possible, to mobilize additional troops, and to evacuate as much as possible of the industrial base east of the Ural mountains, a natural barrier separating European Russia from Asian Russia. Remarkably, all three objectives were carried out with reasonable success.

Because Kharkov was a huge industrial center, there was a colossal effort to relocate its factories away from the approaching Germans in the shortest time possible. Someone in the city government remembered Moshe's organizational skills, and assigned him to a team responsible for the evacuation of the Kharkov tractor factory, which would be turned into an armory and tank factory.

The team worked literally day and night, dismantling the factory and loading parts onto train after train and sending them away to the northeast, over the Ural Mountains. Moshe, Rachel and Rachel's mother were expected to leave on the last train.

Nahum, who had completed his final examinations just a few days before the war, was called to his regional conscription center two days after the war began.

Hundreds of men between seventeen and fifty-five assembled around a small, red-brick building. The process of conscription was extremely simple. Everyone who worked for a factory scheduled for evacuation was to be sent back to help with it. The remaining men lined up and listened to the recruiting officer.

He asked everyone over forty to step forward. "You are to report to Military Base Number 28 tomorrow at 08:00. You will be assigned to units defending Kharkov," he said, and then the older men were sent home.

The officer walked up and down for a few minutes in front of the remaining, younger men, and shouted, "Anyone who wants to volunteer for the Medical Military Academy step forward!"

Nahum stepped forward from his row. He couldn't have explained why he was volunteering. There was no time to think; to analyze the pros and cons. Intuitively, he felt it was the right decision to make.

He looked around and saw three other young men stepping forward. One of them, at the far end of his row, was Felix Berenbaum, who was gazing solemnly at the officer.

"Anyone else?" asked the officer, and one more person stepped forward. "Fine," said the officer. "The five of you, in my office and wait for me there."

"I saw you stepping forward, and decided to join," said Felix, as they stood in the corridor inside the building, in front of the officer's office.

Nahum nodded, watching through the hallway window as the remaining recruits climbed into military trucks, standing shoulder to shoulder in the truck beds. The trucks would take them to their bases, where they would be shaved, given used uniforms and sorted into units.

When the last truck had departed, the officer came back to his office. "I

assume you all finished high school," he said, coolly, looking at the five volunteers.

"I did," said Felix.

"I did." Nahum nodded.

"I did," said other three young men, one after the other.

"Good," replied the officer. "Here are applications to the Military Medical
Academy in Kuibyshev. Fill them out—not here; at home—and bring your
high school diplomas with you. Be here tomorrow morning at ten, with whatever you wish to take with you to Kuibyshev. The train will leave in the early
afternoon. Understood?"

"Yes, Comrade Officer," answered all five.

"Where's Kuibyshev, exactly?" asked Nahum, as he and Felix walked home.
"I know it's on the Volga."

"Somewhere north of Stalingrad," said Felix. "We can stop at my place
and look at my atlas."

Felix Berenbaum's parents were at work. The boys opened the geographic
atlas on the table, and searched for Kuibyshev.

"Here it is!" Nahum pointed his long, bony finger at a small dot north of
Stalingrad, where the Volga made an elbow to the east.

"A long way from home," said Felix.

"What are you going to take?" asked Nahum.

"I don't know. Probably not much. I assume they'll give us military clothes."

"Yep. I'll also take as little as possible."

When Nahum got home, his mother was waiting. "Thank God!" she cried,
"I was told the recruits were taken to the bases right away."

"They were," said Nahum, "but I volunteered for Military Medical Academy." He added, looking at his astonished mother, "I'll be a military doctor, I
guess."

"So, you are going to school?"

"Yep. Here are the papers I have to fill out. We depart tomorrow."

"We?"

"Five of us, from this recruitment center. There might be more who'll go
with us. Felix Berenbaum is going. He volunteered, too."

"Tomorrow," repeated Rachel. "Tomorrow they'll take you away."

"No one is taking me away, Mom. I am going to school; Military Medical
School. I am going to be a doctor, and I am going of my own volition."

"All the same, you will no longer be with me. It's good that Berenbaum is
going with you. At least, you won't be lonely."

"I won't be lonely, Mom, that's for sure. It's a medical school. A Military
Academy. There are probably hundreds of students out there."

"You know what I mean. It's always better to have a friend nearby. Where's the school by the way?"

"In Kuibyshev, on the Volga River."

"Oh, my God! And it seems we are going to Chelabinsk, in the Ural Mountains. I'll die there, without you!"

"Mom, this is a war! We can't plan what's going to happen."

"I know, I know. Nor can we predict our future. Right now, I'm just happy that you are going to be a doctor and you have one more night with the family."

They ate dinner in silence. Only occasional sobbing of grandma Haya interrupted the soundless tension in their dining room. Rachel didn't eat at all. She sat quietly at the table, propping her chin with her two fists, and, with her absolutely dry and wide open eyes, looked at her son, who still wasn't a man enough for her to join the army. At nine o'clock came David Slavutsky, just in time for the after dinner tea. After a few brief phrases, he joined them in wordless tranquility. He left about quarter to ten, just waving at all of them, as if being afraid of breaking the wall of voicelessness.

Next morning, Moshe and Rachel helped Nahum carry his bag to the recruitment center. They were there at ten minutes to ten. At ten o'clock, all five medical-school volunteers were there, waiting for the officer.

The officer came out and told them that a truck was coming any minute to take them to the train station, where they would meet three other volunteers from another recruitment center. Apparently, only two centers in the entire city were giving the recruits the option to enroll in the Military Medical Academy.

"Boy, aren't you lucky?" whispered Felix Berenbaum's father, when he heard this.

"Thank God they are," Rachel whispered back, not paying any attention to Moshe's frown in response to her openly mentioning God.

Near ten thirty, the truck came. Tearful parents helped their children aboard, and ran behind the fume-spitting vehicle for almost half a block, waving their hands and shouting last-minute advice, knowing it would never be heeded.

The train was about two hours late leaving but eventually, around two in the afternoon, Nahum, Felix, and six other volunteers departed for Kuibyshev. They arrived four days later.

The incoming class was made up of three hundred twenty cadets, all boys, most of them from Moscow and other Russian cities. The eight volunteers from Kharkov were the only representatives of Ukraine.

The boys were shown into the dorms, and asked to line up in front of the barbershop, where they were sheared in record time and directed to the bathhouse for hot showers. The bathhouse contained a huge room with just a few showerheads along the longest wall. Along the two side walls there were several faucets with hot and cold water. There were also many benches in the middle of the steamy room. Some people showered along the wall, but most carried their hot and cold water in big tin basins, placed them on benches or on the floor and washed themselves. Some split into pairs, with one person pouring water from tin pitchers onto the other's head and back.

When Nahum went to fetch another basin of hot water, he saw a circumcised man with dark curly hair taking a shower. The man was washing his head and face, and did not see Nahum. Nahum was so astonished to see him that he stood in front of him until the man opened his eyes and stared back at Nahum.

He was as tall as Nahum, but wider in the shoulders, and his torso, arms and legs were covered with short, dark, coarse body hair. Hair grew from his knuckles and earlobes and covered his thighs, chest, shoulders and buttocks. He stepped forward from the shower and wiped his eyes, and his gaze went down Nahum's body, stopping at his groin.

"Jewish?" he asked, and Nahum nodded.

"And you?"

"No, I'm a Tatar. A Moslem," he said smiling, and Nahum heard a distinct accent. "What's your name?"

"Nahum. Nahum Draznin."

"I am Mustafa. Mustafa Dulbeckov. I grew up in the Crimea but, two years ago, we moved to Moscow. My father is an architect, and he got a job there."

"And I am from Kharkov. It's in Ukraine," said Nahum, not knowing how to continue the conversation. "Why are you...?"

Mustafa helped him. "Circumcised?"

"Yeah. I thought..."

"It's Moslem tradition similar to the Jewish one. I guess we do the same. My dad told me about it. I don't really know why. Do you know why Jews do it?"

Nahum had read a biblical story about Abraham and his son, Isaac, in a book called *Tales from the Bible*, but he didn't want to acknowledge that. "No. Just a tradition, I suppose," he answered, and felt much better.

"So it's you and me," laughed Mustafa. "It's gonna be our little bond."

"I'm all for that," said Nahum. He extended his hand to Mustafa.

After the shower, they received their military uniforms right there in the bathhouse. Since a uniform tends to hide the imperfections of the naked human body, everyone looked better in green military shirts and pants. People looked taller, and shoulders and chests appeared broader over waistlines emphasized by black leather belts.

The first week at the Academy was devoted to an intense but abbreviated basic training. Nahum was glad he had played basketball in school. He was in good shape, and wasn't too bothered by two-mile morning runs, mid-morning obstacle courses and afternoon marches and target practice.

Felix, who had never been involved in any physical activities, had a much harder time of it. But the week passed, and the cadets began studying medicine, the main reason they were there. The class was divided into small groups of about twelve people selected in alphabetical order. Nahum Draznin and Mustafa Dulbeckov were in the same group.

The first course was Anatomy. Since the entire class was composed of volunteers who had not had to take any entrance exams, the academic levels of the freshmen were very different. Quite a few cadets were totally unprepared for the rigor of medical school. Even though the professors, faced with the pressure of graduating as many military physicians as possible, tried to pass every cadet, a good twenty percent of them dropped out within the first two months, not being able to master medical Latin or remember the names of the bones, muscle, nerves and vessels of the body. They were immediately transferred to active duty, and sent to the front.

Nahum, Felix and Mustafa did very well. They studied hard, and were among the best students in the class. Anatomy, Physiology, Biochemistry; all were difficult, full of new vocabulary and challenging concepts. The sheer load of classes was enormous. The Academy had decided to jam two years' worth of classes into one academic year in order to accelerate the preparation of military physicians. The cadets had barely time to sleep. They studied on Saturdays and Sundays, and had no breaks. At the end of the second semester, they were told that classes would continue all summer, without any break.

Even though the Russian Army had stopped the Germans near Moscow, defended the surrounded Leningrad and fought for every house in Stalingrad, almost the whole European part of Russia had been occupied, and the Red Army had sustained colossal casualties. The tide of war was far from turning.

On May 1, 1942, the Academy gave their cadets a little bit of free time. May Day was an important holiday in Communist Russia, and there were demonstrations, flags, patriotic songs and displays of military might. In the morning, the cadets marched through the center of the city, parading before local Communist leaders. Then, from eleven-thirty in the morning until three-thirty in the afternoon, they were off duty. They were told to reassemble in the auditorium at three-thirty, sharp.

"I've never been to the center of the city," said Mustafa to Nahum and Felix. "Do you want to walk there for an hour?"

"Say, maybe we can go to the movies. Wouldn't that be great?" asked Nahum, enthusiastically.

"Let's do it!" Mustafa agreed. "I haven't been to the movies for almost a year."

The three of them strolled down the main street of Kuibyshev, enjoying the partly sunny spring day. The trees were still bare, but tiny buds were already swollen, and almost ready to burst into new leaves. The buildings were gray, and still covered by dust and dirty snow. Patches of blue sky were the only color in the city.

"Here's the movie theater." Felix pointed at a two story-building on a nearby corner. "Oh, I've seen this one," he added, as they came to the box office.

Mustafa read out the name of the feature displayed above the box office. "*Six in the Evening, After the War.* I've heard it's very good."

"It's great, but I don't want to see it a second time," said Felix. "You guys go, and I'll just return to the base. That'll give me an hour to catch up with you in Pharmacology."

"You wouldn't mind if we stay?" Nahum asked him, again.

"Oh, absolutely. I don't want to see it again." Felix waved to his friends and walked back toward the school.

"It's about noon," said Nahum, looking at his watch. "We have time. Let's do it."

They bought two tickets for the twelve-thirty show, and went to a street vendor at the next corner to get sparkling water with strawberry syrup. At twelve-thirty, they were sitting in the movie theater watching newsreels, announcements about future releases, and then the feature itself. It felt good to sit in a dark room, sinking into comfortable chairs and watching the black-and-white images on the screen.

The film was very interesting, but seemed to be running a bit long. Nahum looked at his fluorescent watch; it said twelve forty-five, but he sort of ignored it. Maybe ten minutes later, he looked at his watch again—it still showed twelve forty-five. He shook his wrist and stared at the face of his watch. It showed twelve forty-five. He lifted his wrist to his ear. The watch was silent.

He whispered to Mustafa, "What time is it?"

"I don't know, I don't have a watch. We should be fine, though. I think it will end soon."

Nahum couldn't watch any longer. He had to find what time it was. He looked around and spotted a man two rows in front of them in the half-empty theater. He bent over, so as not to obstruct the screen for those sitting behind, and crept over to the man.

"I am sorry," he said apologetically, "can you, please tell me what time it is now?"

The man did not have a watch. Almost in a panic, Nahum left the room and ran to the box office. A big, round clock on the wall showed three-ten. Nahum rushed back to the movie hall.

"Mustafa!" he shouted, forgetting about the other patrons. "Mustafa! It's three ten. We must run!"

Mustafa jumped out of his seat and ran out of the theater. "I can't believe it!" he shouted as they ran. "We are not going to make it. No way!"

The clock showed three forty-five when they ran into their building at the Academy. Roll-call had ended, and their classmates were standing there, still in their four rows. The class commander, a middle-aged major, looked gravely at the two cadets, sweating and panting after their thirty-five-minute run.

"Well, well. Where were you? Why are you late? Cadet Dulbeckov, I am asking you!"

"Comrade Major," answered Mustafa, lowering his head. "We went to see a movie."

"A movie?" roared the Major. "A movie? Don't you know there's a war going on out there? Soldiers are fighting and dying every minute in the fields of combat, and you went to see a movie? With your Comrades spilling their blood, you find time for entertainment? Do you have any excuse, Cadet Draznin?"

"No, Comrade Major, I have no excuse. The truth is, my watch stopped, and we missed the time to return."

"Your watch stopped? And you don't think this is a stupid excuse? Are you going to lie to me about your watch? Shame on you, Cadets Draznin and Dulbeckov! I will relay this incident to the military prosecutors. You will be held responsible for your actions. Meanwhile, I will put you into the custody of the Military Police." He turned to face the rows of cadets, and barked, "Class dismissed!"

He took Nahum and Mustafa to a Military Police barracks, where they were locked into a cell. It was a small, dark room with a narrow window about a foot below the ceiling. A bunk-bed stood by the wall, across from a tiny sink with broken enamel and a toilet stool. A lonely guard was reading a paper in the main room.

"It's all my fault," said Nahum, sitting on the lower bed. "I should have realized my watch had stopped. This is so stupid!"

"Don't cry over spilled milk. I should have been more attentive to the time, too. I don't think they're going to make a big stink about it. After all, we were only fifteen minutes late; not a big deal."

"The Major acted as if we were some kind of deserters."

"Yep, you're right. You never know what's going to happen," Mustafa agreed. "I just hope it's not a big deal."

They both slept poorly. They were tormented all night by anticipation, uncertainty and fear. In the morning, the guard brought them hot water and one slice each of bread.

Somewhere around noon, a young lieutenant walked in, stopped in front of their cell and read them a statement saying that they were accused of being deserters, having been caught after being AWOL.

"The court martial will decide at three this afternoon what the punishment will be," he said in a low voice, and he folded his papers.

"Court martial?" gasped Nahum. "Why a court martial? We were just fifteen minutes late. What kind of crime is that?"

The lieutenant didn't answer. He put the folded papers into his pocket, turned around and left without saying a word.

"They're moving fast," said Mustafa. "I don't like it."

"But court martial? Mustafa, just think of it! A court martial! I can't believe it!"

The court martial was indeed at three o'clock, as the lieutenant had told them. They were led into an almost completely bare room, right there at the MP station. Three officers were sitting at a table across from the entry door: one colonel and two lieutenant colonels. The table was covered with a scarlet runner. The caps of the officers lay on the runner, facing Nahum and Mustafa, who stood at the doorway. The door behind them closed, leaving only two armed soldiers flanking the accused cadets.

"Cadet Draznin," said the colonel, "you are accused of deserting your unit on May 1, 1942. Do you accept your guilt?"

"I was fifteen minutes late, comrade Colonel," answered Nahum, his voice trembling. "I'm not a deserter."

"Were you absent from the unit at Roll Call?"

"Yes. I was..."

"I am interested in 'Yes' or 'No' answers!" shouted the colonel. "Cadet Dulbeckov!" He switched his eyes to Mustafa. "Were you absent from your unit on May 1, 1942?"

"I was also fifteen minutes late. I am sorry."

"Do you accept responsibility for your actions?"

"I do."

"Cadet Draznin, do you accept responsibility for your action?"

"I do."

The colonel leaned over to the officer on his right and whispered something in his ear. Then he leaned to the officer on his left and whispered something to him, as well. Both officers nodded.

"Deserting your unit in time of war is a terrible crime. Had it happened in one of the front-line units, you would have received capital punishment. I hope you realize this." The colonel appeared dead serious. His voice sounded like the voice of the radio announcer who says, "We interrupt this broadcast..."

Mustafa was sweating profusely, his curly hair almost glued to his skull. Nahum felt dizzy, and his legs were giving way.

"This military tribunal," continued the colonel, "with the power vested in it, sentences you, Nahum Draznin and Mustafa Dulbeckov, to one year in a penal battalion on the front lines of our defenses, where you'll serve as corpsmen. With your own blood will you remove this stain from your lives. If you are wounded or killed in action, your record will be cleared, and you will be unconditionally rehabilitated. You will be dispatched to your unit immediately after final exams. Meanwhile, you can return to your dorms and to your classes, but you may not leave the Academy. There will be no appeal. The case is closed."

The colonel gestured to the guards to take the prisoners away.

Nahum and Mustafa walked back to their dorms, still digesting the sentence. The penal battalion was just one step above capital punishment. Penal battalions, like suicide squads, were sent to perform the most dangerous and most physically demanding tasks. Seventy percent of the soldiers in the penal battalions were killed in action, with the remaining thirty percent ending up wounded. Only a wound or death could discharge someone from a penal battalion. Self-inflicted wounds were punished swiftly with a death sentence, which was implemented equally swiftly.

In the dorm, they cried. Sitting on the lower bunk, Nahum buried his face in his palms, with the backs of his hands on his knees. Mustafa fell backward, touching the wall with his head and covering his eyes with inside of his elbow. Neither one could comprehend why such a severe punishment had been dealt out for such a minor incident.

On June 18, 1942, they received written certificates saying that they had completed two years of medical school, even though there was still a month to go. They were allowed to mail these certificates to their families. Nahum included a short note.

Dear Mom and Pa,

The first year of study is over. We worked very hard and completed two years' worth of school in just one academic year. They are sending us to front-line units as medics, and we'll return to school when the war is over. I'll try to

write from my new unit.
  I love you so, so much,
  Yours,
  Nahum

He lied about going back to school, a promise no one had made him, but he felt it would sooth his parents' worries about him. The next day, Nahum and Mustafa boarded a truck traveling south from Kuibyshev to Saratov, where they would be assigned to a specific unit. Felix and a few of their other friends came down to say goodbye. For Nahum Draznin and Mustafa Dulbeckov, the real war had begun.

CHAPTER THIRTEEN

They joined a regiment of other condemned soldiers, all of whom had been sentenced to penal units just outside Saratov, a town on the Volga, south of Kuibyshev and north of Stalingrad. Their battalion was at seventy-percent strength, and every day, new soldiers and officers arrived to swell the ranks. Nahum and Mustafa checked in with the commander.

"Medics?" he said, coming out from behind his broken desk. "Medics, you say? I just had a request for medics...just had it." He went back to his desk and shuffled through his papers.

"Here it is." He pulled out a paper and read it silently. "That's right, we need medics desperately in a unit being formed near Stalingrad. The unit is a priority. So, boys, you're going to defend Stalingrad. How d'you like that?"

He sat down in his chair and began filling out a form detailing their new assignment. "What did you boys do to get into our battalion?"

"AWOL," said Mustafa.

"We were only fifteen minutes late," mumbled Nahum.

"Fifteen minutes, eh? That's all? They must need medics more than I thought." The commander shook his head, and continued toiling over the assignment form. "Fifteen minutes, you said? Wow! You'll have a lot of time on your hands to think about that one. Here's the assignment." He handed the paper to Mustafa. "We'll get you there in a couple of days. Meanwhile, you'll stay with a field hospital unit, Barracks 4."

The field hospital was a hospital in name only. All its medical supplies had been packed in wooden boxes and stored in two large rooms, one box on top of another. The boxes were hand-labeled in black paint. In many places and on many boxes, the paint had washed away, leaving just occasional letters that gave cryptic messages.

The third room was the largest. It served as both clinic and living quarters for the staff. The quarters part consisted of six cots and a massive oak table with two long benches, separated from the clinic by three folding screens with metal frames that supported white, but dirty, linen.

In the clinic part, there were two cots for patients, two small desks with papers piled in total disarray, two metal chests and one large, metal cupboard containing medical instruments, an old scale with a long stick to measure height and several chairs for patients and staff. Between the metal chests, a small metal sink protruded from the wall.

Nahum and Mustafa entered the clinic and looked around. There was nobody there.

"Hi," said Nahum, "is anybody home?"

There was no answer, and they advanced cautiously into the living-part of the room. A large man wearing muddy boots lay on one of the cots, face turned to the wall, knees bent and both fists under the thin pillow beneath his head. He wore a military uniform, but his belt was on the floor next to his cot. His hair was long, gray and disheveled.

"Hello," said Nahum, again. "May we come in?"

"You're already in, aren't you?" answered the man, without turning toward them. "Who the hell are you?"

Nahum and Mustafa looked at one another, and Mustafa said, "We are new medics, temporarily assigned to the hospital."

"We are all here temporarily," sighed the man. Reluctantly, he turned his large head to face Nahum and Mustafa. He yawned, and sat up on his cot, propping himself up with short, muscular arms. "Medics? Welcome to the field hospital of the penal battalion! What an honor!"

His face was swollen, especially the lower eyelids, and his red, meaty nose and wrinkled forehead were covered with blackheads. His greasy, gray hair stuck out every which way.

"Hey, don't get me wrong! I'm joking. I'm the chief doctor at this medical establishment. How do you like this place? Doesn't matter if you don't," he answered himself. "This is it." He rose to his feet and extended his hand to Mustafa. "Doctor Vyasov. I was a major, working in a real hospital, before they assigned me to this pit. They demoted me to unranked soldier, but I am still a doctor. No one can take that away from me!"

Mustafa and Nahum shook hands with doctor Vyasov, and introduced themselves.

"We had finished two years of Kuibyshev military academy at the time when we got into trouble," said Mustafa.

"Sorry to hear that, but…life goes on, my dear colleagues, and the war goes on, as well. May I offer you a welcoming drink?"

He knelt next to his cot, reached under it toward the wall and pulled out a half-empty green bottle. "I have a little bit of pure alcohol left for this happy occasion. Will you join me?"

Nahum and Mustafa, still astonished and somewhat frightened, didn't know what to say.

"Isn't it a bit early?" mumbled Nahum.

"Early for what?" Doctor Vyasov grinned. "It's never too early or too late to have a drink. You either drink it or not. I don't want to waste it." He held the bottle above some tin cups that stood on the table.

"I'll pass," said Nahum, quietly.

"I'll pass, too, if you don't mind," echoed Mustafa.

"Not at all. I don't need these dirty cups, then." Doctor Vyasov raised the bottle and said, "To you, my young colleagues. Welcome to the field hospital," and took a big gulp. "Boy, that's good," he said, plunking the bottle onto the table. "Sit down. Tell me about yourselves, boys."

The next month and a half were hot, muggy and boring. Doctor Vyasov drank constantly, sleeping the rest of the time. "Do you know, boys, why I am the luckiest man on Earth?" he asked them, frequently. "Because you don't drink and I don't have to share my alcohol with you. That's why!" he answered, laughing.

The clinic and the hospital received about two liters of pure alcohol every month. Doctor Vyasov hid the big jar and poured some into the green bottle that he kept under his cot and refilled every day. "I can't stand seeing a dry bottom in my bottle," he told the boys.

Nahum and Mustafa ran the clinic. Every day, each of them saw between ten and twelve patients. Most of the soldiers came in with diarrhea or minor trauma: cuts and bruises. Even though they had no clinical training, Nahum and Mustafa dispensed medications, cleaned wounds and put in stitches. They taught each other, occasionally asking doctor Vyasov to look at a patient. He always did, when he wasn't too drunk.

At the end of July, another medic arrived, a male nurse who had been sentenced to the penal battalion for stealing food rations from hospitalized patients in another military hospital. A week later, when a fourth medic showed up, the base commander walked into the clinic.

"You'll start your training tomorrow," he announced, "and the next week you and your drunken doctor will be shipped to your unit. Enough sitting here in this cushy place. It's time to pay for your deeds."

The training was exceedingly simple, conceptually, but rather harsh, physically. A sergeant made them crawl flat on their stomachs through dust and dirt and puddles, pulling each other along as if rescuing a wounded comrade from the battlefield. This they did on the banks of the river and in an orchard, under burning sun and at night.

"That's all you have to do, boys, pull those wounded out. That's your task, plain and simple; to carry wounded soldiers to safety. Nothing fancy; just crawl in and crawl out. Seek those with light wounds first. They have better chances to survive. I don't want you bringing back corpses. We want people treated and returned to the front. Don't try to treat anybody out there in the field, either. Stop their bleeding with tourniquets, if you can, and carry them back. That's all. Understood?

"Also, put them on your back, face down, so that the chest is firmly on your back and the legs are dragged to your side, as you crawl flat on your belly. That's going to protect you from being killed. We want you healthy; we need you to pull out as many wounded as you can."

After a week of training, when Nahum, Mustafa and the two other men were exhausted, with bruised knees and elbows and the skin torn off all four joints, they were ordered to load the hospital boxes onto three trucks. It took two full days. Doctor Vyasov and a couple of other soldiers helped.

The trucks left the base on Aug 3, 1942, and drove south, toward Stalingrad. Doctor Vyasov sat with the driver of the first truck, the two other medics went in the second and Nahum rode with Mustafa in the third.

Their driver was a short young man with long, bright-red hair, soiled with oil and car grease, who had extremely dirty hands. Nahum and Mustafa, who had taken up smoking when they entered the Academy, offered the driver some of their tobacco. He accepted gladly, even though he had his own. They rolled pieces of old newspaper with tobacco inside them into two-inch-long joints, and lit them up. Soon, the cabin of their truck was filled with smoke that escaped through glassless side windows.

The driver, thankful for the tobacco, was a very talkative man. He seemed unable to stop telling Nahum and Mustafa the story of his life; about his small town, south of Rostov, his family, from whom he hadn't heard in almost year and a half, his work as a driver along the front and his hopes of getting back home and becoming a driver in Rostov.

"After we beat the hell out of the Germans!" he said, emphatically.

Nahum and Mustafa remained silent most of the way. They smoked and listened to the driver, thinking of their own families and of the unknown future awaiting them near Stalingrad.

With stops at a few military bases to fuel the trucks and get some food, the trip took almost two days. Approaching Stalingrad from the north, they could hear the ominous sound of artillery, and see bombs and shells exploding in the sky, mainly west of town. It was particularly frightening at night.

They finally arrived, drove through the northern part of the city, and checked into a unit based between Mamaev Mound and the railroad station, just south of the center of Stalingrad.

Most of the town was spread out along the western bank of the river Volga. The river itself was very wide, probably the widest in Europe. All the way down from Stalingrad to its mouth on the Caspian Sea, it was flanked by low banks, except for a towering, green hill about three hundred feet above sea-level, in the middle of Stalingrad, called "Mamaev Mound." This was probably the most important strategic point in Stalingrad, and, with German troops approaching, Mamaev Mound became the most fortified area in the city.

The field hospital was assigned to a penal company of about three thousand people, stationed between the railroad station and Mamaev Mound. The barracks were actually closer to the station, but the army cleaned out a grocery store about three blocks away for the hospital. Doctor Vyasov and his four medics were the only staff. They unloaded the trucks and unpacked their equipment.

One evening, they were summoned back to barracks to hear the reading of a new order. Order #227, later known as the "Not a step back" order, was issued by the People's Commissar of Defense of the USSR, Comrade Stalin, on July 28, 1942. The order was to be read aloud to every soldier in the Soviet Army. The battalion commander read it through a megaphone.*

The enemy feeds more and more resources to the front, and, paying no attention to losses, moves on, penetrates deeper into the Soviet Union, captures new areas, devastates and plunders our cities and villages, rapes, kills and robs the Soviet people...

The conclusion is that it is time to stop the retreat. Not a single step back! This should be our slogan from now...

So what do we lack? We lack order and discipline in companies, regiments and divisions, in tank units, in the Air Force squadrons. This is our major drawback. We have to introduce the strictest order and strong discipline in our army, if we want to save the situation and defend our Motherland...

From now on, the iron law of discipline for every officer, soldier and political officer should be—not a single step back, without order from higher command. Company, battalion, regiment and division commanders, as well as the commissars and political officers of corresponding ranks who retreat without order from above, are traitors of the Motherland. They should be treated as traitors of the Motherland. This is the call of our Motherland...

THE SUPREME COMMAND OF THE RED ARMY ORDERS:

1.The military Councils of the fronts and first of all front commanders should:

a) In all circumstances decisively eradicate retreat attitude in the troops

---

* The relevant sections of Order #227 are reproduced here in part.

and with an iron hand prevent propaganda that we can and should continue the retreat to the east, and this retreat will not be harmful to us. . .

   c) Form within each Front...penal battalions, where commanding, senior commanders and political officers of corresponding ranks from all services, who have broken discipline due to cowardice or instability, should be sent. These battalions should be put on the more difficult sections of a Front, thus giving them an opportunity to redeem their crimes against the Motherland by blood...

   2. The Military Councils of armies and first of all army commanders should:

   b) Form...well-armed guards (barrage) units..., deploy them in the rear of unstable divisions and oblige them to execute panic-mongers and cowards at site, in case of panic and chaotic retreat, thus giving faithful soldiers a chance to do their duty before the Motherland...

   The order is to be read aloud in all companies, troops, batteries, squadrons, teams and staffs...

   The People's Commissar for Defense,

   J. Stalin.

   The soldiers were silent. They were already in a penal company; that part of their life had been decided for them. They also knew they would have to pay the ultimate price to get out. The lucky ones would only be wounded.

   Nahum looked into the faces around him. They were stern, serious and resolved. One couldn't tell why these people had ended up in the penal company. Some had probably done something wrong, but many, Nahum thought, may have been like him; basically innocent of any crime. He couldn't tell.

   "If the Germans come here, " said the company commander, "we'll meet them here, and we will not retreat. This is where we draw the line. Most of us will die here, on the western banks of the Volga River. Not a single step back. I am not asking you why you are here in this penal unit. That is water under the bridge, and I don't care. But Stalingrad is our unity, our destiny and our way to pay for what we did. It might become our common grave. I call on you to swear with your lives and your blood, to Comrade Stalin and to the Motherland, that we are not going to take a single step back. For Comrade Stalin—Hooray!"

   "Hooray! Hooray! Hooray!" responded the company.

"For the Motherland—Hooray!"

"Hooray! Hooray! Hooray!" shouted three thousand people.

Nahum didn't feel any fear of war, most likely because he hadn't seen any real war, yet. He had settled in to the life of a soldier, but the horror of the war had yet to be discovered. It arrived at the end of August.

On August 23, 1942, the Sixth German Army, led by General Paulus, the same much-decorated army that had taken Paris in 1940, attacked Stalingrad. The attack was part of Operation Blue, a military task envisioned by Hitler to capture the southern oil fields of Russia. Germany desperately needed oil to maintain its military might. Taking Stalingrad would cut off the Russian Army in the east and north, allowing the Germans an unobstructed southern march to the Caspian Sea's oil reserves. On August 23, one thousand German planes dropped incendiary bombs on Stalingrad. The mostly-wooden city was completely engulfed in flame. The next day, in one raid of 600 planes, 40,000 civilians were killed. The battle of Stalingrad had begun.

During the next couple of weeks, the city was completely ruined, reduced to the status of a vast furnace, smoldering and fuming everywhere. The Germans succeeded in occupying almost eighty percent of the city. But what a price they paid! They had to battle for every stone and every house. With bullets, knives and bayonets, Russian soldiers met them every step of the way, and every linear foot of land was defended to the death. The soil of Stalingrad was mixed with human ashes and held together by blood.

Around the railroad station, an area two blocks north, one block south, and several blocks east to the river was still in Russian hands. It was held by Nahum's and Mustafa's penal company and two regular battalions. They suffered terrible losses, and the penal battalion, especially, was decimated.

By the end of September, of the original twenty-seven hundred who had arrived to defend the train station, only one hundred twenty remained alive.

But the hospital continued to function. Every night, when the fighting subsided, the corpsmen, including Nahum and Mustafa, crawled out onto the field, slowly moving from one body to another, trying to identify those wounded who could still be saved. They hoisted wounded soldiers to their shoulders and crawled back to the hospital, pulling them under the occasional bombardment, through sniper-fire and among the many stray bullets that seemed to come from every direction.

After they delivered the wounded soldiers to the relative safety of the field hospital, by now housed under the sky, behind the burnt and broken walls of the brown, brick building, they turned around and crawled out again, to collect as many soldiers as they could in the course of the night.

In the hospital, Dr. Vyasov sorted out the wounded, attending first those who had the greatest chance to survive. He cleaned their wounds with water and scraps of gauze and linen, stopped bleeding with tourniquets and hemostatic clamps that he re-used with patient after patient, sutured wounds and even performed some small surgeries. He did not asked the soldiers their names, and kept no record of his wounded.

When he was done with the wounded, he shouted to his corpsmen the order of their evacuation. Wounded in Group One were dragged eastward to the river immediately and from there evacuated upstream by boat, to the north of Stalingrad.

The fiercest fighting was on and around Mamaev Mound, which changed hands eight times during the battle. By the end of September, it had been held twice by the Russians and twice by the Germans. It was the most important strategic point, towering over the entire city and allowing unobstructed shots at the river to the east and toward the western plains.

It was also the most difficult place in which to collect the wounded. It was relatively far from the hospital, and its slopes were bare, offering no defense from bullets. Whoever was at the top had a clear view of its slopes, and an easy, downhill field of fire.

On September 30, the Russians attempted again to take over Mamaev Mound. After two days of continuous assault, there came a relative nighttime lull. The corpsmen used this time to collect the wounded. The preceding day, the Russian soldiers had scaled two thirds of the hill, reaching some trenches that had been dug previously. Bodies, both dead and wounded, covered the eastern slope of the Mound.

At three in the morning, Mustafa and Nahum were crawling slowly up the hill. It was their fourth outing that night. By now, they knew their routine all too well. Faces to the ground, right hands gripping their handguns, so they could be used in case of confrontation with German corpsmen, bags with tourniquets and linen on the left sides of their crawling bodies. Move right arm and right leg, freeze for a few seconds, move left side forward and freeze again. A few inches at a time.

On the open slope, they were excellent targets for German snipers, even at night. Their task was to crawl up the hill as far as possible, to collect the wounded from the very front line. They reached the trenches and fell inside. Bending over, they began to search for wounded.

It was hard to pass over still-breathing soldiers while trying to identify those with the best chance for survival. They would never forget the eyes of those they left behind. Within five minutes, they had found the soldiers they would carry back to the hospital. They put them on their backs and began their dangerous descent.

They crawled down about ten yards apart. Suddenly, two long bursts of machine-gun fire froze Nahum in place. He knew he had to lie still for a while, because such intense fire in their direction meant only one thing—someone had seen them move. A third burst pinned him down for a longer time. Finally, he turned his head to his left, where Mustafa was, and began crawling. Mustafa wasn't moving.

"Hey," he called softly, "Mu-u-us."

There was no answer.

He waited, and called again, this time a bit louder, "Mustafa."

No answer.

Nahum unloaded the soldier he was carrying, which was against regulations and training, and whispered to him, "I'll be right back, I'm going to check on my friend."

He rose on his hands and knees and rushed to Mustafa. He fell to the ground next to his friend, and extended his hand to touch him. Mustafa didn't respond.

"Oh, God!"

Nahum looked at the soldier Mustafa had been carrying. He was dead, shot in the back by that last burst of fire. Nahum pushed him away from Mustafa, and turned his friend face-up. Mustafa's eyes were closed, and blood was coming from the corner of his mouth.

*Oh, no. God no,*thought Nahum, as he tried to find signs of life in his friend. Mustafa didn't have any. He was dead.

Nahum hugged his friend's head and cried.

Fear and the horror of the war and desperation about his own situation returned with renewed strength. Enormous waves of emptiness and loneliness overwhelmed him. He was again alone in this terrible world, in the middle of a horrific massacre. When he finally let go of Mustafa's head, he felt and saw blood on his hand that had come from Mustafa's neck.

He had been killed by a bullet that had entered his neck below his helmet; a bullet from the burst of fire that had killed the wounded soldier on his back.

Nahum wanted to carry Mustafa's body back to the hospital, but then his obligations to the wounded soldier prevailed. It would be against every possible rule and against his conscience to leave a wounded soldier on the field in favor of a dead body. He couldn't do it.

Nahum stretched his hand to Mustafa's shirt, unbuttoned the pocket on the left side of his chest and pulled out his documents. He put them into his pocket and crawled back to the soldier he had left behind.

"I didn't think you'd come back," mumbled the soldier.

Nahum didn't answer. He put the soldier on his back, and resumed the duty of a corpsman. The darkness of night was lifting, and Nahum hurried downhill, in order to reach the relative safety of the ruined houses at the foot of the hill before dawn. He moved fast, ignoring his usual caution. Another burst of automatic fire stopped him for a minute or two. It was getting lighter, and he had to choose between lying on the field until the next night or taking the chance of being shot at as he was attempting to reach the houses. He had faced such choices before, and twice taken his chances. He felt he needed to reach the hospital.

He moved too soon after the next barrage of bullets. Someone was watching him. As soon as he moved, a new burst showered him immediately. This time, a burning pain ascended from his left leg to his head, tightening all the muscles in his abdomen and chest, and penetrating his brain. He gasped for air, but his chest refused to expand. Under the weight of the soldier on his back, his face sank to the ground and he lost consciousness.

He woke up feeling completely wet, as if he were lying in a puddle. Even his face was wet. He opened his eyes and immediately closed them again, squeezing his eyelids together. The early October sun was high in the sky, blazing down on the eastern slope of the hill.

It must be morning.

He licked his lips and caught a few drops of sweat on the tip of his tongue. He moved his arm, tucking his hand under his stomach. His pants were wet, either from sweat or from his own urine; he couldn't tell which. Only now did he realize that the soldier he had been carrying was still on his back, pressing him into the ground.

He must be dead, Nahum thought, *otherwise, he would have moved.*

Nahum's left leg was numb; he couldn't feel it at all. He tried to reach it with his left hand without moving the rest of his body. He couldn't. As he was deciding what to do, an artillery barrage assaulted his ears. He felt the ground shaking. Twice, soil uprooted by the artillery shells covered him. He didn't move. He fell asleep when the barrage ended, woke up again and urinated through his wet pants, but didn't move until nightfall. All day long, the dead soldier lay on him, as a protective shield.

When darkness came, he moved the man off his back. Suddenly, the pain in his leg came back. He twisted his body and touched his leg; he was bleeding. The body of the dead soldier had been exerting pressure on his wound, and had stopped the bleeding. Now the bleeding had resumed.

Nahum reached for his bag and pulled out a tourniquet. He fastened it high on his thigh, and the bleeding subsided. *Must be a deep wound,* he thought as he began crawling down the hill, dragging his left leg.

After a minute, he heard voices. *Germans!* he thought, and froze again, playing dead.

Indeed, German corpsmen were crawling around, looking for their wounded. Nahum had no choice but to remain still. The Germans went back and forth for several hours. When they were gone, he resumed his descent. He crawled for about a half-hour before dawn. When he stopped, he was still a good hundred yards up the slope, about three hundred yards from the ruins of the demolished houses.

He spent another day lying still on the slope of Mamaev Mound, under criss-crossing fire from both sides. The sky was cloudy, and Nahum began to shiver. He tried to suppress his chills, but that didn't work. Luckily, the snipers didn't see him.

At night, he started moving again, but he was so weak he could only travel a few yards. The numbness in his leg was killing him, but he was afraid of taking off the tourniquet.

He was moaning in pain when someone asked, "Hey, are you Russian?"

"Yes, yes, yes..." answered Nahum repeatedly.

The corpsman crawled closer. "Where's your wound?"

"I put a tourniquet on my leg," said Nahum. "I'm a medic from the Sixteenth Field Hospital; the one by the train station."

"You're lucky," said the corpsman, hoisting Nahum onto his back. "Your hospital was bombed, yesterday. Almost everyone there got killed, including your doctor. No more hospital, Pal. We're pulling everyone straight to the river."

The corpsman pulled Nahum to the ruins. There, still in darkness, two other corpsmen placed him on a stretcher and, bending as low as possible, ran eastward, behind the station. Two other men picked him up, there, and ran to the river, where they put him into a boat. Another wounded soldier was already aboard.

Two men in dark clothes began to work the oars, trying not to splash water as they rowed upstream. Nahum drifted off into unconsciousness, again.

CHAPTER FOURTEEN

T he first and only bomb to fall on Dukora came at four-thirty in the morning on June 22, 1941, the very first day of the war. It woke the entire village. Reb Berl was already up and about, preparing to put on *tefillin** for the morning payer. The huge explosion made him approach the window and peek outside. He saw people piling out onto the main street and looking up at the sky. He went out onto the porch and looked up, as well.

He saw waves of German planes flying eastward, fairly low, just above the pine trees of their forest. In the early dawn, he also saw columns of dark smoke reaching for the gray sky from the burning earth.

"The war! The war has started," people were telling one another. "The Germans are coming."

There was an immediate debate as to what to do in this situation. Obviously, no one in Dukora had any idea where either the Germans or the Russians were. No one could predict the course of the war. No one knew what to do.

"I've heard they're killing Jews and Communists," said one man. "We should probably be heading east."

"I don't believe a word you are saying," replied Reb Berl, stroking his beard. "I know the Germans. They stayed in my house twice. You couldn't have found nicer people. The Polacks are the real killers."

"Reb Berl is right," echoed another man. "Wars come and go, and we are just caught in the middle. No one needs this little *shtetl* of ours."

"You do what you want, Reb Berl, but we are leaving," said the first man. "I know the Germans kill Jews. I'm not going to take a chance."

"So I'll die at home." Reb Berl waved his arm and went back inside.

"Berl," said his wife, shuffling up behind him, "maybe we should go to Minsk, to be with Sam and his family."

Their younger son, Shmuel , or "Sam," in Russian, lived in Minsk, some thirty miles away, with his wife and two children, a boy and a girl.

---

* Tefillin (commonly translated as 'phylacteries') are two small black boxes with black straps attached to them. Jewish men place one box on their head and another one on their arm during weekday morning prayer.

"They'll be just fine," answered Reb Berl. "In fact, they should come here. It's safer in the country." He went straight back to his study, a little room with a small desk and a three-shelf bookcase, put on *tefillins* , one on his forehead and another on his left arm, covered himself with a prayer shawl and said his prayers. He was disappointed that he hadn't done it before going out to see the commotion.

When he finished, he put the shawl and the *tefillins* into their little bags, and placed the bags on the top shelf of his bookcase. He sat at his desk in front of an open Talmud next to the kerosene lamp. He read, mumbling the words that no one but him could understand. To Reb Berl, life in Dukora did not change.

Two days later, a daughter of his next-door neighbor came in.

"Reb Berl," she said, with visible anxiety, "I just came from Minsk, where I live not too far from your son, Sam, and I think I saw his children, your grandchildren, alone, next to the apartment house. I can't tell you for sure. There is terrible chaos in Minsk, so I might have been mistaken, but I thought I'd better tell you, just in case."

Reb Berl didn't bother answering. He went to his barn, pulled out a horse, strapped it to a small, four-wheeled cart and left for Minsk.

As he approached the city, his mare's trot was slowed by throngs of people fleeing the capital of the Byelorussian republic. He was literally the only person going into the city.

People were walking eastward. They were carrying bags, suitcases or bundled blankets filled with whatever they felt they might need in the future. Some were on bicycles, and a few had horse-drawn carts filled with children, the elderly and household goods. Most of them were just walking.

Almost eight hours after he had left Dukora, Reb Berl entered his son's apartment in Minsk. The door was unlocked, and he moved along the dark corridor to the fourth door on the left, his son's room. The apartment seemed abandoned. The doors to individual rooms were either wide open or ajar; the furniture was still there, but he saw no adults. Everyone seemed to be gone. Reb Berl found his grandchildren completely alone.

They sat together on their parents' bed, scared and dirty, eyes and noses swollen from crying. He knelt silently near the bed and hugged them tightly. They began to sob into his rough beard.

He rose to his feet, gathered some of their clothes in a big suitcase he pulled from under the bed, gave them a loaf of bread he had brought with him in a little rucksack, and filled another suitcase with his son's and his son's wife's clothes.

When they went downstairs, the horse and cart had been stolen. Reb Berl

shook his head, and took the suitcase containing his son's belongings back
into the apartment. He wouldn't be able to walk to Dukora with two small
children and two suitcases.

It was around six in the afternoon when they began their march back to
Dukora. There were still thousands of people on the road. Reb Berl carried the
suitcase in his right hand, and gave the left to his five-year-old granddaughter.
His seven-year-old grandson walked next to her. Every twenty or thirty minutes, Reb Berl would pick up his granddaughter and carry her in his left arm.

The boy was a trouper. He walked alone, without a single complaint. They
walked with the crowd until about eleven o'clock at night.

"Let's take a nap for a couple of hours," said Reb Berl. "We are more than
half way to our *bubbie* (grandma)," he added, with a sigh.

Only then, when they were cuddled under a tree some fifty yards from the
dirt road, did he asked his grandchildren what they knew about their parents.

"Mama left for work the night before the war started," said his grandson.

Reb Berl knew his daughter-in-law worked in an orphanage, and stayed
there two nights a week.

"And your papa?" he asked. "Where did he go?"

"Papa left in the morning, when the bombs started falling," answered his
grandson.

"He said he'd be right back," sobbed his granddaughter, hiding her face in
her grandpa's beard.

"He went to Uncle Solomon," said the grandson. "Uncle Solomon had a
horse, and Papa wanted him to come and pick us up."

Reb Berl knew Uncle Solomon. He was his daughter-in-law's brother, a
man who used to ride his horse around town, buying old furniture and old
clothes, "*alte zakhen*," as it was known in Yiddish. He then sold these things
to second-hand stores that re-sold the junk to the public.

"Papa didn't come back," added his grandson. "We went out to look for
him, but the neighbor said he was killed by a bomb just about a block away, as
he was running to Uncle Solomon. We went back and were waiting for Mama
until you came, Grandpa. Do you know where she is?"

"No, I don't." Reb Berl closed his eyes and hugged his grandchildren tightly,
pressing them against his barrel chest. He recited *kaddish*, the mourner's prayer,
for his son.

The children fell asleep, but Reb Berl lay in the dark, thinking that he
would have to go back to Minsk to find his son's body, and bury him according to Jewish tradition.

At three in the morning, when his granddaughter woke up to go to the
bathroom, Reb Berl carefully woke his grandson and said, "Let's start walk-

ing now. That way we'll see *bubbie* very soon." They walked another five hours before they reached Dukora.

Reb Berl and his grandchildren were turning into their street when a column of motorcycles and two trucks filled with laughing, shouting German soldiers, entered Dukora from the north. Fast moving vehicles lifted clouds of dusty gravel high into the air, prompting Reb Berl to stop and cover his face to protect his eyes. When the dust had settled, he saw soldiers running from house to house, herding the residents into the synagogue.

"*Schnell! Schnell! Juden* swine!"

He heard loud screams coming from every direction.

People were being pushed and shoved and kicked and hit with fists and rifle butts. Some were dragged and spit at. Young and old, sick and healthy, all of them scared and devastated, they moved with varying speed and agility, entering the synagogue through its wide-open door.

"*Schnell!*" Reb Berl heard from behind, just as he was hit by a rifle across the back.

He almost fell forward and dropped the suitcase. He turned to face the German soldier, who hit him again with the rifle butt, this time in the stomach. Another soldier was about to hit his grandson. Reb Berl sprang to his grandson and pulled him away from the inevitable blow. He pulled his granddaughter with his other hand, and all three of them ran into the synagogue.

Dukora's small, wooden synagogue was already crowded with people, and Reb Berl saw his wife jammed tightly among the villagers, against the opposite wall.

"Berl!" she shouted, seeing him, as well, but he didn't hear her.

He picked up both children in his arms, and tried to move toward his wife. Suddenly, the soldiers who had pushed the people inside opened fire with their automatic rifles.

Reb Berl hugged his grandchildren to his chest and, out of a protective instinct, turned his back to the oncoming bullets.

Thank God, he thought, *my daughter Fanya lives far away from this hell. Maybe the Germans won't make it to her place.*

He fell, still embracing his grandchildren, his gray beard stained with his and other people's blood, as the torrents of bullets reached the next row of Jews, who also fell, exposing others herded together in the synagogue.

After the massacre, the soldiers poured kerosene over the outside walls and set the synagogue on fire. The fire engulfed the wooden structure, and burned for more than twenty hours, long after the German soldiers had left Dukora on their motorcycles and in their trucks.

* * *

On June 13, 1941, in Dnepropetrovsk, Pavel Rips proudly brought home his high-school diploma. Three days later, on June 16, 1941, he was leaving home for the Sevastopol Naval Institute. In four years, he would become a Red Army Naval Officer, a real sailor, the only thing in the world he truly wanted.

Hershel, Fanya, Rosa and Yakov went to the Dnepropetrovsk train station to see him off. His Uncle Arkady and his wife and two children also came to say goodbye. Pavel took only one small suitcase.

"The Navy will provide everything I need," he said confidently, refusing his mother's advice as to what he should take to school with him.

"Who could have thought, Hershel, that your son would be a Naval officer?" asked Uncle Arkady, joyfully. "You didn't make it."

"I didn't," answered Hershel. "It's a long way from our old *shtetl*, where a Jewish boy could only become a foot-soldier in the Czarist Army."

Fanya cried when she saw her son standing in the doorway of the departing train, but Rosa, Yakov and their cousins laughed with joy for their oldest sibling, and at her tears. They couldn't understand why she would cry at such a glorious moment in their older brother's life.

"Mama, stop it!" said Rosa. "Look at him! He's an adult. He can take care of himself. He'll be an officer."

Fanya didn't answer. She didn't know anything about officers, about Naval school or about the Navy. All she knew was that her son was leaving home and she didn't like it.

Pavel traveled by train, first to Zaporozhye, a relatively small city in Southern Ukraine, downstream from the rapids of the Dneiper River, where he had to change trains to go to Simferopol, a key railroad station on the Crimean peninsula. From there, he caught a bus to Sevastopol and the naval base where his school was located. The trip took two days, and he checked in on June 18, 1941.

Classes would start, he was told, on June 20, 1941, with a month of basic training. Until then, he checked into his dorm. He went through a careful medical examination by naval physicians.

When he received his uniform, he put it on slowly, enjoying the touch of the black-and-white striped undershirt, the mark of the sailor, and polishing his black shoes and every golden button on his coat . But the special moment came when he put his Naval Cadet's cap onto his freshly shaved head. For at least five minutes, he stood in front of the bathroom mirror, looking at the medium-tall, strong young man in his beautiful, dark-blue Naval uniform, the blue-and-white service cap festooned along its peak with gold leaves.

Sevastopol was a small town of about fifty thousand with a long history. It had been adjacent to the ancient Greek colony of Chersonesus, founded in 421 BC. Over the centuries, Cherson had been part of the Roman Empire, until Prince Vladimir of Kiev seized it in 989 AD, used it to force the Byzantine Emperor to honor his offer of his sister, Princes Anna, as Vladimir's bride, and then returned it to Byzantium. While in Cherson, Prince Vladimir accepted the Eastern Orthodox branch of Christianity, and went back to Kiev to baptize his people.

In 1783, the Russians, then ruled by Catherine the Great, annexed the Crimea and began constructing a naval base and a fortress in the town on the southwestern part of the peninsula that they named "Sevastopol." In 1808, the commercial port of Sevastopol was officially opened. Almost fifty years later, after a yearlong siege and many bloody battles, the Russians lost Sevastopol to Anglo-French forces in the course of the Crimean War of 1855. Russia regained control over the city several years later but, by that time, the commercial fleet had moved to other ports on the Black Sea and, from 1894 on, Sevastopol's primary function had been as a naval base.

Basic training started on June twentieth, and the first German bombs were dropped on the twenty-first. The war caught up with Cadet Pavel Rips within a week of his arrival in Sevastopol. All classes had been canceled, but basic training for the incoming cadets continued with increased vigor and seriousness.

After the first day of bombing, the German strategy had become to drop as many mines as possible into the bay, to prevent Soviet ships from leaving the base and from using the bay to hide from German vessels. Regular and magnetic sea mines were floating everywhere. The magnetic mines, drawn to the metal parts of Russian ships and submarines, had previously been unknown to the Russians, and it took them a few months to devise a safe approach to their detection and elimination.

While the Russians continued using Sevastopol's naval base for their infrequent attacks on German and Romanian ports and ships, the Germans were rapidly approaching the Crimea from the west. The battle for the Crimea and for Sevastopol lasted until the end of July of 1942.

The cadets had to wait for the war. The incoming class of 600 young men completed their basic training, and began regular studies. Every day, they had six hours of class work and endured four hours of military and physical training.

The cadets were divided academically into groups based on their major disciplines. Pavel was assigned to a group that specialized in communication. He studied radio, naval and field communication equipment and ways of establishing telephone and radio connections.

Like many other units of the Navy in the Black Sea, the cadets were assigned a specific line in the defense of Sevastopol, a rocky area on the northeastern side of town. Large rocks on the tops of the hills created natural obstacles to the advance of the German troops. Since the Germans had decided to take the Crimea from landward, the Russian sailors were brought ashore to defend Sevastopol from the north.

The people of Sevastopol, as well as the sailors and the cadets, were living in anticipation of a fight. News about German advances and German atrocities was frightening, yet hardening. The sailors' will and resolve were obvious to everyone. They would fight to the death. They were prepared to die for their town, their naval base and their fortress.

By the middle of October of 1941, Sevastopol was almost completely surrounded by the Germans. The sea was the only way in or out. Every day, German planes dropped bombs on the town and mines into its harbor. Cleaning the waterways of mines became an assignment of the highest priority, and associated with great danger.

When, on October 18 of 1941, two weeks before the siege of Sevastopol began officially, the school asked for volunteers to serve on a mine-sweeping vessel, Pavel, who couldn't wait to get to sea, stepped forward. There were more volunteers than the naval commander wanted to draft, but they needed a communications specialist on every ship, and Pavel was selected immediately.

He was assigned to a small minesweeper with a crew of fifteen. They were all sober, serious people. "People in our profession are not allowed to make mistakes," their Captain would repeat. "The very first mistake is our last. There will be no mistakes on my ship."

Cadet Rips was responsible for the maintenance of communications with the naval base and with other vessels. At the same time, he was taught to spot mines in the dark waters of the Black Sea. Most of the mines were spheres covered with little spikes, tethered three or four feet below the surface by anchors on the ends of long lines. Minesweepers had to dislodge these anchors with long hooks, and haul the mines into open water, where they were blown up.

Especially dangerous were the magnet mines. These were new to the Soviets, and they destroyed a great number of Russian vessels before Russian military engineers found a way to disarm them. These mines were attracted to metal, and, immediately after being freed from their anchors, zoomed to the metal underwater parts of the ships and exploded on contact.

The Russians stabilized these mines with metal hooks that were charged with an electrical current by the ship's generator. Electricity blocked the power of the magnets, and the mines could be hauled away and detonated. This dangerous and exciting cat-and-mouse game with mines actually saved Pavel's life.

The nine-month defense of Sevastopol was truly remarkable, mainly because of the sacrifice of the Black Sea sailors fighting on land. At one point, when German tanks were about to break through the defensive lines from the northeast, five of Pavel's classmates and their commander, all of whom had run out of ammunition, threw themselves, with armed hand grenades, under the advancing tanks, blowing them up and preventing their penetration into town. Of the six hundred cadets of the freshman class, seventy-two remained alive when Sevastopol fell. But Pavel was not there.

Pavel took his assignments seriously, with maturity and bravery. He had good hands, and gladly helped with various aspects of work on the ship, whether in the engine room or on the mine-sweeping equipment.

His captain complimented him, one day.

"You are a great Jew," he said, "not like the Jews I knew in my town."

Pavel blushed, but didn't say anything. It seemed to be the norm for everyone to know one good Jew who was not like the "rest of them." Pavel was pleased by his acceptance by his shipmates and his officers, but the collective negative stereotyping of other Jews hurt him greatly. All his Jewish classmates were excellent guys, real patriots, smart, brave and strong. Every Jew he knew was a decent man, a hard worker and a good father, brother or son.

But this wasn't a time for reflection; every minute of their existence was full of danger, and he carried on with the duties of a sailor, a mine-sweeper and a communications specialist.

The besieged Sevastopol finally fell in July of 1942, after nine months of heroic defense. The sea remained the last opening for the evacuation of wounded and the remaining defenders.

During the entire battle for Sevastopol, Pavel's minesweeper had made no mistakes. On the day of Sevastopol's fall, the ship, loaded with two dozen wounded soldiers, departed the Crimea for another port on the southeastern shores of the Black Sea, a small Georgian town called "Poti."

From there, Pavel was taken off his ship and sent to the Caspian port town of Leninakan, where the cadets were reassembled in classrooms to continue their interrupted education. For their naval training, they were assigned to the small but active Russian Caspian Fleet.

The southern part of the Caspian Sea belongs to Iran, a potential ally of Germany that had to be contained, and the Caspian Fleet was supposed to be the guardian against this plausible threat. Pavel stayed in Leninakan until graduation, in June of 1943. At that time, now a Russian Naval officer, Lieutenant Pavel Rips received his new assignment as a naval communications officer with the Baltic Fleet.

CHAPTER FIFTEEN

At the beginning of the war, cities in southern and eastern Ukraine fared a bit better than their western counterparts. The German Army moved forward extremely rapidly, deep into Russia and Ukraine, taking one town after another. A month after the war started, on July 20, 1941, the German troops were less than one hundred miles west of Kiev. On September 21, Kiev fell to the Germans. It took the advancing German army one more month to occupy Kharkov.

During these four months, from the beginning of military action until the city fell, Kharkov was busy evacuating its industrial power eastward. Moshe, Rachel and her mother left Kharkov in August with the plant Moshe had helped evacuate. The factory was destined for Chelyabinsk, a city on the eastern slopes of the Ural Mountains. They were lucky, as their train was not bombed even once. Nevertheless, the ride was slow and they only arrived at Chelyabinsk three weeks later.

David Slavutsky had been drafted into the Army as administrator of the department of dental and maxillofacial surgery at a military hospital that was formed in Tula, a town about one hundred miles south of Moscow. Doctor Evsei Garfinkle, a dental surgeon, who had been chief of one of Kharkov's dental clinics, was appointed to head this department. He also happened to be one of David's major clients in his underground gold business, and he made David his administrator.

Men who had not left with their factories or manufacturing facilities, as well as those who had not been mobilized into the regular Army, were summoned to defend Kharkov in civil-defense brigades. The first task of the civil defense force was to dig trenches along the planned line of defense, three miles west of the city. Brigades of civil defense men, dressed in their ordinary clothes, marched to the outskirts of Kharkov to dig trenches.

Unfortunately, there were more people than spades, and they had to work in shifts. Eventually, they dug miles of trenches, each four or five feet deep. People kept digging even when the sound of German tanks and trucks reached their ears.

The generals believed that the Germans would attempt to encircle the city, and positioned several divisions of the regular Army at the northern and southern ends of town. The central part was guarded by the civil defense, made up of the middle-aged and older men who had remained in town and dug the trenches.

Two days before the battle, it became clear that they had only one rifle for every three men. The order was to fight with shovels, and pick up the rifles of fallen comrades.

On October 24, 1941, the Germans moved into Kharkov in an arrow formation, cutting through the meager civil defense and wedging themselves between the groups of regular Russian troops. The torrents of bullets, artillery shells and bombs decimated the lines of civilians, who only had one rifle for every three defenders. Tens of thousands were killed within a couple of hours of the commencement of this offensive, and hundreds of thousands were captured. Whatever remained of the Russian Army retreated eastward in disarray.

The captured men were kept right there in the field for three days. During this time, the Germans organized hundreds of Ukrainian collaborators into detachments of local police. Unexpectedly, many people volunteered. These were mostly middle-aged men whose families had suffered either at time of the Revolution or shortly after. Ukrainian nationalists who had opposed the Russification of Ukraine made up another group of volunteers. Finally, various criminals found joining the police an easy way to avenge what they considered their "poor treatment by the authorities."

Yurka Gremko fell into in this category. He had worked off and on as an unskilled laborer with a street-paving crew. By the time the war started, he had been arrested three times, for purse-snatching, aggravated battery and theft, and had spent most of the previous two years in jail. He was one of the first to respond to the call of the new administration for a local police force. It was an easy job, he reasoned, with lots of perks and rewards, and so he turned from inmate into law enforcement officer.

On the third day, new recruits into the new police force were walking between the lines of prisoners, looking for Jews and Communists.

"Jews and Communists—two steps forward!" ordered the police commander, through a loudspeaker.

"Jews and Communists—two steps forward!" shouted the Ukrainian policemen, in Russian. The search for victims was their first assignment.

Some people stepped forward. Communists were proud of belonging to the Party, and Jews felt that their appearance gave them away, anyway. Many, however, didn't move. In his new, brown uniform and tall, black boots, Yurka swaggered among the prisoners, trying to identify those who hadn't declared themselves.

"Comrade Rubenstein!" Yurka's face was festooned with a wide smile as he recognized his neighbor. "Didn't you hear the order for kikes like you to step forward? Is anything wrong with your hearing, Comrade Rubenstein?"

Felix Rubenstein remained motionless, looking down at his feet.

"Step forward!" yelled Yurka, "You're an ugly, old, fat Jew! Do you hear me? Step forward!"

Slowly, Felix shuffled forward, almost bumping into Yurka. Equally slowly, he raised his head and looked up into Yurka's face, towering a foot above his own, and spat right into the middle of it. The spit landed on Yurka's nose and dripped down onto his chin.

Yurka gasped and instinctively wiped his face with the sleeve of his new uniform. He stepped back and swung his fist at Felix Rubenstein, drawing blood from his lips and nose. Felix lowered his head again, and stood motionless, staring at the drops of his own blood landing at his feet.

For another hour or so, Yurka and other policemen walked through the rows of prisoners, searching for people they knew, or guessing who might have been a Communist and who might be a Jew. People who stepped forward voluntarily or were pulled out by the policemen were led to the trenches in groups of ten. They stood facing the trenches, hearing behind them the laughter of the firing squads: several groups of cheery, smirking German soldiers with machine-guns.

The Jews and Communists were riddled with bullets in full view of the remaining prisoners, and their dead bodies filled the trenches they had dug just a few days before.

Despite the excitement of his first day at work, Yurka's mood was completely ruined by the silver-colored stain of Felix Rubenstein's spit on the left sleeve of his brown uniform. At the entrance to his apartment house, he ran into Lana Chernenko.

"Wow!" she gasped, at the sight of his uniform. "Boy, you're quick to change sides!"

"What d'you mean, 'change sides?' I've never been on the Communists' side."

"I know, I know," said Lana quickly, realizing she had made a mistake. "I meant you're quick to find a new job. And this uniform sits so well on you. Except you've already stained it." And she pointed at the spot of spit.

"Fucking Jew! This Felix Rubenstein, our neighbor, spat on me," Yurka confessed. "We killed the bastard. I'll just have to wash it off. No big shake. It'll be like new, tomorrow."

"Killed him? Why?"

"We'll get rid of all these fucking Jews and Communists. Whoever's left in town, we'll catch'em. That's the first goal of the new police—to rout them out. Let me know if you see some." And Yurka waved at her, and went to his apartment.

Lana was shocked by this news. Felix Rubenstein had been the father of her friend, Leonid, who was now in the Army, just like her brother, Vasily. She thought she should do something. She didn't know what she could do, but she went straight to the Rubenstein's apartment. Felix's sister-in-law opened the door.

Lana went to Felix's wife and hugged her. "They've just killed Felix," she murmured into her ear. "The Germans and the new policemen have killed your husband." Lana dragged her to a chair, and said, more loudly, as the woman sank in her arms, "Sorry to bring this awful news to you, but I am thinking of you. Tomorrow, they will start plucking out Jews all over town. I guess the stories about the Germans and the Jews are true. They're gonna kill you. What a terrible world."

Felix's wife and her sister were crying silently as they listened to Lana rambling.

"I can hide you at my place," Lana continued, not even realizing the danger of her proposition. "You know I live alone, now. No one will find you at my place. Please, let's go. They'll find you here. Who knows what they're going to do to you? Besides, I don't think the war will last too long. Our Army will return, you know."

She pleaded for half an hour. The women just shook their heads.

"I'm not going anywhere," said Felix's wife. "If they've killed Felix, let them kill me. I'll stay here in my house."

"Thank you for your kindness, but we'll stay together and help one another," echoed her sister. "Thank you very much, though."

Lana left after they promised to come to her in case of real danger. But they didn't come. Next day Yurka and his buddies from the police force took them away and ransacked their apartment. Lana didn't see it happen; she was not at home. No one ever saw the two women again.

* * *

The situation in Dnepropetrovsk was somewhat similar to that in Kharkov. People working at industrial plants and factories which were scheduled to evacuate departed with their employers, young men were mobilized and joined the Army and the rest were left to fend for themselves.

Hershel's brother, Arkady, was chief engineer at the metallurgical plant that was scheduled to relocate to the Siberian town of Tumen. When the evacuation effort began, Arkady made sure that Hershel was hired to dismantle and evacuate the plant. Then, as a plant employee, he was eligible to be evacuated as well. The plant, the equipment and the employees were to leave Dnepropetrovsk in early August, since the town might be taken any day.

On August 5, Hershel, Fanya, Rosa and Yakov were loading some of their household things into a small pick-up truck that had come to take them to the train station. The low bed of the truck was already two-thirds full of someone else's things, and Hershel's suitcases and a couple of boxes were simply piled on top.

Yakov had brought the bicycle that he had inherited from his older brother when Pavel left for Naval school. It was a single-speed man's bike with a tall black frame and chrome handles and pedals. Yakov was too short to reach the pedals from the saddle, so he rode the bike standing on the right pedal, with his left leg reaching the left pedal through the frame. He thought that next year he would be tall enough to ride his brother's old bike in the normal position.

The truck driver refused to take the bike. "There is no room for it!" he shouted. "People are not running away from the Germans to go for a bike ride, for God's sake."

Yakov said he would not go without his bike. He screamed and cried and screamed again, until the truck driver yielded and allowed him to hoist it on top of everything that was already in the truck. Yakov climbed onto the truck, stuffed his skinny body between a box and a suitcase and held on to his bike.

Hershel and Fanya rode in the cabin, next to the driver, and Rosa curled up on their laps. Yakov's fight over his bike added to their anxiety, but pushed the sadness of leaving their home somewhat to the back burner. So many times in their lives, they had had to run away, and so many times they had thought they wouldn't need to do it again. This was especially true here, in Dnepropetrovsk. Hershel had had a good job, they had loved their dream house and the kids had liked their schools and friends, the River Dneiper, and the mild climate of southern Ukraine.

As the truck moved through the pot-holed, cobblestone streets of their neighborhood, Yakov realized he could not hold onto his bike, which was threatening to slide from the truck bed with every bump they encountered. The next moment, the truck hit another pothole, and the bike slipped out of his grasp and tumbled from the truck to the street.

Yakov didn't think twice. He slid from his narrow place between the boxes and jumped off the slow-moving truck to pick up his bike. But by the time he had mounted the bike with his left leg under the frame, the truck was at least a block and half away.

At first, Yakov raced to catch the truck but, realizing that he wouldn't be able to make it, he decided to take what he considered a shortcut to the train station. The shortcut turned out not to be so short after all. The streets he chose were clogged with small trucks and horse-drawn carriages, and a couple of streets had been completely closed by the militia. It took him over an hour to get to the train station.

Meanwhile, Fanya panicked when they arrived at the train station and found that Yakov and his bike were missing from the truck. She couldn't be consoled. "My son, my son," she cried, "where is my son?"

Hershel looked around in total disbelief. He didn't know what to do.

"I told you not to take the freaking bike," said the truck driver. He began unloading boxes and suitcases onto the sidewalk.

Rosa was scared, as well. Throngs of people with boxes, suitcases, sacks, bags, small children and elderly relatives were crying, swearing and pushing everywhere.

"Our train is on Platform Five," said Hershel. "Fanya, stop crying and sit here. He'll show up, trust me," he added firmly, even though he wasn't at all sure whether or not Yakov would make it to the station. "Rosa and I will start carrying our bags to the train." He took a box and a suitcase, and Rosa took a smaller bag, and they went to the right of the train station building, across the tracks to Platform Five.

The train was already there, its open-bed cars loaded with factory equipment covered with canvas. At the back of the train, there were four boxcars for the people traveling with the equipment. Most of the space in these cars was already occupied by people who had arrived earlier, and by their personal items.

Four or five soldiers on the platform were checking for papers authorizing their bearers to board this train. The soldier who checked Hershel's papers said he had seen some space in the last car. Hershel and Rosa went there and squeezed their bags inside. Luckily, people were reasonably accommodating. Rosa stayed in the car, and Hershel returned to Fanya and their remaining bags.

Fanya was still in despair. She sat on her boxes, crying and lamenting her fate. She didn't want to move. Hershel spent five minutes trying to convince her to go to the car, saying that he would come back to search for Yakov, but she would not go.

At that very moment, sweating and panting, Yakov showed up at the train station.

"Mama, Papa!" he yelled, as he approached along the sidewalk. "Sorry! My bike fell off the truck and I had to jump down to pick it up."

"Idiot," said his crying mother, and turned her face away. With renewed energy, she stood up, grabbed one of the suitcases and walked off toward the railroad tracks.

"She's right," Hershel said to Yakov. "You gave us a helluva scare. Stay here with the remaining boxes, and I'll be right back." He carried two large suitcases away, leaving Yakov guarding the two remaining boxes and his bike.

After ten minutes, Hershel returned to fetch the remaining bags and his son. The bike would not fit into the crowded car, but because this boxcar was the last car in the train, Hershel was able to pull a rope from one of his suitcases and tie the bike to the back of the car.

"I guess your brother's bike will travel with us to Siberia," he said to his son, who was helping him tie the bike to a metal railing at the end of the car.

The car was crowded with people and their belongings. People were sitting on the floor or on their bags, suitcases and boxes. They were mainly workers from Arkady's factory, with their families.

The Rips family had a lucky spot against the wall of the car, and Fanya and Hershel were able to lean back against it. The car had no windows and, when the sliding door was closed, air and light were able to enter through the many cracks and slits in and between the wooden slats of which it was made. The train traveled slowly and made numerous stops, mostly for no apparent reason and in the middle of nowhere.

Even though no one knew whether the train would stop for one minute or ten minutes, people jumped off at every stop to relieve themselves, because there was no bathroom on the train. There were two long stops, for over an hour each, at railroad stations. Hershel and Rosa went to fetch hot water from the stations, Fanya remained inside to guard their belongings and Yakov stationed himself at the back of the train to watch his bike. Otherwise, the first day of journey was uneventful.

At the dawn of the second day, the train was bombed by German planes. With the sound of the approaching planes, the train would stop, and the crew and passengers would jump out, run away from the train and lie down in the grass and shrubs, or behind trees, rocks and the natural ruggedness of the land. Germans planes filled the sky like big, dark birds whose droppings brought death and destruction of incredible proportions.

There were two bombing raids, that morning, but the train and passengers were lucky. Except for a couple of near-misses, the bombs missed the train and the people scattered around it.

The sound of the third raid woke them at dawn on the third day. Someone opened the sliding door, and people began jumping into gray fog. Yakov really didn't want to wake up, so Rosa pulled him, and followed her parents. The family sitting next to them was also rushing off the train, but one woman with a baby and a toddler waved her hand, saying "Whatever will be will be."

This time, the airplanes came down very low. One could clearly see the dark-brown helmets of the pilots in the cockpits. Instead of bombing, the planes used their machine guns to strafe the ground around the train. The screams of wounded and frightened people resonated with the sounds of airplane engines and machine guns. Parents covered children with their bodies, while others instinctively covered their heads with their arms, leaving their bodies exposed to the rain of bullets from above.

Only one bomb was dropped in this raid. It scored a direct hit on the Rips' car, the last car of the train. When the raid was over and everyone slowly raised their heads and began tending the wounded, crying over the dead and staring at the train, they saw a pile of twisted metal, burned wood and the remnants of many suitcases in the place where the last car had been.

There was no trace of the woman with two children, and no trace of Yakov's bike. The metal frame of the car, with its wheels broken, was still attached to the car in front of it. The engineers unhooked the destroyed car and motioned to the people to get back aboard.

People buried their dead in shallow graves, and carried the wounded into the cars. The train continued eastward, pulling its valuable load, grown heavier with sorrow, fear and despair.

CHAPTER SIXTEEN

The instant Nahum opened his eyes, he felt a searing pain in his leg and lower back. He was lying flat on his back in the bed of a truck, next to another wounded soldier, whose only signs of life were the loud moans emanating from his windpipe at every bump of the road.

There were two other soldiers in the truck, sitting next to the reclining pair of wounded and leaning against the side of the truck-bed. One soldier's arm was tied to his chest with rolls of dirty gauze. The other had a thick bandage on his head that also covered the upper part of his face. The driver and another wounded man with a head-bandage were in the front of the truck.

They were going to the hospital some ten miles away, along a muddy dirt road peppered with bumps and potholes. The driver seemed to feel that the speedy delivery of his wounded to the hospital was much more important than avoiding the rough spots in the road.

They arrived at the hospital in the middle of the afternoon. Nahum was taken into a large room, where he waited for triage. His leg was very painful, but at least he wasn't on the wooden floor of the truck, bouncing over every obstacle of the rugged terrain. After about an hour, a young doctor approached him.

"Where are you from, soldier?" he asked, cutting open Nahum's pants with a sharp knife, in order to see the wound.

"I am a medic from Stalingrad."

"Medic?" The doctor grinned. "Let's turn you on your stomach, so I'll be able to see what you've got." He and a nurse gently held Nahum's leg while Nahum, moaning loudly, turned onto his stomach.

"I was a student at the Kuibyshev Medical Military Academy before they sent me to the front line."

"Hey, that's my alma mater!" said the doctor. "I graduated last year."

"I just did a year. One for two, to be exact."

"You have a deep wound, my man. A lot of debris, and the wound looks infected. Can't tell what's going on with the bone. I'll see while I'm cleaning it. If any bone is crushed, we may need to amputate it." He bent over Nahum, and added, "I'll take you right away, medic. What's your name?"

"Nahum Draznin."

"I'll do my best. Listen, we're almost colleagues, eh?" And he patted Nahum's shoulder.

Indeed, an hour later, Nahum was wheeled into an operating room. Surgery lasted about an hour, as well. It was done under local anesthetic, and the surgeon tried constantly to engage Nahum in conversation, but he was still in a lot of pain, and could barely maintain consciousness.

"You are lucky," said the surgeon. "The bone is not broken. Might get infected, though; you had a lot of dirt in your wound. Aside from that, I cut out a big part of your calf muscle; it was shattered, anyway. Tied the vessels that were still bleeding. Hopefully, the nerves are intact. If we can avoid osteomyelitis, an infection of the bone, you'll be hopping around in no time."

Nahum stayed in the hospital for two week. He was indeed very lucky. His bones did not become infected, but there was a secondary infection at the stitches. The doctor looked at his wound at the end of two weeks, and said, "I'll send you to a large hospital in Chelyabinsk for further treatment and rehabilitation. I don't want to discharge you and run the risk that your infection will spread to your bones. Let's play it safe."

That evening, Nahum and twenty-two other wounded soldiers were evacuated to Chelyabinsk by train.

He knew that his parents were in Chelyabinsk. The last time he had written them a letter had been in June, before he joined the penal battalion. He hadn't heard from them, either, so he sent them a short note from his hospital bed in Chelyabinsk:

Dear Mama and Papa,
I've been wounded, but don't worry, it wasn't serious. I am now recovering in Chelyabinsk Military Hospital. Hope to see you soon.
Love,
Nahum.

Two days later, Rachel received the letter, and half an hour later, she was at the hospital. She was extremely happy to hear that Nahum was alive. It didn't really matter to her how lightly or how badly he was wounded. He was alive, and that was all that mattered. She found her son in a large room containing twelve metal beds, all occupied by wounded soldiers.

All the soldiers in this ward were out of immediate danger, and lying there healing their wounded limbs. Most of them still couldn't get out of bed. There was one nurse assigned to this and an adjacent ward who was constantly busy, and couldn't possibly attend to all the needs of the wounded soldiers. Rachel, who wanted to stay with Nahum for as long as possible, volunteered to help the nurse in the large ward.

She gave the soldiers water, bedpans and spoons, and fluffed their pillows, covered them with blankets and helped them with their medications. Apart from short breaks at night, she spent almost two weeks in the room, until Nahum was discharged.

His wound had healed, leaving a huge scar in place of his calf muscle, but the bone remained intact, as did the remaining vessels and nerves. Without the calf muscle, his leg was extremely weak, and flexion in his ankle was only partly restored.

"You must exercise your leg constantly," said the doctor, upon his discharge. "You ought to be able to build up new strength in whatever muscle you have left. Also, the more you flex your ankle, the better it will eventually become. It's mainly up to you to restore your leg's function. Meanwhile, crutches will support you on your healing leg."

Nahum stayed home for a week, and went to the local military registration office to find his next assignment. The officer looked through his papers, including the hospital discharge summary, and said, "They think you need four to six months to recover fully. There is a medical school here in town. If they admit you, I'll let you enroll and finish your training. The Army needs doctors. If they don't accept you, you'll go back to the front in six months. Fair enough?"

"Fair enough, Comrade Major," answered Nahum, enthusiastically. He was certain the school would admit him. He couldn't see why not.

As it turned out, he was correct. The Dean of the Medical School was delighted to see a man from the front lines, a former cadet of the Military Medical Academy and a student with excellent grades, who wanted to enroll in his Medical School. He met Nahum at the door to his office, helped him to a chair, held his crutches and offered him a cigarette.

"We certainly have a spot for you. Most definitely. If we don't admit soldiers who have risked their lives for the Motherland, then whom shall we admit? You are a priority for our school. With your grades, I would think you should do well as a third-year student, even though we are at the beginning of the second semester. You think you can handle returning to books and classes?"

"I think so," said Nahum, confidently. "If you want, I can start the second semester right now, and take the first-semester final in about a month."

"Oh, that would be perfect. You know what? You can take the tests any time during the second semester. I'll let our professor know that it's totally up to you when you wish to take a test. You don't know how much a real soldier from the front line could add to our class. All that experience and maturity!

Our students' lives will be enriched."

The very next Monday, Nahum showed up for classes. As before, he found the learning process enjoyable, and not at all difficult. He quickly went through the material from the first semester, and by the end of April, he had successfully passed all of the first-semester finals. Also by the end of April, he was walking with only one crutch supporting his weak side on stairs or uneven terrain.

Socially, however, he had hard time finding friends among his classmates. Even though the difference in age was imperceptible—he was only a year or so older than the majority of students in his class—he was the only one who was in the Army and the only one with combat experience. The students related to him as if he were much older, and outside their group.

He wasn't too bothered by this; he knew he had to catch up with his studies, and spent all his time doing just that: studying, studying and studying.

*   *   *

The Rips' train slowly approached the station. The last couple of miles had been particularly slow and tedious. The train had barely moved. When it had finally stopped at the Tumen railroad station, and the doors of the cattle cars opened into the short Siberian daylight, the passengers piled into the small, brick-and-wood building of the train station.

Inside, at two long desks, sat local representatives, directing the arriving refugees to various living accommodations. The Rips family was sent almost to the center of the town, to a room in a small log house that already housed three other families.

Because only one of their suitcases had survived the bombing, it was a relatively easy walk from the train station to their new quarters. Luckily, Hershel had a job, and his meager salary would take care of their most immediate needs, such as warm clothes and a few pots and pans.

Rosa and Yakov enrolled in the neighborhood school, and the school year began, as usual, on September 1, 1941. This was to be the last year of school for Rosa, but Yakov had two more to go.

The children at school accepted the refugee students matter-of-factly. Most locals realized that wartime demanded various sacrifices. They wouldn't have minded the influx of refugees into their community except that they had to accommodate the newcomers in their houses, giving up their rooms and sharing their kitchens and bathrooms with strangers who would be staying in Tumen for an unknown period of time.

Rosa was only five foot two, and the teacher asked her to sit at the front of the class. Rosa didn't mind at all. In addition to being short, she was near-sighted, but she did not want to wear glasses, thinking that she was not as pretty with them on her cute, round face.

She picked the front desk of the middle row. She shared her desk with Vasselina Ugrumova, a local girl who was as short as Rosa, and nearsighted. She wore large, black-rimmed glasses to see the blackboard.

"I've heard they are going to bring Jews to Tumen," said Vasselina to Rosa, one day, as they were walking home from school.

Rosa looked at her with astonishment, not understanding what Vasselina's excitement meant. "I know," she answered, "Jews are being killed by the Germans. They can't stay where they are."

"I've never seen a Jew," said Vasselina. "People say they have horns."

"Horns?"

"Yes. Two small horns. Father Eremei showed us a picture of a famous Jew, Moses, I think his name was, and he had two small horns. Father Eremei told the people in the church that all Jews have these horns. I'd like to see them."

Rosa was absolutely shocked. She couldn't think of anything to say. She had never seen a picture of Moses; she hadn't even heard the name. But, she realized, she didn't know of any famous Jews. She only knew her family and her school friends in Dnepropetrovsk.

"Did you ever see Jews where you used to live?" asked Vasselina.

Rosa stopped suddenly and said, "Vasselina, I *am* a Jew." And, seeing the astounded, terrified eyes of Vasselina, she bent her head and patted it with her palm.

"See? I have no horns. Jews don't have horns. They are people, the same as you are. Touch, touch here, Vasselina."

She moved her head towards her classmate, grabbed her reluctant hand, and pressed it against her head. "See, see, there are no horns."

Vasselina drew back her hand and shouted, "I don't believe you! Father Eremei said Jews have horns. He knows. You are not a Jew!"

They were standing in the middle of the sidewalk staring at one another in mistrust and disbelief.

"Fine," said Rosa, "if your Father Eremei knows, so be it." She turned away from Vasselina and ran home.

When Hershel returned home, Rosa asked him, "Papa, who was the famous Jew, Moses?"

"Oh, my goodness," said Hershel. "I haven't heard his name for quite a while. He was the man who led the Jews from Egypt, where they had been slaves, to Israel, where they became free people, again. On the way, believers say, he received the Torah from the hands of God. Why do you want to know?"

"A girl in my class said he had horns, and therefore all Jews have horns. She said there was a picture of him that showed his horns. Is this true?"

"Oh, Jews don't have horns; you know that! I haven't seen the picture, but I was told there was a picture or a statue of him, somewhere in a foreign land, showing him with two small horns. People say the artist wanted to show the rays connecting him with God or with Heaven, but made something looking like small horns."

"Why don't these people like us? Why do they make up these horrible stories about horns?" lamented Rosa.

"Religions are funny things, Rosa. They unite some groups of people, but also instill hatred between groups. The best thing is not to believe."

"We are not religious, but we are still Jews. How come?"

"One day we'll all be the same, and we'll all love each other. That day will come."

Rosa switched the angle of her questioning. "If we all are going to be the same, why do you tell us we must marry Jews?"

"Because that day has not yet come. We are not yet accepted. This is precisely why Jews should marry Jews." Hershel left the table, ending the conversation.

The Russian winter of 1941 was one of the coldest and snowiest in living memory. Tumen was no exception. People were hungry, angry and determined to survive. Since October, 1941, Hershel and Fanya had received only one letter from Pavel. By the time Rosa graduated from high school in June of 1942, they had no idea where he was or whether or not he was still alive. Even though Hershel worked hard, his meager salary was barely enough to feed his family. But he wanted to see his daughter continue her education.

He often told her and Yakov, "There's no future for you without education. I see so many smart people around me who would have been so much better off in life if they had had education. Without the diplomas of higher education, you are nothing. As long as I'm able to work, I will support your education."

In Tumen, there was only one opportunity for education, a teachers' school, so Rosa applied there. She would have been perfectly happy to become a teacher; she hadn't even thought about going to school away from home.

But her Uncle Arkady and his family were moving to Chelyabinsk. He had been promoted to the position of Chief Engineer at a very large metallurgical plant, and was leaving in July. His daughter, Rosa's cousin, who was a year younger than Rosa, asked her to move with them, and to go to school in

Chelyabinsk.

"There are so many more schools there, so many students, so many more young people. I'm going to go to medical school next year. Why would you want to be a teacher? Let's become doctors. You go this year, and I'll join you next summer. You'll live with us or in the dorms. So much better than being a teacher!"

To Rosa, this sounded both convincing and exciting. She liked the idea of becoming a doctor, even though she had never thought about it before. Being in a town with many more students also appealed to her. Tumen was a pretty boring place, after all. But she didn't know how her parents would react to her new idea.

Fanya just shrugged her shoulders. She still in shock from losing her Dnepropetrovsk home, and hated Tumen and Siberia and their communal living. To her, any place was better than this cold, Godforsaken Siberian town.

Surprisingly, Hershel wasn't opposed to the move, either. He actually liked her choice of medical school.

"The most important thing for me, Rosa," he said seriously, "is that you finish your education. I don't want you to drop out. If you promise to stick with your schooling until the very end, I don't mind letting you go. My brother is there, and he'll help you with whatever you might need. As long as you keep your word not to quit."

"I promise!" said Rosa, happily, not seeing any reason why she would quit school.

The next day, she sent her documents to Chelyabinsk Medical School and, a month later, heard that she had been accepted. The letter advised her that school would start on September first, and she must be there a week beforehand, for orientation. It was also decided that, for the first year, she would stay with her uncle and aunt, and could decide later about moving to a dormitory.

Rosa arrived in Chelyabinsk in August, 1942 and, on September 1, became a medical student. Fourteen months and six days later, on November 6, 1943, at a school dance in honor of the twenty-sixth anniversary of the Bolshevik Revolution, Rosa Rips met a tall, slim medical student.

There were easily a couple of hundred people at the party. The student brass band was playing tangos, foxtrots and waltzes. Some couples were dancing, but a lot of the men were standing along the right-hand wall of the hall, and many women were lined up along the opposite one.

Rosa wore a blue dress that hung to the middle of her shins and had three buttons at the neck, two of which she left unbuttoned. Because she was only five foot two, she wore shoes with at least two-inch heels. She had come with her cousin, a freshman at the school. Both girls loved to dance, and, one after another, boys invited them onto the floor.

About an hour into the party, Rosa noticed a tall student with bushy black hair, wearing a green military uniform without epaulets or insignia, who was standing alone at the wall, leaning on a crutch under his left arm. He was tall, and she could see his eyes, forehead and untidy black hair from the dance floor. He smoked and gazed randomly at the dancing couples.

A couple of times, their eyes met, at first just for an instant. But, after a while, he was watching the short, energetic Rosa all the time. Whenever she looked at him, while twirling about the dance floor with different partners, she would meet his eyes. She smiled, and he smiled back.

Half an hour later, when the band was taking a smoke-break, she approached him.

"And you don't dance because...?" she asked, with a wide smile.

"Two reasons. One is fairly obvious," he answered, lighting up a cigarette. "I was wounded in the leg, and it hasn't quite healed, yet."

"And the less obvious reason?"

"Less obvious to you, but to me, it is also straightforward. I don't know how to dance. I've never tried."

"You and my brothers! I love dancing! I'm Rosa, Rosa Rips, a second year student." She offered him her hand.

"Nahum Draznin. Fourth year student." He shook her hand.

"And what happened to your leg?"

"I was wounded just over a year ago, now. It's getting better. My plan is to walk without crutches by January."

"That's when I'll start teaching you how to dance!" laughed Rosa.

"I'm willing to try." Nahum smiled. "I know you like dancing and the party is still young, but it's a bit boring for me, here. Do you mind if we just go for a walk?"

Rosa turned to the dance floor and searched for her cousin, who was still dancing in the crowd. "I came with my cousin. I'm living with my uncle's family, you know, and I can't leave without talking to her. Wait for me here; I'll be back."

"I haven't moved from this spot in an hour and a half. I'm not going to go anywhere," replied Nahum.

Rosa dashed to the dance floor to find her cousin and, five minutes later, returned to Nahum, who was still leaning against the wall, puffing rings of smoke from his cigarette.

"We can go, if you want. I'll meet my cousin at home. By the way, you smoke a lot. Every time I look at you, you have a cigarette."

"Nasty habit, I know," said Nahum, as they meandered through the crowd to the checkroom. "It helps me think, I think," he added. He put on his dark-green military overcoat and she her black coat with the gray rabbit-fur collar, and they walked out of the building.

In Chelyabinsk, November was almost a winter month. It was cold. Neither of them had any headgear or scarf, and they raised their collars to protect their cheeks and ears from the cold wind.

"We are not going to walk for too long in this weather," said Nahum, shivering from the cold.

"Why don't you just walk me home? My uncle's apartment is not too far away," said Rosa, who was also very cold, especially her legs.

"With pleasure."

Rosa's Uncle Arkady indeed lived about twelve blocks away from the school; about a twenty-minute walk. Luckily, there seemed to be less wind in the narrower residential streets, and they felt more comfortable.

"May I see you tomorrow?" asked Nahum, as he shook her hand at the door to her apartment building.

"I'll be in the library, studying," said Rosa, "some time after three o'clock."

"I have classes until five. Will you wait?"

"I will," said Rosa, and she disappeared behind the door.

She liked this lanky student in military clothes. He was different from her other friends; calmer and more intelligent, with a distinctive sense of humor.

Nahum walked home slowly, thinking about how much energy, vitality and joy of life this girl possessed. In the depressing times of war, those were rare qualities.

They saw each other daily, mainly in the library after classes and in the evening, when he walked her home. A week later, she invited him to meet her Uncle Arkady.

Nahum came on Thursday, around eight o'clock, wearing his green military clothes, black shoes and gray overcoat. He was still using one crutch. He sat at the dining table with Uncle Arkady and Aunt Frieda, and her cousin served tea with small, homemade biscuits.

"Rosa was telling us you were wounded on the front lines. Where did it happen? Where were you?" asked Arkady.

"In Stalingrad. Just over a year ago."

"My goodness. That was a real tough spot," sighed Aunt Frieda.

"My mama thinks I was lucky that I came out alive."

"I would definitely agree with her," added Aunt Frieda. "Wouldn't you?"

"Oh, I'm with her. In retrospect, it was pure luck."

"Were you a medic?" asked Arkady.

"Yes. I did a year in a Military Medical Academy before being sent to the front."

They sat at the table for almost three hours, and talked about the war, the recent success of the Soviet Army, medical school, Nahum's life in Kharkov, Arkady's life in Dnepropetrovsk, their lives since evacuation and their family ties. They "clicked." They liked each other, listened to each other's stories with attention and interest, and made optimistic projections about their own and their country's futures.

"Very nice kid, Rosa. Very nice," said Uncle Arkady after Nahum left, and he held out his fist with his thumb up. "Great kid."

At the end of the next week, Nahum proposed to Rosa. "I love you and I want you to marry me," he told her, when they were sitting alone across a library table. He extended his arm and put his hand over hers, looking straight into her eyes.

"We've only known each other for two weeks!" gasped Rosa, even though she felt she loved him, too. "That's such a short time."

"I feel I know everything I need to know about you. What more can I possibly uncover? You have a big heart and all the energy in the world. You are there for your friends, and I hope to be one of them forever. I love you today as I will love you three months from now. What's the point in waiting?"

"Maybe one of us should finish school? I still have three and half years to go, but you; you will be done in year and a half. Can't we wait until then?"

"What difference would it make? If you agree to marry me, let's do it now. We'll go through school together. Why wait? This is my commitment to you. I want to be with you. I don't want to wait. Will you marry me?"

"Do you need to ask your parents? By the way, I haven't even met them."

"If you agree to marry me, we'll go and meet them right now. I don't need to ask them. I know they'll support me, and they'll love you. We will just tell them we are getting married."

Rosa was silent. Everything was like a dream or a fairy tale: the prince, the speed with which she had fallen in love, the happy ending. She had drifted off in' this fantasy world when she was awakened by his touch and his voice.

"Rosa, Rosa, I love you. Will you marry me?"

She looked into his wide-open blue eyes and said, softly, "Yes."

He dropped his face onto her hand and began kissing it. She ran her other hand through his hair and pulled his head toward her.

"Yes," she said again. "I'll marry you."

CHAPTER SEVENTEEN

R achel was immediately enchanted by Rosa's energy and vitality. The short, slim girl, a few months shy of her nineteenth birthday, felt a bit timid, following Nahum into Rachel and Moshe's home. But her shyness didn't last long. With friendly encouragement, Rosa's gregarious personality came to the fore.

What Rachel liked most was Rosa's description of her family: her parents and her two brothers. The pride and love of her siblings and parents were so prominent in her stories that Rachel not only noticed them, but actually turned her head to Moshe and said, in Yiddish, "She loves her family; it's a good sign."

Rosa, who had grown up in Celiba and Dukora speaking Yiddish with her mama, and her grandparents, burst into laughter.

"I understand Yiddish very well," she said, with a ringing laugh. "It's my 'mama-loshen.'"

And they all laughed.

The next morning, Rosa wrote a letter to her parents.

Dear Mama and Papa,
Several weeks ago I met a wonderful person, Nahum Draznin, who proposed to me yesterday. AND I AGREED!!! WE ARE GETTING MARRIED!!!
He is absolutely wonderful, tall and handsome, with big blue eyes. He is also the smartest student in the school. He is a fourth year student and recently returned from the front. Uncle Arkady met Nahum several times and he can tell you how great Nahum is. I know you will love him as much as I do the minute you see him. I also met his parents and they are very nice as well.
Mama and Papa, I am so excited! I wish you were here with me!
Love you so much,
Yours,
Rosa

The next week, Rosa and Nahum applied for a marriage license. They filed their petition with the local civil authorities, and were told to come back in a month, to be registered as husband and wife.

"These are the rules," said the woman at the marriage registration desk. She accepted their papers without even lifting her eyes to theirs. "You have to wait a month."

"Not a big deal," said Nahum, as they walked out of City Hall, somewhat disappointed with news of the marriage rules. "It'll give us time to request a family room in the dorms. Besides, we are getting married for life, and what is one month, in the life of human beings?"

Meanwhile, in Tumen, Hershel read Rosa's letter to Fanya. "'We are getting married!'" he read, in a low voice. He put the letter down.

"*Oy, mein Gott!*" said Fanya. "I knew she should have stayed at home."

Hershel didn't reply. He remembered how he had traveled to Dukora to ask Reb Berl's permission to marry his daughter. It had been a bit old fashioned, he realized, but it was a good tradition. It was the right thing to do. *How can you not ask the father? Who is this Nahum, anyway? And Rosa, too, not a question, not permission, just like that—"we are getting married." That's it; a fact.* He should go there, to find out what was going on.

"Is that it? Anything else in the letter?" asked Fanya.

Hershel lifted the letter and finished reading. "'...*wish you were here with me! Love you so much, Yours, Rosa.*'"

"Arkady liked him. Maybe he is not such a bad guy," said Fanya.

"It doesn't matter!" replied Hershel, sternly. "First of all, they should have asked us. Just to show some respect, if nothing else. And second, I don't want her to drop out of school. Getting married; having children—she'll never finish. She'll never be a doctor. I'm going to Chelyabinsk. I must stop this nonsense."

A week before Rosa's marriage, Hershel arrived in Chelyabinsk.

"Papa!" Rosa jumped to hug her father, as he walked into Arkady's apartment. "I'm so happy you're here!"

Suddenly, she noticed the stern look on her father's face. "Papa, what's the matter? Has anything bad happened? Is everyone fine?"

"Well, everyone's fine," answered Hershel, walking into the room. "We're worried about you. It's your marriage that brought me here."

"It's a good deal, brother," Arkady chimed in. "She got the best groom in the world. You're a lucky man, my brother."

This spontaneous interjection of Arkady's calmed Hershel. *Maybe it is the best thing for Rosa,* He thought. *Why does she need to ask me?* But instead, he said, "I don't really care how good he is. I don't want you to get married."

"Why not, Papa?" Rosa was shocked.

"I'm telling you, Hershel, he is the best Jewish boy you can find," added Arkady. "I'd be thrilled to have a son-in-law like him."

"He may well be, but that's irrelevant. Rosa's too young. It's too early for her. She must finish school, first. Remember, you promised me? Remember? That you'd finish school?"

"I do, and I will finish school."

"You are not even nineteen. You don't know what you are doing."

"So? Mama was eighteen when she married you, wasn't she?"

"And she did not know what she was doing. Besides, I was firm on my feet and I did ask her father whether I could marry her. Did anyone ask me?"

"I'm sorry, Papa," cried Rosa. "You were not here; we couldn't ask."

"Is that what's bothering you, Hershel?" Laughed Arkady. "Come on, brother. In the middle of a war, a thousand miles away from you, young people fall in love and want to get married, and you want them to search for you? Forget it. You'll see Nahum and you'll understand how lucky you are."

When Nahum came in, Rosa was still crying and Hershel fell terrible, but he didn't want to yield. He looked at Nahum briefly, and lowered his eyes. *My God! He's an invalid!* he thought, seeing only Nahum's crutch.

"It's just a wound," said Nahum, guessing Hershel's fear. "It's getting much better, and I won't need support after the first of the year. I'm glad you came. I always wanted to ask your permission to marry your daughter." He sat down.

Silence filled the room. Then Rosa lifted her face, Hershel straightened his shoulders, and Arkady's face melted in a huge smile.

Hershel avoided a direct answer. "And how do you plan to support your-selves? You are both students, aren't you?"

"We receive small stipends from the school. We hope to get a dormitory room for families, and my parents will help. They live here in town. I have a year and a half to go, and then I'll be working."

"Don't you need to go back to the Army?"

"I might, particularly if the war goes on."

"Rosa, do you understand this? That he might still go back to the front? Who knows how long you might be waiting for him to come home? Do you understand?"

"I do, Papa. I do."

Hershel stayed in Chelyabinsk for two days. Before he left, he said to Rosa, "I know you are in love, and I bless your decision. I just want to tell you that it's never too late to change your mind. You are so young."

"I love him, Papa. Everything will be fine."

Hershel kissed his daughter, and returned to Tumen. "I blessed them, but I'm not happy about this," he told Fanya. "I don't think it's a good decision, but what do I know?"

He didn't tell Fanya that Nahum was on crutches. By the time she sees him, he probably won't need them.

By the end of December of 1943, Nahum and Rosa had become husband and wife. They had no wedding. They walked into the City Hall, signed their names in the Marriage Registration Book, received a Marriage Certificate, and walked outside—husband and wife. By that time, the course of the war had become completely different. Russian troops had liberated Kharkov, Dnepropetrovsk and Kiev, and were moving toward Minsk and Leningrad. In 1944, people, schools and factories began returning to the liberated areas.

Nahum and Rosa applied for transfers to Kharkov Medical School for the fall of 1944. Nahum had one and Rosa three years to go before graduation. They and Nahum's parents returned to Kharkov in July, 1944. They left behind the grave of Grandma Haya, who had died in Chelyabinsk a year before.

Except for the shattered windowpanes in most of the flats and bullet marks on the façade of the building, their apartment house was surprisingly well-preserved. Only the upper floor of Entrance D had been demolished by the heavy bombing. When the Draznins arrived, repairs were already underway. They nailed bed sheets over the broken windows, and waited patiently until city workers came to put new glass in the window frames.

Rosa and Nahum took over the small room with the balcony, and Rachel and Moshe put their bed in the large room, where Grandma Haya's bed had used to stand. After the dormitory room, Rosa was delighted to be in her own apartment with their own bathroom and toilet. Rachel and Moshe were also extremely happy to return to their old place. It was one of the happiest days in their lives.

Some of the old neighbors were coming back, as well. Some who had stayed in Kharkov during the occupation looked at the returning neighbors with fear and uncertainty. They were terribly afraid of being accused of collaborating with the Germans. For most people, such accusations meant serious trouble.

Maria Ivanovna Pilman returned to her apartment only to find it occupied by a family who had moved into the empty flat in 1941, immediately after Kharkov had fallen into German hands. These people didn't want to move out, and they shut the door right in the face of Maria Ivanovna, who, crying inconsolably from the abuse and frustration, came to stay with the Draznins.

The next day, Nahum went with her to the newly formed regional Communist Party center, and argued that the mother of an officer of the Russian Army should be allowed to move back into her own apartment. Arkady Pilman was a Major in the Army, and still on active duty. Three weeks later, the squatters were evicted, and a tearful, grateful Maria Ivanovna moved back in. But she had no information about her husband, David Maximovich, who had been arrested, back in 1937.

Yurka Gremko had left Kharkov with the Germans. During the occupation, he had risen in the ranks of the local police force, and become Chief of the regional division. He was known in Kharkov as a notorious torturer and killer, and had simply been unable to stay in the city when the Russian Army came back. His mother, Varvara Mikhailovna, was still living in the apartment house, and working full time as janitor, sweeping sidewalks and washing stairwells.

Lana had also left with the Germans. Throughout the occupation she had flirted and slept with German officers, to make money to survive the misery of the war. When the Russian Army had been about to enter Kharkov, she had decided to move to Kiev, a city where she'd be a total stranger, without the baggage of her past behavior. She had known that some girls who made a living in similar ways had moved all the way to Germany, but she hadn't wanted to leave Russia. Changing cities had seemed to her enough. Her brother, Vasily, a tank commander, had been killed in action, her mother had still been a prisoner in one of the Siberian labor camps, her alcoholic father was dead, and nothing had been keeping her in Kharkov. She had left.

No one knew anything about Leonid Rubenstein. His apartment remained empty and its windows broken, allowing snow, rain and sunshine to enter easily.

The night before she left Kharkov, Lana had gone to the Rubenstein apartment and left a small envelope with a short letter in a crack in the wall, beneath the windowsill. *To Leonid*, she had written across the envelope, and stuffed it into the largest crevice.

When Leonid came back, in 1946, the apartment was still empty, still had broken windows and was terribly weather-beaten. It was almost a miracle that no one had moved in. Leonid, like Vasily, had been serving in a tank division. In 1942, his tank had been hit, and he had barely escaped with severe burns on his face, scalp and hands. He had spent months in hospitals and survived numerous infections, but his skin had been replaced by ugly scar tissue.

He had volunteered to go back to the Army, but, despite the suicidal ideation that outrageously crazy behavior on the front lines , he had survived his delirious courage and been discharged in early 1946.

He walked into his filthy apartment and looked around. It was totally empty, it was dirty and it looked almost completely destroyed. Leonid slowly walked around, as if measuring the size of the rooms. Finally, he saw an envelope sticking out of the crevice under the window. He pulled it out.

To Leonid, it said. He opened it and read a short paragraph scribbled on a page torn from a small notebook.

I don't know whether you'll return home, but I must tell you what I know about the fate of your parents. I felt you need to know, if you do come back. Yurka Gremko killed your father as soon as the Germans came into town. His body is in one of the mass graves on the outskirts of Kharkov. Your mother and her sister were taken to the Ghetto, and I don't know whether they survived. I doubt it. The war is a terrible time, and our generation had the worst of it.

Yours,

Lana

Leonid spent the night on the floor of his messy apartment. At dawn, he took his gun, and went to see Yurka's mother. Varvara Mikhailovna was already up and ready to go outside to clean around the building. She opened the door and looked at Leonid without recognizing him.

"Yes," she said. "What d'you need?"

"Leonid Rubenstein," he said, pushing her inside. "I came to pay my dues." He shot her twice in the chest. As frightened neighbors popped out of their doors to see what was going on, he put the gun into his mouth and pulled the trigger.

The 1944-45 academic year at Kharkov Medical School started in September. In February, Rosa found out that she was pregnant. It was a great cause for celebration. Nahum and his parents were as excited as Rosa was. In April, she would turn twenty, and in October, they would have their first child. She wrote a letter to her parents, who, by this time, had returned to Dnepropetrovsk.

Yakov, now eighteen, had been accepted into engineering school, and Pavel, twenty-two, was still serving in the Navy, on the Baltic Sea.

Having received Rosa's letter, Hershel decided to visit her in Kharkov. It was only six or seven hours from Dnepropetrovsk to Kharkov, and on April the 8th, Rosa's twentieth birthday, Hershel boarded the train. He hasn't celebrated his children's birthdays for five years. The last one he remembered was Rosa's fifteenth in 1940. He bought her favorite vanilla ice cream. It was still cold in Dnepropetrovsk in early April, but he bought her an ice cream cone over Fanya's objections who was convinced that cold ice cream in the cold weather would result either in sore throat or a week of running nose, a high price to pay for a ten-minute pleasure.

April of 1945 was cold as well. Dirty snow was covering the street of Kharkov, but the roofs of the buildings were already clear of snow. Hershel wore a winter coat with a narrow fur collar and a wool cap with short flaps covering his ears. He had only a small suitcase and decided to walk from the train station to the Draznins. It was at least an hour walk, but he arrived early, around three in the afternoon, and knew there would be no one at home until about five o'clock.

When Rosa came home shortly after five, she found him sitting on his suitcase in front of the apartment house entrance D main door.

"Papa!" She exclaimed happily. "What a great surprise! I am so happy you came!"

"How are you, my sunshine?" he asked Rosa, hugging her carefully, suddenly remembering she was pregnant.

"I'm fine, Papa. I'm very happy, and I feel good in their family. They love me and treat me very well."

"I'm so glad to hear you say that."

"You don't need to worry, Papa."

"That's what parents do, isn't it?"

At the dinner table, Hershel didn't talk much. Rachel and Moshe were meeting him for the first time, and they tried to initiate conversation on several occasions, but Hershel seemed completely disinterested in maintaining it, regardless of topic. Instead, he seemed to be studying their faces and their non-verbal behavior. He ate very little, citing lack of appetite and a dull headache. After dinner, he asked that his mattress be placed in the kitchen, refusing to sleep in either Rosa's or Rachel's room.

Next morning, Hershel woke up earlier than anyone else in the house and, when Rosa came out of her room, he said, "I'm leaving, my sunshine. I'm going back to Mama."

"Why, Papa? You just came! Why can't you stay a little longer? Maybe another day?"

"No. I came to see how you are; what your life is like. I see you are happy and content, and that's all I need to see. I'll go home knowing that you are happy—what else can a father ask? You are happy, so I'm happy."

He left as soon as everyone got up.

That evening, at dinner, Rachel said to Rosa, "An interesting man, your father. Doesn't talk much, eh?"

"*Er iz a bisele zudreit* (he is a bit crazy)," commented Moshe, in Yiddish, forgetting that Rosa understood it perfectly.

Before anyone could blink an eye, Rosa jumped to her feet and pounded her fist on the table. "He is my father, and you have no right to speak badly of him. Good or bad, my family is my family, and no one, absolutely no one, is allowed to say a bad word about them in my presence. Never!" This time she slammed her palm on the table, and quickly left the room, leaving the astonished Nahum, Rachel and Moshe at the dinner table.

She cried on their bed until Nahum and Rachel knocked at the door and walked in. "Rosa, my dear," said Rachel, "we have never said anything disparaging about your family, and we will never do that. It was just a bad joke. Moshe didn't mean to insult you, believe me." She bent over Rosa and kissed her on her head.

A baby boy was born on October 1, 1945. Three months later he became seriously ill. He was hot, couldn't sleep and cried, literally non-stop. Rosa, who had planned on returning to classes after a short maternity leave, decided to take a year off. She also chose not to tell her parents about her decision to interrupt her schooling. She remembered how afraid her father had been that she might drop out of school. She thought she'd tell them later, when she'd gone back.

The baby, named Boris, after Rosa's Grandpa Reb Berl, continued to be extremely sick. Nahum brought home a private pediatrician, who diagnosed severe middle-ear infection. Antibiotics were not available in Russia, at that time, and the pediatrician recommended seeing an ear specialist, suggesting possible surgery to drain the infection.

Nahum went to the best specialist at the Medical School, who examined little Boris and said that surgery ought to be performed immediately. He operated the same evening.

He made a long incision behind Boris' left ear, cutting through the soft bone to allow the pus that had accumulated in the middle ear to drain. The surgery saved Boris' life. Rosa stayed in the hospital with her baby who, to everyone's delight, recovered very quickly.

At that time, Rosa made another important decision—to switch from medical to dental school. Both medical school and a future career in medicine required weekend and night calls that would take her away from her son. As a dentist, she reasoned, she would be home all weekends and all nights.

Transferring from one school to another was relatively easy. A more difficult task was writing her father about it:

Dear Papa,
One little boy is recovering well after his urgent surgery. He is eating well and gaining weight. Because of his illness I took this year off, but I will be returning to school next fall. I've made a decision to switch to dentistry, simply because it will allow me to avoid night and weekend calls and spend more time with the family. I will be a dentist. It's almost the same as a physician.

Love,
Rosa

She reread her draft, and crossed out the last sentence; it sounded too defensive. *I'm sure he'll understand*, she thought as she dropped her letter into the mailbox, even though she wasn't certain at all.

Meanwhile, Nahum had been drafted into the Army for two more years. Because the war was already over and he had previously served in the front lines, he was assigned to the Internal Security Forces as a physician in a camp for German prisoners of war. It was a terrible job, involving very little medicine. His clinic had almost no medications, and no one in the Internal Security Forces or among the camp commanders cared about the lives and well-being of the German prisoners.

Tens, if not hundreds, of them died daily from disease, malnutrition and torture by either guards or other prisoners, and no one was overly concerned.

Nahum found the job depressing and demeaning. His medical skills were totally unnecessary for the work he was expected to perform. He was actually surprised that he felt no animosity or anger toward the German prisoners. He could no longer associate these pitiful men with the monsters who had inflicted such incredible suffering on his countrymen. If anything, he wanted to help to those who made it to his dilapidated clinic.

He spent most of his time reading medical journals that he checked out from the Medical School library, and thinking about his future plans. From his reading, he, unexpectedly, developed in interest in endocrinology, a medical specialty that was dealing with problems of the glands, such as the thyroid, the adrenals, and the pancreas. The more he read, more fascinated he become, particularly with the ways these little glands affected growth and development of human beings. The endocrine glands produce biochemical substances, called hormones, and either excess or deficiency of these hormones caused incredible problems in person's health. If diagnosed timely, these problems could be reasonably well controlled. He thought endocrinology seemed to offer challenging diagnostic puzzles and, at the same time, realistic therapeutic hope. It also stimulated his curiosity as to how and why these endocrine problems develop in the first place. Intellectually, he was greatly intrigued. By the time he was discharged from military duty, he was firmly convinced he wanted to become an endocrinologist. He made his professional choice.

CHAPTER EIGHTEEN

I n May of 1945, two weeks after the capitulation of Germany, Colonel Doctor Evsei Garfinkel and his administrative assistant, Captain David Slavutsky, were returning to Russia from Germany. The war had taken their dental unit from Tula to Riga to Warsaw and, eventually, to Germany.

Now they were going to Moscow for a week of vacation and reassignment. David had only his large rucksack with him, but the doctor was carrying two sizable suitcases. When the train approached the border-crossing between Poland and Russia, a group of border-patrol soldiers boarded the car in which the doctor and David were riding.

As if anticipating trouble, the doctor leaned over to David and said, "If they ask whose suitcases are these, tell them they are yours. Whatever happens, I'll take care of you for life."

David didn't understand what doctor Garfinkel was referring to, but he nodded agreeably.

As if they were working on a tip, the soldiers and their officer walked straight up to Dr. Garfinkel. "Colonel Garfinkel," said the officer. "Where is your luggage?"

Silently, the doctor pointed to David's rucksack. The soldiers opened the rucksack, and the officer searched through its contents. Not finding what he was looking for, he asked, "Whose suitcases are these?"

"Mine," said David, meekly.

"Open them, Captain," ordered the officer.

The first suitcase David opened contained clothes and personal items, but the second one was full of gold watches and dental crowns and bridges.

"It's your lucky day, Colonel," said the officer, as he and his soldiers led David away and carried off "his" suitcase.

Within a month, David had been sentenced to fifteen years at hard labor for unlawful possession and illegal transfer of gold. During the investigation and at the trial, David repeatedly insisted that the suitcase was his, and that Dr. Garfinkel had had no idea what was inside.

Three months after David was convicted and sent to the labor camp, Dr. Garfinkel paid a visit to the Draznins. He brought with him a medium-sized suitcase full of money.

"All you need to do," he said to Moshe, "is to take this suitcase to a dentist in Moscow; Dr. Posner. That's it. Your mission ends with this. Posner will take care of the rest."

"What's `the rest?'" asked Nahum, deeply concerned about what had happened to David.

"The rest, my friend, is that Posner will take this money to the personal secretary of Mikhail Ivanovich Kalinin, President of the USSR. Every month, our government announces amnesty for certain prisoners, and this personal secretary to our President prepares a list of the lucky ones. I found out that he accepted bribes to put a name on the list. Once a month, Mikhail Jovanovich signs whatever list is on his desk; he doesn't even read the names. Posner has dealt with the secretary before, but I don't know whether directly or indirectly. He said it should work."

"What if it doesn't?"

"I'm risking a lot of money, but I have a Plan B. I've found a way to get to a doctor in the camp. We are going to pay him to declare David sick and request his release from jail because of health problems. One of these plans should work."

"Are you planning to pursue them at the same time?" asked Nahum.

"Yes. I don't know which one will hit the target, and, as you know, I promised to take care of David. I will stand by my word."

The next week, Moshe traveled by train to Moscow with the suitcase full of money. He was petrified just at the thought that the authorities might have learned about his mission and that someone might ask to see what he was carrying in his suitcase. Yet, when Nahum, seeing how afraid his father was of taking the money to Dr. Posner, had offered to go to Moscow in his place, Moshe had flatly refused.

"If they catch you with money, your career is finished and your life is ruined. If they catch me, I have very little to lose," he had said to his son.

Moshe boarded the train five minutes before departure, and put the suitcase on the upper berth, about six feet away from his seat, as if it wasn't his at all. But he watched it carefully for the entire twelve hours of the train ride. He was carrying another, smaller suitcase containing his clothes, the one that he would acknowledge in case of search. He put this second suitcase under his feet.

In Moscow, Moshe took the suitcase with the money to Dr. Posner's home, and gave it to the doctor himself.

"From Evsei Garfinkel," he said softly, barely moving his dry lips, and the doctor nodded silently.

Moshe left and went back to the train station to catch the return train to

Kharkov. Only when the return train had departed from Moscow did Moshe's fear subside. He felt as if a huge burden had fallen from his shoulders.

Six months later, David Slavutsky was released from the camp. The Draznins never learned which of the two plans of Dr. Garfinkel had worked. It didn't matter, for they never saw Dr. Garfinkel again, and David didn't want to discuss the matter. He returned to his typewriter-repair shop, and resumed his normal life.

*   *   *

Kharkov was the second city in the Soviet Union to have an Institute of Endocrinology, the first being in Moscow. The Institute of Endocrinology in Kharkov had a large research division and a clinical branch that included a hospital and an outpatient clinic. The academic leader and Physician-in-Chief of clinical operations was a famous internist-endocrinologist, Victor Moiceyevich Kogan-Yasny, who was also a professor at Kharkov Medical School. Nahum made an appointment to see Professor Kogan-Yasny a month before his discharge from active duty.

Professor Kogan-Yasny was punctual, and saw Nahum at exactly eleven am., the appointed time.

"So, why do you want to become an endocrinologist?"

"Several reasons." Nahum was ready for this question; he had asked it of himself on numerous occasions. "From the point of view of biology and science, I find the discovery of hormones fascinating. Tiny concentrations of hormones produced in an endocrine gland are capable of influencing the entire organism. I am sure more hormones will be discovered in the future, which will make the science of endocrinology even more appealing.

"From the clinical standpoint, there are a variety of conditions resulting from hormonal imbalance. Endocrinology is not only heart problems or lung problems; all the systems in the body can be affected. To me, it's much more challenging, clinically.

"Finally, I would like to be involved in clinical research and, from what I've read in the medical journals, endocrinology is the best field in which to combine clinical work and medical research."

Professor Kogan-Yasny listened attentively. "You said you read medical journals. I thought you were an Army doctor. Aren't you?"

"Yes, I am. Fortunately, my assignment leaves me a lot of days with a lot of free time, and I read medical journals that I check out from the school library."

"Have you attended my lectures at the Medical School?"

"Unfortunately not. I was at Kharkov Medical School for only a year. I've studied at Kuibyshev Military Medical Academy and in Chelyabinsk."

"Do you have any ideas as to what you would like to do?"

"I'm open to any ideas, but I've read something recently that attracted my attention."

"What's that?"

"I've read that radioactive iodine is being used to diagnose thyroid problems, and I wouldn't mind studying that in more detail."

Professor Kogan-Yasny liked this idea very much. He'd read articles in foreign medical journals about the use of radioactive iodine in the West, and thought it would be very appropriate to bring these techniques to his clinical department. He also liked this young doctor who was reading medical literature while in the Army. That indicated interest and intellect.

"I will give you this opportunity," said Professor Kogan-Yasny. "When can you start with us?"

"In a month," answered Nahum. "As soon as I finish my tour of duty."

"I will assign you to our Internal Medicine Section. You need to be a good general physician first, in order to become a good endocrinologist. In terms of research, I want you to develop your idea, and I will be your research mentor. You and I, young man, we'll start using radioactive iodine here in Kharkov."

Professor Kogan-Yasny came to Nahum and offered his hand. "I'm looking forward to it."

"I am, as well, very much. Thank you, Professor Kogan-Yasny."

Nahum began working at the Kharkov Institute of Endocrinology in the summer of 1947, as a Junior Research Associate.

Six months later, Felix Berenbaum joined the Institute's Department of Physiology. Felix had graduated from the Military Medical Academy in 1944, and served in the Army until December of 1947, when he had returned to Kharkov.

Felix did not enjoy clinical medicine, and didn't really want to work with patients, so the position of Junior Research Associate in a non-clinical department was exactly what he wanted. He was very grateful to Nahum, who had told him about the opening in the Department of Physiology.

There were several other Junior Research Associates at the Institute, and every one of them was working diligently, trying to collect research material for his or her dissertation. That was the goal—to write and defend the dissertation for the title of Candidate in Medical Science. This dissertation was a first obligatory step on the way to professorship.

In mid-January of 1948, on his way to work through the snow-packed streets of Kharkov, Nahum met Felix several blocks from the Institute.

"Did you see today's *Pravda?*" asked Felix.

"No, I haven't seen a paper today. Anything exciting?" said Nahum, smiling. He usually read the paper at lunch.

"Mikhoels was killed in Minsk in a freak accident; hit by a car."

Solomon Mikhoels had been the greatest actor in Russian Yiddish Theater; one of the most famous Jews and arguably one of the best actors in the country. During the war, Comrade Stalin had appointed Solomon Mikhoels President of the Jewish Anti-Fascist Committee, a political action body composed of the most prominent Jewish writers, scientists and military and civil leaders in Russia. In this capacity, Mikhoels had been sent on a seven-month tour of England, North America and Mexico, to raise funds to fight the Nazis.

"What was he doing in Minsk?" asked Nahum.

"Who knows?" said Felix. "The paper said he was dead at the scene. The state funeral is planned for tomorrow. What a tragedy!"

Nahum didn't answer. An auto-pedestrian accident in a relatively small town five hundred miles away from Moscow that killed the most famous Jew in Russia sounded suspicious, but freak accidents do happen, he thought. The state funeral also meant official recognition and government support.

"Just an accident," he told Felix, as they walked through the gates to the Institute. "Terrible things do happen, Felix. Life is so fragile."

He didn't think much of it until a barrage of articles in the Russian press began attacking Jewish intellectuals, calling them "rootless cosmopolitans." The name implied that they really didn't belong to the motherland, Russia, and instead were part of an international Zionist organization devoid of national pride and country-specific ties.

In July, almost all the members of the Jewish Anti-Fascist Committee were arrested, including the poets, Itzik Feffer and Peretz Markish, a world-renowned scientist, Lina Shtern, and the director of the major Moscow hospital, Boris Shemolovich. At the same time, Jewish literature was being removed from bookstores and libraries, and the last Jewish schools in the country were ordered closed. Jewish theaters, professional and amateur drama groups and choirs were closed as well. In November, 1948, the Jewish Anti-Fascist Committee was officially dissolved.

Jews in Russia were terribly frightened. Afraid to discuss the issues, Nahum and his Jewish colleagues immersed themselves deeper in their work.

Institutions of higher education were in a particularly depressed mood. At this time, on average, close to forty percent of the academic faculty in the largest Russian cities were Jews. The Kharkov Institute of Endocrinology was not an exception. More than half of all the scientists at both senior and junior levels were Jewish.

"It's good that the Jewish schools are finally closed," said one of the research associates, in the cafeteria, during lunch. "We need to be assimilated into the greater Russian culture, and not to maintain this *shtetl*-like environment."

Nahum lowered his eyes to his plate. He was determined not to get drawn into such conversations.

"Yiddish is a dying language anyway," agreed another one. "Theater, poetry; just a waste of time and effort."

During his days in the Army, Nahum had learned to listen more than he spoke. It was hard, because he was an ardent debater and almost always had his own strong opinion, but he had learned to restrain himself. The anti-Jewish propaganda in the press bothered him a lot, but he still didn't quite understand the issue. He, too, thought that Jewish schools and Yiddish institutions were remnants of their old life. He had grown up surrounded by Russian culture, Russian literature, Russian poetry and Russian film and theater. He was an assimilated Jew.

Now he was struggling to understand why this powerful Russian culture was turning against him and people like him. He sensed and felt vicious, blunt anti-Semitism in all the rhetoric about "rootless cosmopolitans." He realized that this was more than just a fight with the remnants of the old Jewish culture, but he couldn't grasp the extent of it, and certainly had no idea how to deal with it. For now, the only escape he saw was his clinical and research work.

Also in 1948, Rosa completed dental school and joined the staff of the municipal dental clinic, where she worked from eight in the morning until four in the afternoon, every day. Little Boris went to daycare not far from their apartment house.

In December, Rosa received a letter from her mother saying that her father, Hershel, had been arrested for embezzlement of funds from the agricultural cooperative where he had worked after returning from Tumen.

Their old house had survived the war, and Hershel, Fanya and Yakov had returned to Dnepropetrovsk in 1945, and settled there, once again. Yakov had continued his education at the engineering school, and Hershel had signed up with the agricultural cooperative on the outskirts of town. A financial review of the cooperative in early 1948 had revealed that large sums of money were missing, the books were in disarray and produce was being sold outside governmental contracts. All the administrative officers of the cooperative had been arrested, even those who had had nothing to do with the books or finances.

Hershel was Chief Agriculturist and a member of the administrative structure. He was accused of conspiring to embezzle the funds, and sentenced to a three-year term in jail, without visitation rights. He began serving his time in a prison outside of Dnepropetrovsk.

Four months into his term, he either stepped on a nail or hurt his foot in some other way, so that the plantar surface of his right foot became red and swollen, and extremely painful. Within a week, the redness had involved all his toes and the dorsal surface of his foot, and ascended to his shin.

He asked to see a doctor. They told him that the doctor came to the prison twice a week, and he'd be able to see him on his next visit, in two days. The next night, he developed chills, became intermittently hot and cold and was sweating profusely and unable to stand.

The guards carried him to the jail's infirmary, where the nurse measured his temperature and found it very high. After smelling acetone on his breath, she measured the sugar in his urine. It was also off the scale.

She made a diagnosis of diabetes. She gave him aspirin to reduce his fever, and waited for the doctor to come, the next morning. He examined Hershel and found his foot completely blackened, with the skin broken and oozing pus. His shin was red all the way to the knee, changing to bluish-dark-purple toward the ankle. His breathing was deep, fast and laborious. He was unconscious.

The doctor re-checked his urinary sugar and found it again very high.

"He had diabetes and gangrene of his right foot extending halfway through the shin," concluded the doctor. "He is in a diabetic coma," he said to the nurse. "Nothing is going to help now. Even amputation of his infected leg wouldn't save him. Let him go."

Hershel died before nightfall. He was buried in the cemetery attached to the jail, and a letter about his death containing a statement from the prison doctor about the cause of death, was mailed a month later to his widow. The letter also said that his grave, Number 13742, was in Row "L."

When Rosa found out what had happened, she went to Dnepropetrovsk and took her mother to the prison cemetery. Pavel didn't come. An officer in the Russian Navy couldn't even think of asking to visit the grave of his inmate father. He thought he would come during his regular vacation time.

Rosa and Fanya found the cemetery, and then Row "L" and grave Number 13742. The grave was relatively fresh, and covered with yellowish clay. A small wooden obelisk showed only the grave number; no name. The women looked at other graves and saw no names there, either. Once again, they compared the number on the obelisk with the number in the letter, and decided they had the right spot.

Standing next to the grave, they cried, hugging each other shoulders. *What a terrible end for such a wonderful man*, thought Rosa, but she didn't say a word. *At least he knew I had finished my dental school*, raced through her mind, as they left the cemetery. *I promised him, and I did it.*

Nahum finished writing his dissertation in 1952. It was the first large study in Russia to investigate the use of radioactive iodine in clinical endocrinology. Professor Kogan-Yasny was very proud of his pupil, and recommended that Nahum defend his thesis at Leningrad Medical School.

It was customary to defend dissertations in another institution, and not where the dissertation had been written. Where to defend was generally the choice of the person who had written the thesis, and his or her mentor. Professor Kogan-Yasny knew academic physicians in Leningrad, and felt they were sufficiently open-minded to accept such a novel clinical paradigm.

Nahum and Professor Kogan-Yasny wrote a request to the Leningrad Medical School, and Nahum's work was accepted for defense in September of 1952.

In August, 1952, came the trial of the members of the former Jewish Anti-Fascist Committee and other intellectual Jews. All these "rootless cosmopolitans" were accused of being British, American and Zionist spies. Ten of them were sentenced to death and, on August 12, 1952, the poets, Peretz Markish, Leib Kwitko, David Hoffstein and Itzik Feffer, the novelists, David Bergelson and Der Nister, and Dr. Boris Shemolovich were executed at Moscow's Lubianka jail.

The death sentence of Lina Shtern was commuted to exile and life in prison, probably because she was too famous abroad, being a world-renowned scientist. Twenty people were sentenced to long prison terms, and more than eighty others were jailed for relatively short times.

Professor Kogan-Yasny called Nahum to his office. When he came in, the Professor locked the door and sat in his chair, preparing to talk. He even opened his mouth to start a sentence, but caught himself and said, after a short pause, "I'm walking home for lunch. Do you mind walking with me to my apartment? I have a question or two to ask you about your dissertation."

Without waiting for Nahum's answer, he went to the door, unlocked it and stepped outside. He didn't speak until he was about a block from the Institute.

"Not a good time, Nahum. Not a good time for your defense. I'd say not a good time for anything." He added, mumbling, "I'd recommend we postpone your defense until next spring. Let's say next April or May."

"Do you think we should do that, in the light of the last trial?" asked Nahum, carefully.

"And you don't?"

"Wouldn't it be too obvious?"

"Leave it to me. I'll tell them I don't feel well enough to travel, and I want to be there during your defense."

"I'll trust your judgment, Professor."

"I don't know whether I'd trust it myself, but if you do, let's postpone. A smart young Jewish scientist is a great target, right now. We shouldn't give them that opportunity."

"But why? Victor Moiceyevich, why are they so anti-Semitic?" fired Nahum, encouraged by the unexpected openness of his mentor.

Professor Kogan-Yasny stopped, turned to Nahum and put his hand on his shoulder. "I live in this gray building. Thanks for walking me home. I'm just too old and too scared even to think about it. And I wouldn't recommend that you think about it, either." He turned away and walked into his house.

The new date for Nahum's defense was set for the end of April, 1953. On January 13, 1953, the newspaper *Pravda* announced that a group of high-profile academic physicians had been arrested as Zionist spies. The article, titled "Killers in White Gowns: Vicious Spies and Killers Under the Mask of Academic Physicians," accused Doctors Vovci, B. Kogan, Feldman, Grinshtein, M. Kogan, Etinger (who had died in jail earlier), Egorov, Levin and Pletnev of being "a band of inhuman beasts," and the killers and poisoners of several Communist leaders. It said that these doctors, through the previously-executed "spy," Dr. Boris Shemolovich, were tied to the Zionist spy, Solomon Mikhoels, who had been recruited by a Jewish organization named "Joint."

The article went on to tell the readers that a patriotic Russian physician, Lydia Timashuk, had discovered several vials of poison that these killer-doctors wanted to use in an attempt to kill other Soviet leaders, including Comrade Stalin.

For her vigilance, Dr. Lydia Timashuk had been awarded the Order of Lenin, the highest honor in the Soviet Union. The entire band of physicians, concluded *Pravda*, had been arrested and rendered harmless.

Within the next two weeks, several prominent Jewish physicians were arrested in Leningrad and Kiev. Two days later, Professor Victor Moiceyevich Kogan-Yasny was taken straight to jail from his office at the Kharkov Institute of Endocrinology. All the research associates stood silent in the hall as their mentor was led unceremoniously away.

Nahum was in shock. Like everybody else, he stayed at work until the end of the day, but just sat in his small office, staring out the window.

"Victor Moiceyevich has been arrested," he told Rosa, as he walked into their apartment.

"Your dissertation!" gasped Rosa.

"To hell with the dissertation, even though I've worked so hard on it. What's going to happen to him? And to us? And to all the other Jewish doctors?" He hung his coat in the closet, and added, "What is going on with the world?"

"I've heard from people," said David Slavutsky, when he came that evening for dinner, "that they are building barracks for Jews in Siberia. They'll send us all out there."

"I can't believe this!" said Rosa. "It's impossible."

"Those are the rumors," David insisted.

"We just have to live as if nothing has happened," announced Moshe. "There's nothing any of us can do."

"Papa's right," Rachel agreed. "Life goes on. We've gone through so much, and this too will be behind us. Let us go on living."

They did. Nahum continued to prepare for his defense; it was still scheduled for the end of April, in Leningrad. Rosa worked in her clinic. They now had two children; a girl named Tatiana had been born in August, 1952. Rachel and Moshe also went to work at their usual places.

The time was very tense, but nothing important happened until March 5, 1953, the day Comrade Stalin died.

For the Soviet people, it was a sudden and major event. People cried everywhere. Spontaneous demonstrations in his support and in his honor were erupting in every corner of the vast country. However, in many families, hidden from the eyes of neighbors, there was a colossal sigh of relief.

On April 4, 1953, the newspaper *Pravda* published a revelation—all the arrested doctors were innocent, the plot had been a complete fabrication and all of them had been released immediately.

Nahum ran to see Victor Moiceyevich. His wife opened the door and let Nahum in. He saw a terribly elderly-looking man who had lost an enormous amount of weight in the four months he had spent in jail.

He cried when he saw Nahum. They hugged. "Oh, Nahum, please, be careful; they broke several of my ribs," he said, wiping his eyes and nose.

Nahum went to Leningrad alone, because Professor Kogan-Yasny still wasn't able to travel.

"Go alone, Nahum. You don't need me there. I'm convinced you'd do equally well whether I'm there or not." Professor Kogan-Yasny shook his head when Nahum begged him to go to Leningrad. "Your work is excellent and no one knows this subject better than you."

"It may well be, but I wish to see my mentor in the audience." Insisted Nahum.

"I appreciate what you say, but I'm simply not fit to travel. Physically, I wouldn't be able handle it. Yet another delay is not warranted. You must go."

Nahum realized that his frail teacher was truly unable to make a trip and went alone. The defense went perfectly well. The committee liked his work and enjoyed listening to his presentation, and everyone was duly impressed by his ability to answer questions. They voted unanimously to approve his dissertation.

That night the very first phone call he made was to his mentor.

"Victor Moiceyevich, as you said, it was accepted unanimously. I am the happiest man alive!"

"Congratulations! You should be proud of your work."

"I wouldn't have done it without you."

"So, I'm proud of you, too." Joked Professor. "I'll tell you something else when you come home."

Nahum returned to Kharkov not only triumphant, but because of his innovative work, a rising star of Russian endocrinology. When a couple of days later he came to see Professor Kogan-Yasny, he said, "You promised to tell me something else when I phoned you from Leningrad. What is it?"

"Oh, just something I can't tell over the phone – Mazel Tov, my friend,

Mazel Tov!"

CHAPTER NINETEEN

Professor Victor Moiceyevich Kogan-Yasny was never reinstated. Re-Reinstatement was promised on several occasions, and he waited, first patiently and then impatiently, but equally without success. He was told that various administrative snafus had prevented his reinstatement and that, nevertheless, it should happen any day. After six or seven months, he was finally told that, because he was close to retirement age, he would not be reinstated. Well-deserved retirement was his best option, he was told.

A month after his successful defense of his dissertation, Nahum was invited to meet with the Director of the Department of Human Resources of the Institute. The Director and the Secretary of the Institute's Communist Party organization were waiting in the Director's office.

After a brief salutation and expression of congratulations, the Director said, "We've been thinking about your future, Dr. Draznin, and thought it might be a good time for you to become a member of the Communist Party. I'd say the Party needs people like you; bright, energetic and talented. What do you think, Ivan Fedorovich?" He turned to the Secretary.

Ivan Fedorovich was a former X-ray technician who had risen in the ranks of the Party to become Secretary of the Institute's Party organization. It was now his full-time job.

Ivan Fedorovich cleared his throat, and said, "Dr. Draznin is an excellent candidate. And, you know, we don't offer membership to everyone. It's an honor reserved for people like you."

"I...I am honored," said Nahum. "I feel it is a great honor. Is there anything I should do?"

"First of all," said the Director, "you should submit an application; a request to be considered. This is a formality, you understand. The Membership Committee will look at your file, and will invite you for an interview. Once you pass that stage, the rest is easy. I am very glad you are serious about this. We want you in. Isn't that right, Ivan Fedorovich?"

"Absolutely. We want you in," repeated Ivan Fedorovich.

"Well," said the Director, escorting Nahum from his office, "why don't you bring your application to me in a day or two, and we'll go on from there."

"I suppose it ought to be good for my career," Nahum said to Rosa and his parents, when he got home.

"Most certainly," agreed Moshe.

"I'm always apprehensive when you start getting into politics," sighed Rachel.

"There is no politics. It's membership in the Party," replied Nahum.

"The Party *is* politics."

"He should join," Moshe insisted. "So many more doors will suddenly open. For a Jew who is not a Party member, it's tough to make a career."

"What do you think, Rosa?" Nahum looked into her eyes.

"I think Papa's right. You should do whatever you think would be best for your career."

Nahum nodded. Two days later, he knocked at the office door of the Director of Human Resources.

"Oh, Dr. Draznin! Come in, come in."

"I've brought my application, and I wonder whether I can leave it with you?"

"Certainly. Let me have a quick look at this."

The director extended his arm from behind his desk and took the application from Nahum's hand. He put it down on his desk and read it attentively.

"I'd say…oh, sorry, Dr. Draznin, please sit down." He gestured at the chair. "I'd say this is a great letter. I wouldn't change a thing."

"Thank you," said Nahum, softly.

"You know, I meant to tell you, I've met here with a couple of people, kind of senior people in our Party organization, and they've suggested that I ask you to do one more thing."

"Surely. Please go ahead." Nahum was on guard, but couldn't guess what was coming.

"We've got some information that you got into trouble while in the Military Academy. Don't! Please, don't say anything." He raised his hand. "It was all corrected, and you were completely absolved of it, but people felt you need to do a little extra to demonstrate your commitment. Nothing really major."

"How did you know?" Nahum snorted. "It's not in my file. It shouldn't be there. I paid for that, and it should have been erased."

"Oh, Dr. Draznin, in real life nothing ever disappears. There are always people around who have seen something or have heard something. The rumor mill, as they say. But that's all behind us. If you are willing to do a couple of small things for the Party, there won't be any problem with your application."

"What would you like me to do?" asked Nahum, still terribly upset.

"You are the most popular person at the Institute. You have a lot of friends, your colleagues like you and our senior professors adore you. You meet people, you talk with people; you mix so well with everyone . I would like to ask you to take mental notes on what people say, what they discuss and what opinions they express. And then you and I would meet weekly, and you just tell me what's going on. You know, I love to feel the pulse of this place."

"You are asking me to be an informant?" asked Nahum, sinking into his chair.

"I wouldn't say an 'informant.' Hopefully, there's nothing to inform about, in this Institute. Just an observer; a vigilant member of the Party.

"By the way, as soon as you are admitted into the Party, we're thinking of promoting you to the rank of Senior Research Associate. What do you say?"

"I need to think about it," mumbled Nahum.

"Think about it? What is there to think about?" The Director smiled. "Such a small favor for being made a member of the Party."

"I still need to think about it." Nahum had pretty much regained his composure. "I'd love to help, but I do need some time to digest your offer. Please give me a couple of days." He stood, preparing to leave.

"If you insist," said the Director, coldly. "Don't take too much time. If I were you, I wouldn't procrastinate for too long." He handed Nahum his application. "See you when you are ready, Dr. Draznin."

Nahum left the Director's office and went straight to see Felix Berenbaum. Felix's laboratory was on the second floor, near the end of a long corridor. The door was open, and Felix was in, working on his experiments.

"Felix!" said Nahum. He wanted to whisper so no one else would hear him, but his voice came out as loud hiss.

"Yes, I'm here," answered Felix, from behind the laboratory bench.

"Felix, did you ever tell anyone here about my trial in Kuibyshev?"

Nahum watched Felix like a hawk, trying not to miss even the smallest sign in his behavior.

Felix didn't reply. He stared at Nahum, thinking what to say.

"Felix, tell me the truth! Did you tell this to anyone?"

"I...I sort of did," mumbled Felix, finally. "They were asking me about my life, and I told them we were together in Kuibyshev. That's it. I didn't say anything about your trial. I swear I didn't."

"What else did you tell them?"

"I told them we were separated in '42, when you left for the front. That's it! Believe me, Nahum, that was it." Felix's face was red, and his eyes seemed fearful and lying, but he insisted that he hadn't said anything about the trial.

Silently, Nahum stared at him in disgust and pity, watching his moving lips and frightened posture. He turned away, and walked out of the laboratory. He was absolutely convinced he knew the source of the information. He slammed the door as he stepped into the corridor, and the sound of it drowned out the sound of Felix's prattling.

Nahum wanted to tear up his application right there in his office, but he restrained himself. He arrived at home furious.

"They want me to be an informer. A snitch! Can you believe it? Like lousy Berenbaum!"

"Berenbaum? Isn't he your friend?" asked Rosa.

"Not any more. I am tearing up my application, and never again will I apply to that organization!" He pulled his application from his pocket and tore it into pieces.

"Maybe you should talk to the Secretary of your organization first," suggested Moshe.

"No, that's the end of it. I don't want to get involved. Never," he said, emphatically.

A month later, Nahum ran into the Director of Human Resources again. They greeted one another politely and parted. A month after that, the Director came to Nahum's office. Nahum, who had just returned from the clinic, hung his white coat on the coat rack and sat down in his chair.

"Sorry for intrusion, Dr. Draznin," said the Director, poking his head in the door. "May I come in?"

"Certainly, do come in."

"Just a quick business visit." The Director walked in. "You may have heard we are going through a reduction in force in our Institute. The administration met yesterday, and decided that you are overqualified for your position."

"I don't understand," said Nahum, in astonishment. "Overqualified for what? To see patients? Or to do research?"

"You have already defended your dissertation, but you are still a Junior Research Associate."

"That is fine with me."

"You should have been promoted, but unfortunately, we have no openings," said the Director, ignoring Nahum's remarks. "I regret to inform you that we have to let you go. You don't need to come to work tomorrow. Today is your last day. I am sure that, being the smart, resourceful person you are, Dr. Draznin, you'll find a position elsewhere without delay." His smile accompanied his sarcastic statement. "Please clear your office by the end of the day."

He walked out without waiting for Nahum's reply.

Nahum could not find a job. Young, mid-level Jewish physicians were being laid off at every hospital and every research organization. At the Institute of Endocrinology, only three remained employed. One of them was Felix

Berenbaum. The rest, like Nahum, were desperately searching for positions elsewhere.

His search continued for almost a year. Every day, he wrote letters to various organizations, first in Kharkov, then in all the major Ukrainian cities, and eventually, in most of the cities in the European part of the USSR. At the end of the year, when he was ready to write to Asian cities such as Almati and Tashkent, he received a letter from Riga, from the Latvian Ministry of Health.

He was told about an opening at one of the seaside resorts for a physician to care for the guests of the resort. There would be no research, no real patients, no endocrinology and certainly no academic career. But, after a year of being unemployed, this was a real job. Nahum went to Riga to investigate.

Before he left Kharkov, he sent another letter to the Minister of Health of the Byelorussian Republic, in Minsk. *This will be it*, he thought, *this will be my last letter*. He wrote it in the morning and mailed it on the way to the airport to catch his flight to Riga.

Dear Comrade Minister, he wrote.

I am a 31-year old Jewish physician-endocrinologist, a Candidate of Medical Science and a pupil of Professor Victor Moiceevich Kogan-Yasny, and I am currently looking for employment. My preference would be a challenging and/or academic position where I can combine clinical and research endeavors with teaching or administration. I know that Byelorussia lies within the area of endemic goiter, but I am not aware that any endocrine services are offered to your population. I would be delighted to come for an interview, should you have any potential opening.

Sincerely,
Dr. Nahum Draznin

He addressed the envelope to Comrade Insarov, the Minister of Health, Minsk, Byelorussia, dropped it into the mailbox and forgot about it.

He returned from Riga in an upbeat mood. "It's a great place; a wonderful resort on the shores of the Baltic Sea." He described it to Rosa and his parents. "Sandy beaches, lots of pine trees, charming old buildings. They have a little house for the doctor and the family, right on the premises. They also have a dental clinic in a nearby town, less than ten minutes away by bus."

"What about the language?" asked Rosa. "Don't they speak Latvian?"

"Yes, they do, but they all also speak Russian, and certainly the guests of the resort are overwhelmingly Russian. It shouldn't be a problem. I may even be able to do some clinical research." He added, "Quite a few of the guests have diabetes, and I might be able to do something with them." He couldn't completely resign himself to the idea of losing his research interests.

The next day, he wrote to Riga accepting the position, and advising them that he would arrive within a month.

They decided that he would go alone, and Rosa and the children would join him a couple of months after he had settled in. A week before his scheduled departure, a letter came from Minsk. Rachel pulled it out of the mailbox.

"You know, Rosa," she said, as she handed the letter to her daughter-in-law, "maybe we shouldn't even show it to Nahum. If it's a rejection, it would open an old wound. If it's an invitation for an interview, why bother? He has already agreed to take a job in Riga."

"I can't withhold from him," said Rosa. "Even though you are probably right, I'll let him see it. I can't make these decisions for him."

Comrade Insarov, the Minister of Health, had invited Nahum for an interview.

Dear Dr. Draznin,

Thank you for your letter. We have been thinking about organizing endocrine clinics and services in Byelorussia, but didn't have anyone to lead the effort. You might be the man we are looking for. Come and see me as soon as you can.

Yours,
Insarov
Minister of Health

Nahum left for Minsk the next day. A day later, he called home. "I am taking the job in Minsk. This is a dream job. They're entrusting me to organize clinical endocrine services and continuing medical education and research for the entire Republic. There will be an outpatient clinic and a small, ten-bed inpatient unit, and I will be in charge of everything. I will be building endocrinology from the ground up. It is an unbelievable job!"

"What about Riga? You are supposed to start there in three days, aren't you?" Rosa asked.

"I've just called them and canceled. I can't pass up such an opportunity as Comrade Insarov is giving me. I'm telling you, it's a dream."

Nahum stayed in Minsk, and assumed his responsibilities immediately. Almost a year and a half later, at the end of December of 1955, Rosa, Boris and Tatiana joined him in Minsk.

The Ministry of Health, which had been so generous in providing Nahum with an exceptional job, could not arrange an apartment for him. They put him into a queue of physicians and medical school faculty, to receive an apartment when one might become available in several years.

It took Nahum about a year to find the right bribeable people among the city fathers to procure a small room of approximately two hundred square feet in a two-room apartment in an old two-story building in the center of the city.

The apartment had a tiny kitchen and a very small toilet with a stool and a sink. A single woman, a retired elementary-school teacher, was living in the second, much smaller, room.

The Draznins lived in this room for four years.

Nahum enjoyed his work tremendously. Being the only properly-trained endocrinologist in the entire Republic, with its seven-million population, made him a local celebrity almost overnight. He saw a lot of patients, and trained other physicians to provide adequate care for patients with diabetes and thyroid problems. He embarked on new research projects and hired young physicians to build and expand his research group.

After three years, he convinced the Minister of Health to create a Department of Endocrinology at the Minsk Institute of Continuing Education, to attract those who wanted to become endocrinologists from all corners of the Soviet Union. At that time there were only two such departments in the country, one in Moscow and the other in Kharkov. Minsk became only the third place the country to provide formal specialization in this field. Nahum was named Department Chairman.

However, because the initiative to create the Department and to appoint Nahum its Chairman had come from the Minister of Health, the Director of the Institute of Continuing Education disliked him immensely. The Director, Dr. Savchenko, felt strongly that Nahum had been forced upon him, and that he should have been consulted before the decision about the Department was made. By the time Nahum realized why Dr. Savchenko was so cold toward him, the damage had been done.

In 1961, Nahum was ready to defend his second dissertation and become a Doctor of Medical Sciences, the next obligatory step in becoming a Professor. He planned to defend his dissertation in Voronezh, a Russian city southeast of Moscow. He had picked Voronezh on the advice of his consultants, who felt that there were several people in the Voronezh Medical School with great expertise in the field of Nahum's interests.

And indeed there were. Nahum's formal and informal meetings with these scientists were extremely helpful and productive. He was ready to go there for his formal defense.

Dr. Savchenko was tremendously upset when he learned that Nahum was going to defend his dissertation. Even though Dr. Savchenko was about three years older than Nahum, his own dissertation was not yet ready. He just couldn't stand the thought that the faculty member he liked least might become a Professor at his Institute. Dr. Savchenko approached his Director of Human Resources, and asked him to call Kharkov, where Nahum had come from, and find whatever he could about Nahum Draznin.

In two weeks, a copy of Nahum's personnel folder from the Kharkov Institute of Endocrinology was lying on the desk of Dr. Savchenko.

"I've got him!" exulted Dr. Savchenko, full of malicious joy. "This folder has plenty in it to stop this smart-ass Jew boy from defending his dissertation!"

The defense went extremely well. Nahum presented it with his usual clarity, and handled the questions with confidence, knowledge and respect for the people posing them. It lasted about two hours.

After all the questions had been exhausted, Nahum left the room to wait outside while the Committee deliberated. He went out of the building into a charming courtyard to smoke a cigarette.

The deliberations started in a positive way. The scientists who understood the subject matter provided strong support for his work. Others were ready to follow the lead of the specialists, when the Chairman of the Department of Communist History said, "Yesterday, I received a letter from the Director of Dr. Draznin's Institute. The Director questions the moral character of Dr. Draznin. I realize it's strange, but he asked me to share his letter with you, even though it has nothing to do with Dr. Draznin's research.

"Apparently, Dr. Draznin was court-martialed, during the war, for being a deserter. He was sentenced to serve in a penal battalion. He was wounded and his record was cleared. Nevertheless, the fact remains, his reputation as a solid citizen is questionable. He was later asked to join the Communist Party and refused.

"Not a good sign," added the Chairman of the Department of Communist History, putting the letter away. "I personally will vote against his dissertation, and I think you should do the same. I don't want our school be marred by such a person."

The balloting was secret and, with no further discussion, the members of the scientific committee cast their votes. The secretary of the scientific committee counted the "Yeas" and "Nays."

"We have nine votes "Yes" and nine votes "No,'" he announced solemnly. "The defense has failed."

Nahum was heartbroken. He couldn't comprehend what had happened. No one, not even his strongest supporters, would talk to him.

"You never know, with secret ballots," said one of the members of the Committee, as he walked past Nahum to exit the room. Only several weeks later did Nahum find out what had happened, through the same consultant who had advised him to go to Voronezh.

"How could you do such a thing?" shouted Nahum at Dr. Savchenko, running into his office. "How could you write such a malicious letter about me? Why? You have no right to do this!"

"I don't even know what you are talking about!" shouted Dr. Savchenko, rising from behind his desk. "I didn't write any letters about you. Whoever told you that was just lying! I don't give a darn penny about you. How dare you come here and criticize me?"

"I know what you did," answered Nahum. "This is terrible, treacherous and deceitful. I hope I can catch you with your hands in the pie!" Nahum ran out of the office.

Dr. Savchenko slowly stretched in his chair, again, and raised his fist. "Yes!" he said with satisfaction. "Yes!"

Two years later, Nahum defended his dissertation in Vilnius, Lithuania. The Lithuanian scientists and the faculty at the Institute of Experimental Medicine received him warmly and with great support. The committee voted unanimously in favor of his work. A year later, he became a full Professor at the Institute.

Dr. Savchenko had also moved on. He replaced the retiring Comrade Insarov as Minister of Health of the Byelorussian Republic.

In 1964, the Moscow Institute of Endocrinology was forming a delegation of Russian endocrinologists to attend an international meeting in Buenos Aires. Envisioning broader representation, the Director of the Moscow Institute included Professor Nahum Draznin in the delegation. An invitation went out to Nahum, and a request for support in obtaining an international passport for him went to the Byelorussian Ministry of Health.

For two months, there was not a word in reply from the Ministry. After a second request, the Minister sent a letter to Moscow.

In reply to your request to support an application for an international passport for Professor Nahum Draznin, we wish to inquire whether a Byelorussian candidate could be considered for inclusion in the delegation instead of Professor Draznin.

Professor Alexander Savchenko,
Minister of Health

The Director of the Moscow Institute of Endocrinology replied, sending a copy to Nahum:

*The Byelorussian candidate will certainly be considered, providing he or
she has scientific credentials equal to those of Professor Draznin.*

A month later, Nahum received a letter from the Ministry of Health stating
that, unfortunately, there was not enough time to process his request for the
international passport by the time of the departure of the delegation.

"Why is it that being Jewish in Russia is a perpetual punishment?" said
Nahum to Rosa, when he finally realized he was not going to Argentina.

"It's not necessarily a punishment for being a Jew. Savchenko just doesn't
like you. I think your Minister is using your Jewishness simply to hide his
jealousy."

"That's awful, what you just said. It actually means that anti-Semitism is
better-accepted in our society than jealousy. It's like the famous joke: one guy
tells another, 'Let's go beat up some Jews and some bicyclists.' And the other
guy asks, 'Why bicyclists?' Jews have done so much for this country, and yet
government-sponsored anti-Semitism is still a part of our life.

"Look; I am a Professor, a doctor and a teacher, and I am treated like a
prisoner in my own homeland. Will there be an end to it? Ever?"

CHAPTER TWENTY

Zhitomir, a town about one hundred miles West of Kiev, lies in the fertile land of the central Ukraine. Historically, however, it was just outside the Ukrainian border, until it was annexed to Ukraine and Russia in 1793. Prior to that, Zhitomir was a major administrative town of the vast western Ukrainian region known as Volhynia.

Zhitomir was settled by Vikings in 1240, the followers of Prince Rurik, who himself settled in Kiev. Zhitomir was an important trading post on the way from Scandinavia to Constantinople. A hundred years later, the territory was taken over by Lithuania (1320) and, almost two and a half centuries afterward, was ceded to Poland, in 1569. It remained in Polish hands until the second division of Poland, in 1793.

By 1900, approximately 80,000 people lived in Zhitomir, one third of whom were Jews. Zhitomir became one of the prime centers of Jewish life within the pale of settlement. Two printing houses in Zhitomir published one half of all the Hebrew-language literature in Eastern Europe. While Jews lived all over town, poor Jews dwelt in Podol, an area of slums and shanty houses not far from the Teterev River, a tributary of the mighty Dneiper.

Esau Lerman lived in one of these shacks with his wife, Chaya-Shira, his five-year old daughter, Shiba, and a newborn son, Jehuda. When his son was only a year old, Esau died, presumably of tuberculosis, but no one really knew why. His widow, an uneducated poor woman, started doing laundry for other people who could afford her services financially but had no time or insufficient physical strength to do it themselves.

She had very few customers and, most of the time, she and her children remained at home, hungry, waiting for someone to bring a load of laundry. A couple of years later, she remarried, but her second husband was as poor as the first, and she continued doing laundry for other people as if nothing happened in her life. Indeed, the only thing that had changed in her daily existence was that she had given birth to another girl, and was now taking care of three children.

Jehuda grew up in the streets of Podol, the poorest part of Zhitomir. In some mysterious way, he taught himself the Russian language, and one day, after finding a discarded school textbook of arithmetic, he became obsessed with learning mathematics, and began methodically solving problem after problem from his textbook. Several problems were beyond his abilities, and he asked his mother to give him a little bit of money to pay a math teacher, who explained the solutions to him.

At the age of fifteen, he discovered a large group of German Baptists living on the outskirts of Zhitomir. They had been there since 1860, living in a large German-speaking colony, engaged in trades and handcrafts.

Fascinated by their language and culture, Jehuda embarked on the study of German. In two years, he was fluent enough to converse with the Volhynian Germans. At seventeen, he spent a year and a half preparing to take the high-school-leaving examinations, obviously without attending school at all.

He passed all the required tests with the highest marks, and was ready for higher education. With mathematics and physics still his favorite subjects, he decided to apply to Moscow Engineering Academy.

Jews required special permits to live in Moscow, and he didn't have one. Without a permit, Jehuda traveled to Moscow to take the entrance exam, and slept on a bench in the park, putting a couple of books and his coat under his head as a hard pillow.

The entrance exams lasted three days. Jehuda had no problems with any of the subjects, except for a seemingly simple mathematical problem. The question was, *How many laborers would be needed to finish a construction job in five days, if one worker toiling alone would have been able to do it in twelve days?* Jehuda's reasoning was straightforward. One worker, who could finish the entire assignment in twelve days, appears to accomplish one twelfth of the assigned job in one day. A certain number of workers must accomplish one fifth of the job in one day in order to finish this work in five days. Dividing one-fifth by one-twelfth, he found that two and two fifths of a laborer would be needed to do one fifth of the work daily, and to finish the entire work in five days.

How can it be, he asked himself, *that the answer contains a fraction of a laborer? I must have made a mistake.* The question resonated in his head. He worked on this problem for almost an hour, always getting the same answer, but ignored the other problems on his list, sweating from anxiety and not believing his answer.

Finally, frustrated to the point of feeling crushed, he wrote his crazy answer—two and two fifths of a laborer—and turned his attention to the other problems, in order to complete his test.

That night, he couldn't fall asleep on his park bench. Either the moon was too bright or the pillow too hard; he had not a trace of sleepiness. He thought he had failed the test, and scolded himself for wasting his money by coming here and not being able to solve such a simple written problem. He was disgusted with himself until the next morning, when he learned he had received the highest mark for his math test.

How stupid, he thought, *the answer must have been a fraction of a laborer! Oh, well; that's life.*"

There were fifteen Jewish boys who had passed all the tests with the highest grades, but the school had allocated only four spots for Jewish students. The quota was set at four percent: four Jewish students in a class of one hundred freshmen.

The Dean pulled names from a hat, in a simple lottery. At the end, Jehuda's name remained in the hat.

"Next year, you might be luckier," the Dean announced to the eleven disappointed Jewish kids, who were greatly superior to at least ninety percent of the non-Jewish candidates.

Jehuda returned home and took a job as a tutor in math and German, and also in Latin, which he had also mastered to fluency. He applied to the same Moscow school twice more, only to lose the lottery both times. Meanwhile, several of his non-Jewish pupils had been admitted to various schools, which added to his frustration.

At the age of twenty-three, he made a radical decision—he would go to Germany to study. Unexpectedly, the knowledge of German that he had picked up as a child growing up in the slums of Zhitomir was making a huge difference in his life.

Jehuda had saved most of his money from tutoring, and he traveled to Heidelberg to enroll in an engineering school. That, however, proved to be a mistake. Despite having a brilliant mind for mathematical problems, he discovered that he had no patience and was all thumbs at drawing. After three months, he transferred to Munich University Medical School.

Even in liberal Germany, proud of its Enlightenment, he found that the majority of German students did not accept their Jewish classmates as equals. The German students spent a great deal of time drinking beer, chasing pretty girls and fighting duels with their sharp swords. A facial scar from an opponent's sword was viewed as a proud mark of their school years.

The Jewish students came to school to study, but the German and Austrian Jewish students cared little, if at all, about their Eastern European brethren. Contemptuously, they called all Eastern European Jews "Polish Jews," collectively, regardless of what part of Eastern Europe they came from, and considered them "uncultural intruders" into their assimilated German culture. Upon graduation, Jewish students who were not German citizens received their medical diplomas, but no license to practice in Germany. They were expected to go back to their own countries.

That was just fine with Jehuda, who had no intention of staying in Germany or assimilating into the German culture, though he had actually grown to like and respect it. In 1914, just before World War I, he returned to Zhitomir with his MD and PhD degrees.

Pre-Revolutionary Zhitomir was a sleepy town that had its share of violence: there were several pogroms that killed innocent Jews, a hatred of the Volhynian Germans and a violent animosity between Ukrainians and Poles. Most of the doctors in Zhitomir were Poles who watched with great anxiety what was happening in the war and in turbulent Russia.

The year he came back, Jehuda proposed marriage to Miriam Kirchik, sister of two former pupils whom he had tutored before departing for Germany. Miriam was a high-school-educated Jewish girl who was delighted to have the tutor of her brothers as her suitor. Her father, who had been brought into her family as a "*kestkind,*" a man who was supposed to study the Torah and sire children, had no objections. Her older brothers were duly impressed that young Dr. Lerman was requesting to marry their sister, and they were married the same year.

Professionally, Dr. Lerman joined a Polish physician, Dr. Dovner, in his neurological and psychiatric practice. His choice of practice was not surprising. At that time, both specialties had been attracting the best intellectual minds in Germany and France, the two great rivals in science and medicine at the beginning of the Twentieth Century. As a student and as a young doctor, Jehuda had been greatly impressed by advances in these blossoming fields and stimulated by ardent debates with free-thinking students and faculty in Munich.

When he returned to Zhitomir, he found the only neurologist in town, a semi-retired man called Dr. Dovner. Dovner was cynical, frustrated and emotionless. He worked short hours, played the flute at home and collected rent from a row of houses he owned along one of the best residential streets in town. Jehuda decide to join him, with the hope of growing into his new fields and Dovner's practice.

Two years later, when it became absolutely clear that Zhitomir would join Soviet Russia, all the Polish physicians left town, leaving a huge vacuum in the health-care field. Dr. Dovner left Zhitomir as well, abandoning his patients and his real-estate holdings.

Young Dr. Jehuda Lerman took over his neurological and psychiatric practice, and became the only logical choice to head the Zhitomir Psychiatric Hospital.

In 1916, the Lermans had their first child, who died three years later of scarlet fever. Even though child mortality was high and deaths were to be expected, the death of a first-born son was devastating.

At the end of June, 1922, they had a second child, also a son, whom they named Victor. By this time, the new Communist-led government had taken firm hold in Ukraine and in the town of Zhitomir.

The first Chief of the newly organized regional Health Department was an uneducated, but highly opinionated, man. He could read a simple text, but wrote with numerous grammatical errors, and knew only elementary arithmetic: adding and subtracting to one hundred. A quick look at the Health Department budget convinced him that too much money was being allocated to the psychiatric hospital.

"What?" he shouted. "We spend money on crazy people? At a time when we don't have enough for normal citizens? Lock them up and let them die," he proclaimed, and completely eliminated the budget of the psychiatric hospital.

Dr. Lerman was incredulous. "These are sick people." He attempted to reason with the man. "Mental illness is not different from any other disease. These people must be treated."

Ignorance prevailed over reason, and the funds were withdrawn. The Chief of the Health Department left enough money to pay for a drastically reduced staff at the hospital, and for minimal maintenance of the building.

Stymied and despondent, Dr. Lerman went home, and refused to go to work. He declared a strike.

After a couple of days, word of the scandal reached the Secretary of the Zhitomir Communist Party, whose brother suffered from schizophrenia, and happened to be locked up in the same hospital. After a short delay, the Secretary ordered the funds for the psychiatric hospital restored, albeit at a reduced level, and Dr. Lerman returned to his duties.

Jehuda bought a new house in a better, cleaner, wealthier part of town, where several Jewish physicians had bought homes, as well. The house was relatively small, and the Lermans, who by this time had a little daughter, as well as Victor, built a sizable addition, with extra bedrooms and a study. Old apple, plum and pear trees surrounded the house and shaded the porch and the entire backyard. Lilac, raspberry and gooseberry bushes grew along the back fence.

Victor grew into a happy, frenzied, light-hearted, somewhat carefree boy. Dr. Lerman insisted that he attend a public Russian-language school, where academic requirements were not too stringent, and Victor placed in the middle of his class without any apparent effort.

When he was twelve or thirteen, the Jewish schools in Zhitomir were ordered closed, and Victor's class had to absorb a large influx of Jewish students. On the one hand, this was an eye-opener to Victor, who was suddenly

222   Boris Draznin

encountering much better students than anyone he had known previously. These newcomers were so much ahead of him that he thought they were math and science geniuses. On the other hand, for a while, he lost his self-confidence.

"How can I ever compete with these guys?" he said to his father, one evening. "They are so much smarter."

"I don't believe they are," answered Dr. Lerman. "They apply themselves to study, while you twiddle your thumbs and fritter away your time. You can be as good as they are, if you put your heart into it."

"I can never do it. They are so smart, particularly, in math." Victor shook his head.

"Fine. They are better in math. Prove, then, that you can do well in history, literature, or—you know what?—in German. That's right. If you can speak to me in German by the end of your school year, I'll buy you a new bike and you'll get your confidence fully restored. Agreed?"

Victor shrugged his shoulders. He wasn't confident at all that he could handle this task. But he started. German was the foreign language he was taking in school. He had books and dictionaries and his notes. His father also had German books and his medical texts, as well as some old newspapers. As Victor learned new words and phrases, the task seemed to get a bit easier every month. By the next June, the end of the school year, he could maintain a reasonable conversation with his dad and, to his great surprise, he could understand the Heinrich Heine poetry that his father recited by heart.

"I am proud of you," declared Jehuda. "You see what you can do when you make an effort? Keep your skills; don't let them disappear."

"I won't."

"I wonder whether you can tackle English." asked Jehuda. "It's going to be more difficult, because you are going to be doing it all on your own. You have no teachers and no one to help you."

"Why do I need English? Who speaks English, around here?" asked Victor, sarcastically, but then he remembered his new bicycle, and thought he might get something else for his efforts.

"Why do I know Latin? The language is dead, but the knowledge stays with you. Besides, from what I can see, English is becoming stronger as an international language in science and medicine. Even German articles refer to the increasing number of English papers. One day, it might become very useful."

Victor didn't like to be pushed, but he decided to try. He got a few self-teaching guides to English from his father's library, and embarked on his new task. His father was right; without the help of teachers and practice at school, it didn't go as easily as German had, but it certainly moved along.

* * *

Some time in 1938, while perusing the newspaper, Victor asked his father, "Isn't it surprising how many enemies of people we still have, so many years after the Revolution? It seems that every day, more and more are discovered, and in high circles, too."

Jehuda, who had never brought up this subject for discussion, looked at his son over his eyeglasses, put his paper aside and responded, "Let me tell you something, but you should never discuss it with anyone else, unless you wish to become an orphan." He leaned across the table as if he wished to minimize the strength of his voice. "There are no enemies of the people or enemies of the state. Whenever a new ruler rises to power, whether he is a new king or a new dictator, he kills the top echelon of followers of the previous ruler. This is what Stalin is doing. He is ridding himself of Lenin's circle.

"You tell anybody that I told you that, and I'll be gone. You tell anyone that you deduced it on your own, and you'll be gone. This is for you to understand, but not to share. We live in dangerous times."

The same year, Jehuda's mother, Victor's grandmother, Chaya-Shira, was killed by a neighbor who, like a character in Dostoevsky's *Crime and Punishment*, thought that the old woman had money hidden in her dilapidated house. He broke in at night and suffocated her with a pillow. Not finding any money in the house, he spent what he had on a bottle of vodka, drank it all night, and, in the morning, confessed his deeds to other neighbors and to a policeman.

After the funeral, when they came home from the cemetery and washed their hands, Jehuda said solemnly, "For all the problems we acquired with the Communists, if they were not here, these bandits would kill all the Jews in Russia."

Later that year, Victor's other grandmother died, and his grandfather, who was totally incapable of living alone, moved in with the Lermans. He was given a small bedroom where he placed his little desk and an equally small bookshelf full of old, tattered Hebrew books.

Grandpa spoke only Yiddish, and spent his days at his desk, reading his books. Several times a day, he turned south, toward Jerusalem, placed his shawl over his head and prayed, singing something in Hebrew and moving his body back and forth, occasionally bending his knees. To Victor it looked both strange and funny. Many times, he would stand behind his grandpa, who was oblivious of his presence, and mock his praying movement, barely holding in his laughter. Grandpa never looked back. Either he was truly unaware of his grandson's presence, or he simply ignored the silly boy.

In the summer of 1940, Victor left for Leningrad, to take the entrance exams for the Leningrad Medical School. First, he had thought of going to Kiev, as it was much closer to Zhitomir; not quite a hundred miles to the east. But he had finally decided to try his hand in Leningrad, mainly because two of his mother's brothers, former pupils of his father, were now living in Leningrad, so he would have a place to stay during the entrance tests and possibly during the school year, if he were not assigned to the dormitory.

For the first time in years, he studied really hard. Physics, chemistry and biology all needed to be reviewed carefully and remembered well. He did very well—his four "As" and one "B" got him into Medical School.

There was no quota at that time, and about a third of the incoming class were Jewish kids. Victor was expected to do well, but he exceeded everyone's expectations. He was brimming with self-confidence, and his family back in Zhitomir was proud and delighted.

When Victor, now a young man over six feet tall, walked into the auditorium for his first lecture, he stopped in the doorway and studied the faces of his classmates who had arrived earlier. In the second row of the amphitheater, he noticed a tall, slim girl with a long, brown braid who had already carefully organized her notebook, a pencil and an eraser in front of her sharp elbows.

Wow! he thought, *What a pretty girl!*

But she was sitting too close to the lecturer for him; Victor preferred the last row, where he was not that visible.

Later that month, he met her in the library, where she studied daily after classes. Her name was Judith Elkin, but everyone called her Dina. She was a very serious, studious girl. She had finished high school with a gold medal, the highest honor in the school, and been admitted to Medical School without entrance exams; just an hour of discussion with the admission committee had sufficed. She remained the best student in her class, as well. She sat up front at every lecture, always took notes and asked questions, completed all her assignments on time and fully and never, ever missed even an hour of school.

Dina had grown up in Leningrad, and lived with her parents in the center of the city, near the Nickolsky Cathedral. Victor asked if he could walk her home after they had studied in the library, and she said yes. He tried to do that every day, even though he detested staying in the library for so long every evening.

He told her about his life in Zhitomir, his pranks at school and with other boys in town, about his father's love of medicine and medical research, about his wonderful bike and about his studies of German and English.

She told him that she had been born in the very small Byelorussian town of Rogachev, somewhere on the Dneiper River, and had moved to Leningrad when she was six years old. Neither of her parents had any formal education, and both of them worked in retail. They lived in a huge, eighteen-room apartment on the third floor of a large and ornate apartment house.

Before the Bolshevik Revolution, an aristocratic Russian family had lived in the flat, but now eighteen families called it home. Each family had one room and a little table with a kerosene burner in the common kitchen. There was one bathroom in the apartment for all eighteen families. They used the sink to wash and brush their teeth, and all used the same toilet. The large, white-enamel bathtub was never used, as everyone used to go once a week to the public bathhouse, a block away, to take a shower or a bath. Dina's family actually had one of the largest rooms; almost four hundred square feet.

Dina's father, Abraham Elkin, was an exceptionally quiet, modest man. The youngest of four brothers, he had never learned to fight for his place at the table or in the food line. After his parents had died and his brothers had left Rogachev, some to Leningrad and some to America, he had left his family home and moved from the small town, where there were no jobs, to Leningrad, where one of his older brothers had found him a retail sales job.

His wife, Dina's mother, was an energetic woman who was the dynamic force in the family. Her name was Miriam, but she was called Maria. She worked not far from home, in the meat department of a medium-sized grocery store, and her work allowed her to be the *de facto* breadwinner of the family.

By the end of the academic year, Victor and Dina had become truly good friends. They saw each other almost daily, and always on the weekends. Victor met her parents and went to dinner with them on many occasions.

In June of 1941, classes ended, and Victor went back home to his family in Zhitomir.

"I will be back no later than the middle of August," he told Dina, holding her hands in his. "The summer will pass quickly, and I'll be back in no time. I'll write to you, I promise."

"I'll write to you, too," Dina assured him. She wanted him to stay, but knew he had to go home to his parents.

Ten days later, when Victor was still searching for the perfect time to tell his parents about Dina, German bombers attacked Zhitomir. The same day, Dr. Jehuda Lerman was mobilized and made Chief Physician of the Military Psychiatric Hospital that had been formed east of Kiev, and now was moving to the Ural Mountains.

The family of Dr. Lerman, his wife, their son, Victor and their fourteen-year-old daughter, Lena, left Zhitomir the next morning.

Victor wrote to Dina daily, mailing his letters from every train station they passed, with no idea whether the letters would ever make it to Leningrad. He also listened to the news, a helpless observer as the Germans advanced toward Leningrad.

The psychiatric hospital had finally settled in Novosibirsk, a Siberian town some one thousand miles east of the Urals.

Victor had not received a single letter from Dina. By the middle of winter, he had heard that Leningrad was surrounded by German troops and people were dying of cold and hunger. In with three or four of his letters, he put chunks of frozen butter, and mailed them to Dina. There was no response and no way of finding out whether she was still in Leningrad or whether or not she was still alive.

He was desperate, heart-broken, and inconsolable. He was lost; completely lost.

CHAPTER TWENTY-ONE

D ina and her parents stayed in Leningrad, as did almost three million of the city's inhabitants. The Germans began to approach Leningrad in September of 1941. The German generals, who needed their tanks on the Ukrainian and Southern fronts, decided to pull their heavy guns away from Leningrad, and not attack the city, but, instead, to encircle it, placing it under what they thought would be an quick and effective siege.

By the end of the first week of September, the city was completely surrounded, with only a single waterway through Lake Ladoga connecting the besieged city with the rest of the territory still in Russian hands.

The nine-hundred-day siege of Leningrad was unquestionably the most tragic period in the city's history. The suffering and heroism of the people who remained in the city became legendary. People had no heat, no running water and almost no food. By the middle of winter, the food ration was one quarter-pound of bread per person per day. In a span of just two months, January and February of 1942, over 200,000 people died of starvation and exposure.

Frozen bodies remained on the streets. There were rumors of cannibalism, but no one in the city thought of giving up. To the defenders and citizens of Leningrad, death was preferable to surrender.

A month before the war had begun, Dina's mother had changed her job, accepting a position as administrator of a technical school for metal craftsmen. With the siege, classes in the technical school, as well as in the medical school, were canceled, and the students and faculty joined the rest of Leningrad in digging anti-tank trenches and putting up defensive obstacles around the city.

Dina's father, Abraham, was mobilized into the Leningrad civil defense force, and assigned to guard one of the few factories still functioning. The Elkins were exhausted, but lucky to be alive.

In February of 1942 came an order to evacuate the technical school, so it could be used to prepare young people in the eastern part of Russia to enter the skilled work force. At dawn on February 27, the Elkins, with other students and those faculty who had survived the siege thus far, boarded heavy trucks for the trip across the ice of Lake Ladoga into Russian-held territory. "The Road of Life," as this passage came to be called, was used to bring meager supplies into the city and to evacuate people from besieged Leningrad.

It was dangerous. The lake was frozen solid, but German artillery shells blew large holes in the ice that sometimes were covered with only a thin new layer through which trucks could easily fall into the icy water. But the convoy carrying the technical school made it to safety without problems. Two days later, the school was put on trains and sent eastward.

They were told that the school would be deployed in Novosibirsk. The Elkins had never heard of the town before. The train ride to Novosibirsk lasted over three weeks.

March is still a cold month in Novosibirsk. Standing on the platform in the light of the weak early-afternoon Siberian sun, huddling from the cold and waiting to be directed to their apartment, Dina's heart sank and froze somewhere inside her chest. Then she looked up and saw Victor coming slowly toward them.

"Victor!" she shouted, not really believing that it was he.

"Dina!" came back to her, as he suddenly saw her and froze to the spot.

Apparently, for almost two months, he had been coming daily to the train station, hoping, without any rational reason, that one day she might show up. And now she had.

In January of 1942, Victor had enrolled in Novosibirsk Medical School as a second-year student. The school was not too far from the train station, and, every afternoon, Victor would stroll through the station, looking at arriving passengers and searching for Dina.

The next day, he took her to the Medical School. She was allowed to enroll for the remainder of the semester, and had to take final tests for the entire year so she could start third year the next fall. Life began anew.

Victor was living with his parents and younger sister. Their grandfather had died in December, 1941, probably of starvation. He had refused to eat non-kosher food, and lived for a while on bread and water. He had read his books, prayed and never complained about anything. Then, one morning, he didn't wake up.

*   *   *

"How can a people like the Germans, with such great traditions of enlightenment and rich humanistic culture become so incredibly barbaric and inhumane?" Victor asked his father, one evening, while they were listening to classical music on the radio.

"This will be one of many puzzles for future historians," answered Jehuda. "I'd say that Germans are an exquisitely obedient and disciplined group of people. They proved capable of blindly following their leaders. Also, Europeans are brought up in the traditions of nationalism. It was only natural for the German people to buy into the idea of their national and cultural superiority."

"And anti-Semitism?"

"That's what unites the Catholic, Lutheran and Eastern Orthodox churches. Christianity, from its inception, had to separate itself from Judaism, its religious and cultural predecessor, and the separation assumed this violent form. Besides, not having their own country didn't help the Jews. They remained foreigners, even among the people with whom they shared the land for generations."

"But Russia is not a religious state, and yet we also have plenty of anti-Semitism."

"I've always thought, and still do, that elimination of religious tensions would be the greatest feature of Soviet Russia. I hope, in your lifetime, you will see equality of the Jews with everyone else in this country. Until that time, you have to be the best to be successful."

Victor tried. He was one of the brightest students in his class, and the only one who knew foreign languages and could read foreign medical literature, a feat that everyone else found absolutely incredible.

In 1944, when Victor and Dina graduated from medical school, the war was still in full swing, but now the Russian armies were on the offensive and pursuing the German troops. The front line moved to the western border of pre-war Russia. All graduates of medical schools were mobilized into the Army and, in order to stay together, Victor and Dina decided to get married immediately after graduation, hoping to receive a joint commission. They got their marriage certificate a week before receiving their military assignments.

As a couple, they were assigned to a large military hospital that moved westward with the advancing Russian troops. They had to catch up with their hospital in Romania, northwest of Odessa, a Ukrainian town on the Black Sea. They arrived in Odessa by train, from Moscow, and joined a group of fifteen physicians assigned to various hospitals in Romania and Hungary.

They traveled as a group to the Romanian border. The truck dropped them off at a border control point and left.

The officer at the border collected their documents and disappeared into his booth. He came back after twenty minutes, to announce that their documents lacked an important stamp, and that he would not be able to let them through.

"What stamp?" gasped a short, woman physician, a Captain, who was commander of their fifteen-person group. "We received these papers in Moscow. We are the doctors and the hospitals are waiting for us. You must let us through!"

"No, I won't." The officer shook his head. "This is an international border. This is not a joke. You don't have stamps authorizing passage, and I won't let you through."

"What shall we do, then?"

"I don't know. Go back to Odessa and ask them for proper stamps." He returned to his booth, and would not discuss the subject any longer.

The fifteen doctors were at loss. The truck that had brought them to the border was gone. It was getting dark, and the closest village was about a mile away. They walked to the village, still arguing as to what they should do next.

On the porch of the first house in the village sat another border patrol officer, a young man with a bushy mustache. He was smoking a cigarette.

He gave them a friendly greeting.

"I don't think the village has room for fifteen of you. Where are you guys going?"

"We are going to Romania to join our assignments, but your colleague out there," the Captain pointed, "didn't let us through. He said we are lacking an important stamp in our documents."

"Let me see your papers," asked the friendly officer. He examined the papers carefully and said, "He is right. There should have been a stamp right here." And he pointed at the assignment papers. "But not to worry; it's a minor thing. A pack of cigarettes from each of you, and I'll let you through tonight. My shift starts at two a.m. Come before dawn, though, while it's still dark."

They slept in a haystack, digging themselves deep inside the wet mass to escape the drizzling rain, until two in the morning, when they returned to the border checkpoint. The friendly officer collected a pack of cigarettes from each of them and waved them through.

"Go, go, Doctors, quickly, before anyone sees you."

They walked across the bridge over the Danube River from Russia into Romania, not even seeing the river in the darkness below their feet, and, in three hours, made it to the military command post in the Romanian town of Galati, as they were supposed to do. There they stayed for a day, drying out and having hot meals, and there they received their individual assignments.

Victor and Dina found their assigned hospital in Romania, and joined its surgical staff. Over the next several months, they moved with this hospital from Romania to Hungary and then to Austria, entering Vienna in 1945. In June, Dina, now an expectant mother, was discharged from her military duty and sent back to now-liberated Leningrad, where her parents had returned from Novosibirsk.

Victor, meanwhile, was transferred to another hospital, this one in Budapest. One day, while walking through the streets of the Hungarian capital, Victor saw a store selling antique and used books, with an older man sitting behind the counter, reading an equally old newspaper.

Victor walked in. When the bell on the door rang, the man raised his head from the paper and, seeing a Russian officer, greeted him in broken but understandable Russian. Victor answered in German, asking if he could look around.

"Of course!" was the answer. "Anything in particular? Maybe I can be of help?" The man spoke perfect German.

"Old medical texts or English-language textbooks," said Victor.

"I have both." The owner waved his arms and walked out from behind the counter to the shelves. "What's your name, Officer?"

"Victor Lerman. I'm a doctor with the Russian hospital."

"Lerman? Must be Jewish? My name is Farkas. Leon Farkas. I'm Jewish, too."

Mr. Farkas was a man of a medium height, with a large tuft of dark-black hair growing on the top and back of his head, leaving a tall, bold forehead ascending almost to the middle of his skull.

"Where did you learn German, Doctor Lerman?" asked Mr. Farkas, in a friendly way. "So unusual for a Russian soldier, don't you think?"

"In school, believe it or not, and at home. My father insisted that I study languages. And you? Do you understand English, Mr. Farkas?" asked Victor. "I would like to take lessons."

"I certainly do," said Mr. Farkas. "I speak several languages, and English happens to be one of them. I'll be happy to teach you what I know."

"I have no money, but I can pay with cigarettes and sugar," offered Victor, who received several ounces of sugar and a pack of cigarettes a day as his military ration. He saved both, as he didn't smoke and used very little sugar.

"I'll take it," agreed Mr. Farkas.

They met twice a week for hour-long lessons, mainly reading medical texts and reciting English grammar. After the English lessons, they conversed in German. Mr. Farkas told Victor about his life and the life and fate of Hungarian Jews, many of whom, surprisingly, had survived the war. Mr. Farkas said they had not been deported to concentration camps until 1944, although enough time had still been left before liberation for a great number of them to perish before the war ended. He had lost his family in a concentration camp, but he himself had survived and returned to his bookstore and the tiny, two-room apartment attached to it. He lived and worked on the ground floor of a three-story building sandwiched between two taller ones on a small street two blocks from the Synagogue.

Mr. Farkas also told Victor about Palestine, and the prospects for the Jewish state bounded by Jerusalem and Tel-Aviv, Haifa and Beer-Sheba. One evening, he made an offer.

"If you wish to go to Palestine, all you have to do is change into civilian clothes, here in my apartment, and my friends will smuggle you away, via Romania, to Italy and then to Palestine. It's that simple; all you have to do is just change clothes."

"I can't," replied Victor, confidently. "My family is back in Leningrad and my parents are in Zhitomir. I can't leave. I can't drop everything and disappear."

"If you ever change your mind," said Mr. Farkas, gently, "I'm here to help for perhaps another year or so, and then I'll move there, myself. To remain in Europe is too painful for me."

He never brought it up again, and they continued their English lessons until Victor's discharge from the Army in 1946.

In the hospital, Victor befriended another young Jewish doctor, Vladimir Berger. Vladimir, five years older than Victor, had graduated from Kiev Medical School two weeks before the War began. He had become a surgeon, and served first in the small field hospitals and then in large, stationary medical centers, where he did traumatic brain surgery. His war experience had made him an excellent trauma neurosurgeon.

In 1944, Vladimir had visited Kiev, his liberated hometown, still in ruins and disarray. He had found a deep crater at the site of his parents' house, left by one of the first bombs to hit the city, before dawn one morning in 1941. His parents had been inside.

He had also learned that his older sister, two cousins and their families had died in Babi Yar, now a mass grave of over one hundred thousand Jews who had been killed outside Kiev.

At the age of twenty-eight, he was the only member of his family left alive.

His happiness at the liberation and inevitable victory of his country, which he had joyfully shared with the rest of Russia, had yielded to a profound depression, as he left Kiev to join his hospital.

Vladimir couldn't sleep, and had lost his appetite. Eventually, he found salvation in his work, spending up to twenty hours a day in the operating room. He took a liking to Victor, and, after learning that Victor's father was a psychiatrist, confided in him as if the son of a psychiatrist were the psychiatrist himself.

"I can't tolerate violence anymore," he confessed. "I am dedicating my life to repairing what violence has done to people. I tend to their wounds and, with every new patient, I hope this one will be the last wounded soldier of this terrible war. My family were the best people in the world, and look what happened. They were wiped from the face of this world for nothing; for no reason at all. I mean my parents were killed for nothing, and the rest of my family were killed because they were Jewish.

"We were so close to one another. My nieces, my nephews, my cousins; life was ahead of them, and now they are gone as if they never existed. It is so profoundly *wrong*."

Victor listened carefully, not really knowing how to help. Occasionally, he tried to direct their conversation toward Vladimir's own life; his future, his health and his sanity. It didn't help.

In November, 1945, Victor was awakened by the sound of two gunshots coming from the back yard of the school building in which hospital was located. Screams and commotion reached his window, as well. He quickly put on his shirt and pants, and was ready to go out when someone knocked at his door.

It was Vladimir, wearing his white coat over his military uniform. He looked lost, and held a handgun in his right hand.

"I've just killed two people," he announced, softly. "The two soldiers behind the machine shop."

Victor was paralyzed. He stared at his pacifist colleague in disbelief.

"A group of our soldiers was raping a Ukrainian girl. You know, one of those brought here by the Germans as slave laborers. I happened to be passing by. I walked out to have a smoke and just stumbled upon them. She was screaming and asking for help. I told them to stop. One hit me in the face, she screamed louder and I pulled my gun and shot him. And then, I don't even know what possessed me, I came closer and I shot the other one, the one who was on top of the girl. I shot him in the back, between the shoulder blades. I'm sure he is dead. Victor, I've killed two people. I used violence in response to violence; something I abhor so deeply. Now they are going to kill me. Full circle. Violence breeds violence. Help me, Victor. Help me."

"Did anyone see you coming here to me?" asked Victor.

"I don't think so."

"You have no family back home, is that right? No one?"

"No one; absolutely no one."

"Here is an address," said Victor, writing on a torn piece of paper. "Go to this man. 'Mr. Farkas' is his name. Tell him you are from me, and he will help you to go to Palestine. You'll be safe. Go. Leave your white coat in the stairwell and go. Hurry!"

Vladimir hesitated. "I don't speak Hungarian."

"He speaks a little Russian. Tell him, 'I am a Jew, from Victor. I want

Palestine.' That's all you need to say. Hurry! Remember—'I am a Jew, want Palestine.' He'll help." He almost pushed Vladimir out the door.

Victor looked down at the street from his window. He saw the shadow of Vladimir, without his white coat, moving rapidly to the corner and disappearing in the night.

He sat on his bed for five minutes more, and then went to the emergency room, to find what had happened with the soldiers Vladimir had shot.

The next day, Major Vladimir Berger was denounced as a murderer and deserter, and the Military Police looked for him all over Budapest. He was never found.

Victor returned to Leningrad in 1946, when his daughter, Elena, was seven months old. Dina had just begun specialization in pediatric infectious diseases, with her mother at home to help with the baby.

Victor, who had decided to become a neurosurgeon, went to the Institute of Neurosurgery named after Andrei Lvovich Polenov, a famous Russian neurophysiologist. He had an appointment with Professor Bondarchuk, chief of the second surgical department.

"What kind of special skills do you have?" asked the Professor, as if it would be just a waste of time to interview this young doctor, fresh from military service.

"I've been a surgeon in the Army."

"So has every other able military doctor in the Russian army," interrupted Professor Bondarchuk. "Anything else?" He seemed ready to end the five-minute interview.

"I am fluent in two foreign languages."

"Fluent in foreign languages? Do you mean you can read in...what language?" Professor Bondarchuk suddenly focused on Victor.

"German and English. Yes, I can read and speak both German and English."

"I need a man just like you," smiled the Professor. "What did you say your name is?"

"Victor Lerman."

"You'll start next week, Victor Lerman. In my department."

Professor Bondarchuk had no intention of teaching Victor neurosurgery or even allowing him into the operating room. He was writing a textbook on neurosurgery, and needed references from foreign medical journals and books. Every day, Victor had to go to the library to read German and English medical books and journals and take notes from the foreign literature on an assigned theme. In the afternoon, he had meetings with Professor Bondarchuk at which he went over his notes, which the Professor would then use for his book. This lasted for six months, until Victor received a letter from his father, who knew what was happening, telling him to transfer immediately to another department, because, according to Jehuda, he was simply wasting his time.

By this time, Victor had met and had several conversations with the chairman of another department, Professor Isaac Savelievich Babchin, who agreed to take him into his group. Professor Bondarchuk was outraged, but couldn't do anything. Victor went to work for his new mentor.

In 1948, Comrade Stalin initiated another purge, starting in Leningrad. Unlike the purges of 1937, this one acquired a clear anti-Jewish tone within the first eighteen months. Leningrad's Jewish medical community became one of its first victims.

A newly appointed Chief City Physician, Dr. Gookasian, arrived from Moscow to institute new policies. The new Party line specified that every academic physician should be properly qualified for his or her position. However, this benign statement was twisted against most young and mid-level Jewish physicians. They were found either "overqualified" or "underqualified," and relieved of their duties. In the Polenov Institute of Neurosurgery, over ninety percent of Jewish doctors were fired. The same was happening in every medical facility in Leningrad.

Everyone knew what was happening. Everyone understood why it was happening. No one could say a word. Even in their own homes, people were afraid of mentioning the subject.

"Hush! The walls have ears," Dina's mother used to say, and she would put her index finger to her lips.

Victor and Dina were let go at the end of 1950.

"You are still young; someone may hire you," said Doctor Glickman to Victor, as he was clearing out his office. "I am fifty-two; not even a slim chance; not a gleam of hope."

Indeed, no one was hiring. The Jewish medical community was decimated. Fortunately, no one was arrested. At least, not until January of 1953, when the "doctors' plot" was revealed publicly in the Communist newspapers.

Meanwhile, those fired doctors who could find jobs in provincial Russian cities and towns moved away from Leningrad, the cultural gem of Russia. Those who couldn't move remained unemployed.

Dina was given the option of going to Archangelsk, a Northern port town on the shores of the White Sea. Victor was given no mandatory assignment, and he tried desperately to find something in a better place.

In 1951, already an unemployed neurosurgeon, he presented some research at the All-Russian Neurosurgical Congress in Moscow. His boss, Professor

Isaac Babchin, was sitting in the audience next to the President of the Byelorussian Academy of Sciences, the neurophysiologist, Nicolai Grashchenkov.

"Excellent presentation," said Grashchenkov to Professor Babchin. "A terrific young clinician-scientist you have in your group."

"He is terrific, but he's no longer in my group. He's just been fired. There's nothing I can do. An excellent scientist without a job."

"I am developing neurosurgery in Minsk. Send him to me, and I'll see what I can do."

By the end of the day, the President of the Byelorussian Academy had interviewed and hired Doctor Victor Lerman.

"We are very keen on establishing a strong neurosurgical presence in Minsk. We have recently hired two neurosurgeons, and both happen to be Jewish. I want you, too," said Professor Grashchenkov firmly, when he noticed the uneasy smile on Victor's face. "But I cannot hire you through our Institute of Neurology and Neurosurgery," he added, matter-of-factly. "We already have too many Jewish doctors, there. However, I'll ask my friend, the Director of the Institute of Agriculture, to hire you. It shouldn't matter to you where your check is coming from, should it?"

"Oh, by no means. It won't bother me at all. I am so grateful to you for giving me a chance," answered Victor, sincerely. He promised eagerly, "I am defending my dissertation next month, and I will come immediately after that."

The next morning, he phoned Dina in Archangelsk and his father in Zhitomir to tell them this wonderful news. "I'm going to be a neurosurgeon in an academic institution. And it's in Minsk. It's kind of provincial, but it's a capital city. It's going to evolve. I am sure I'll find something for you, Dina, as soon as I arrive and meet people."

Dina wasn't too optimistic. She had also defended her dissertation, but was still working as a regular doctor in the Department of Pediatric Infectious Diseases. She wanted an academic position and she wanted to do research, but there was no hope, in that Northern city, with its minimal academic medical infrastructure.

Six months later, with the help of Victor's new boss, Professor Grashchenkov, Dina was hired as an Assistant Professor of Pediatric Infectious Diseases at Minsk Medical School. The same year, they received a room in a large apartment that they would share with three other families, and they brought their daughter Elena to Minsk from Leningrad, where she had been staying with her grandparents.

They were happy. They had survived the lay-offs, both of them now had academic jobs in the same city, they had their own room and their daughter was about to enter elementary school in one of the major, if a bit provincial, cities of the Soviet Union. What else could one wish for?

CHAPTER TWENTY-TWO

Winter in Zhitomir can be stunningly beautiful. By the middle of December, snow covers the town, and stays white and crisp, with individual flakes reflecting the rays of the sun like tiny diamonds that play with light. The roofs of the houses are covered with a seven-to-ten-inch-thick snow blanket, and large banks of snow separate the narrow sidewalks from the plowed streets. Equally high snowbanks surround porches and gardens, in front of and behind the houses.

The snow begins to melt in March, and the healthy Ukrainian winter is replaced by a wet, dirty, icy early spring that, by April, reveals white and green flowers and juicy, succulent buds.

Victor tried to visit Zhitomir at least once a year but, occasionally, up to eighteen months passed between his short visits. This time, he arrived in February of 1953.

Two weeks before Victor's arrival, Doctor Jehuda Lerman was removed from the position of Medical Director of the Zhitomir Psychiatric Hospital that he had occupied for so many years. He was told that he was approaching retirement age, and that a new and younger Director would be needed to lead the hospital into the future.

He was transferred to a neighborhood clinic, where he was given the title of Senior City Psychiatrist. The clinic was located about ten city blocks from his house, in an old, four-story, rust-brown-brick building. The clinic's Medical Director didn't like having psychiatric patients in his building.

"They frighten both the staff and other patients," he pronounced to his underlings.

But he couldn't argue with the city's decision, and, instead, directed his displeasure at the old psychiatrist. He gave Doctor Lerman an office on the top floor.

"I know it isn't easy to negotiate the stairs all the way up to the top," he said to Doctor Lerman, with a note of sarcasm in his low voice, "but the view's well worth the effort."

The view toward the Teterev River, over the roofs of one- and two-story houses, was indeed magnificent. However, it wasn't too pleasing for an older doctor with intermittent chest pain and shortness of breath. Jehuda walked up the stairs every morning, slowly, but at a steady pace, trying to avoid stops and not reveal his shortness of breath, even though, on occasion, he was barely able to hide his struggle. He was too proud to let anyone see it.

Victor and his father were drinking their after-dinner tea in Jehuda's study. Light from a black desk-lamp gave bright illumination only to the surface of the desk. The bookcases along the walls stood in the dim remnants of light that barely reached the perimeter of the room.

Sitting on a small couch, holding a cup of tea in his hands, Victor asked his father, "Do you really think they were trying to poison Stalin?"

Jehuda lifted his cup to his lips, took a small sip of hot, strong Georgian tea and placed his cup back on the saucer. He looked straight into Victor's eyes and answered, "It would be awful if they did, but it would be many-fold more dangerous if they didn't."

"You mean if they were falsely accused?"

"Yes. That is exactly what I mean. I cannot believe those people are criminals or spies. Those Jewish doctors are afraid of hurting a fly, if you ask me."

"If they are innocent, we'll be facing a catastrophe," Victor agreed. "It's going to be another wave of anti-Jewish terror."

Jehuda summed up. "We will be facing a catastrophe. We most certainly will. I'm glad you understand."

"Sometimes I wish I didn't. It would be easier to live in this country not realizing what's going on."

"We have no options. First of all, there is no way out. Second, I'm not sure life is better anyplace else. You know the famous English proverb about the grass that is always greener..."

"...on the other side of the fence," said Victor.

"Precisely."

Victor returned to Minsk depressed. Even though there had been no arrests or mass dismissals of Jewish doctors in Minsk, the situation was tense, and a sense of unpredictability permeated their lives. Jewish doctors were silent, and never discussed either the doctors' plot or any of their feelings with anyone else, not even other Jewish doctors. The fear was overwhelming.

The announcement of Comrade Stalin's death in early March of 1953 brought only momentary relief. No one knew or could possibly predict what kind of events would follow the death of the Great Leader. No one knew who would come to power or which way Soviet Russia would turn. Only when, on April 4, *Pravda* published the statement that the doctors' plot had been a complete fabrication, and all those doctors who had been accused of crimes they had never committed were immediately released, did Victor feel his fears and tension subside substantially.

In 1954, both Dina and Victor turned their full attention to their professorial aspirations and to their second dissertations. Professorial positions were again an attainable goal.

In 1959, they finally received their own, non-shared, individual apartment. It was a two-room flat with a small kitchen and bathroom. Victor and Dina used the smaller room as their bedroom and study, and placed a small wooden desk in front of the window and a queen-size bed against the opposite wall. Their daughter, Elena, slept on a pullout couch in the larger room, which also contained a dining table with six chairs, a cupboard and many bookshelves. When they had company, Elena slept in their bed until the guests had departed. Most of the time, the family ate at the small dinette in the kitchen, and used the dining table as a desk for one of the parents or for Elena, who did her homework there.

During the same year, Victor thought often of applying for the vacant position of Director of the Institute of Neurology and Neurosurgery at the Byelorussian Academy of Sciences, but he was told early in the recruitment process that the job was reserved for a "real" Byelorussian, and that Jewish doctors need not apply.

At that time, the Byelorussian Republic was undergoing an interesting transformation. The first generation of Byelorussian peasants who had completed their higher education immediately before or after the War, was slated to replace the Jewish professors at the University and in other centers of higher learning. These people came to be known as the "national cadre," and had a distinct priority in hiring, even though they were much less qualified than the well-educated Jewish "intelligentsia."

But such were the ground rules of the new policy of promoting Byelorussians. The rules were very popular among the locals and criticized by the Jews, although they accepted them reluctantly.

The Jewish people of the Soviet Union, who retained nothing of their religious Jewish heritage, were made second- or even third-class citizens in their own towns and republics. Even though the immediate danger to their lives had passed with the passing of Comrade Stalin, the official policy of limiting Jewish involvement in higher education, internal and international politics and leadership positions remained in effect, as strong as ever.

In 1959, Doctor Jehuda Lerman had a heart attack. He was prescribed complete bed-rest for almost a month. After he recovered, he returned to work in his clinic, where his office was still on the fourth floor of the clinic building. It was taking him almost half an hour to climb the six flights of stairs, as he now spent a considerable time at each landing, fighting shortness of breath.

He never complained, as he believed the Medical Director was well aware of his limitations and, if he wanted to, could easily have assigned him an office on the ground floor.

Outraged, Victor did complain, and wrote a number of letters to various authorities in Zhitomir, to which he received polite answers promising to switch Doctor Jehuda Lerman's office to one of the lower floors as soon as appropriate space opened up. It never did.

Doctor Jehuda Lerman died in his sleep during the winter of 1961.

* * *

In December of 1955, weeks before moving from Kharkov to Minsk, Boris and his grandmother, Rachel, were returning home after seeing a play at the Children's Theater. They were riding in a cold tramcar at about ten o'clock in the evening, when a drunken man in a long, dirty black coat climbed into the car.

He could barely stand. As the tram moved ahead, shaking and rolling along the tracks, the drunken man's body swung from side to side until he finally caught the pole in the middle of the car. Suddenly, his hand slid down the slippery surface of the chromed pole, and he fell into the seat just in front of Rachel and Boris, on top of a frail, old man.

"Oh, shit!" the drunkard swore, as he was trying to get back to his feet.

The old man attempted to help him, and pushed him away and upward, but the drunken man took his push for an unfriendly gesture. The car jerked again, and he was thrown back onto the same old man, who extended his both arms to protect himself from the falling body of the drunk.

"What the fuck are you doing, pushing me? You are an old, lousy Yid!" screamed the drunk, assuming the old man was Jewish. "The Germans should have finished you all, fucking parasites!" He bent over and pulled the old man off his seat into the aisle.

The old man fell to the floor of the car. No one moved to help. No one wanted to deal with the drunk, who now plunged into the old man's seat, stepping on and over the old man's body, shouting, "I'll kick your ass, lousy Jew! Where did you hide during the war?"

The old man, who may or may not have been a Jew, didn't reply. He slowly crawled away and rose to his feet a few yards away. Mutely, he moved along the aisle toward the driver of the tram, who kept his eyes on the road, pretending not to see what was going on inside the car. The people in the car turned their faces to the windows, also pretending not to hear or see a thing.

Rachel, who was now sitting immediately behind the swearing drunk, grabbed her grandson's hand and pulled him to the door at the middle of the car. "We'll get out at the next station," she said, "and walk two blocks."

The car stopped, and they got out. They walked in silence, still holding hands.

By this time, ten-year-old Boris knew that he and his family were Jewish. Like his father, twenty-five years before, he had learned about being Jewish in the classroom. Also like his father, he didn't like being Jewish, because, for him, it had no meaning other than being different from his classmates and neighbors.

He had felt better when he found that his best friends in the class, Sasha Cherniak, Marina Chernina and Vova Val, were Jewish, as well.

"Grandma," he asked, "why was that man swearing at the Jews?"

"He is drunk; just a drunkard. I don't think he knew what he was saying. Don't pay attention to drunken hoodlums."

"But you didn't want to stay in the car," Boris persisted. "Did you think he might beat us up?"

"No, no. I didn't think so," Rachel lied. "I'm telling you he is a pathetic, miserable drunk. It's better not to get involved."

"Is that why no one defended the old man?"

"I guess so."

They didn't talk until they reached their apartment house.

"Grandma, why don't they like us?" he asked, as they were climbing the stairs.

"Smart people do," answered Rachel. "Always deal with smart people and avoid the ignorant."

"How do you know who is smart and who is ignorant?"

"You'll figure it out as you grow older. It's not that difficult."

Seven months later, after they moved to Minsk to join Nahum some time in the summer of 1956, Boris read *The Count of Monte Cristo*, a book he had found on the bookshelf in the Minsk apartment. He was fascinated with the story of the falsely accused sailor, Edmond Dantes, who had escaped from an unbreakable prison, the infamous Chateau d'If. Dantes found an incredible treasure, became Count of Monte Cristo, the richest man in Europe, and then plotted and executed a brilliant revenge. The Count was a great role model; an incredible example of righteousness.

"I will get revenge on everyone," thought Boris, closing the cover of the book, "everyone who abuses Jews. I'll pay them back, one by one, exactly like the Count, including that terrible, drunken man in the tramcar."

"Papa, where did you get this book?" Boris asked Nahum, that evening.

"This one, I bought," said Nahum. "I love to read, and while I was here alone, and the evenings were too long, I had hours to read."

"But we don't have that many books." Boris pointed at the short, narrow bookcase standing between his couch and his sister's bed.

"Most of the books I've read, I checked out from the library. They have thousands of books. You can take home a couple, read them, return them and check out new ones."

"Can we go to the library?" asked Boris, enthusiastically. "Is it like a book-store?"

"Only larger. And you must return a book after you read it. The concept is to let you borrow a book for a certain number of days. I'll show you. We'll go there this Saturday," Nahum promised.

The city of Minsk had one large public library. It was located in a huge build-ing built in the neo-classical style, with massive columns, an impressive entranceway and a cupola-covered vestibule. The library was named after Comrade Lenin—the Lenin Library. Each floor of the five-story library con-tained a number of rooms, their content organized by subject: History, Art, Medicine, Classical Literature, Engineering and others. Each room had long, wide tables made of dark wood, surrounded by equally massive wooden chairs.

People sat in these chairs, quietly reading books. The walls of each room were lined with file cabinets containing thousands of index cards, on which were recorded book titles and names of authors, filed in alphabetical order and cross-referenced to other drawers. People searched through the index cards, copied the titles of the books they wanted onto special request sheets and handed the requests to the librarians, who sat at a special desk located on the central wall of each room.

The librarians sent the requests to the back rooms of the library, where the books were stored. There, away from the public, other library workers pulled the requested books off the shelves and brought them to the librarians, who then gave them to the requesting parties. The entire process usually took about twenty minutes.

Nahum patiently showed Boris how the system worked. They finally chose four books from the index cards: *The Three Musketeers*, by Alexandre Dumas, *A Journey to the Center of the Earth*, by Jules Verne, *The Invisible Man*, by H.G. Wells and *The Last of the Mohicans*, by James Fenimore Cooper.

"These are all fantastic adventures," said Nahum to Boris as they approached the librarian's desk. "You'd love them. I guarantee it."

"We allow only two books at a time per customer," said the librarian, a middle-aged woman with large butterfly glasses that sat on the tip of her nose.

"That'll be fine," replied Nahum. "We'll get a library card for my son. Two books for me and two for him."

"I still remember my first library card," smiled the librarian, and she pulled an application form from the drawer. "Family name?" she asked Boris, as she prepared to fill it out.

"Draznin," answered Boris, proudly, looking forward to having his own library card.

"First name?"

"Boris."

"Father's name?"

"Nahum."

"Date of birth?"

"October 1, 1945."

"Ten years old. What a wonderful age," said the librarian.

Boris who wanted to appear older, corrected her. "I'll be eleven in less than three months."

"Don't rush time, young man." The librarian shook her head. "Your birthdays will come in due time. You'll get older whether you want to or not. Nationality?" she asked, as she came to the fifth line of the application.

Boris was dumbfounded. Why? Why did she need to know his nationality? His face flushed and he raised his eyes to his father, who also remained silent, refusing to help.

He heard the librarian's voice from behind the desk. "Jewish, I presume?"

He looked at her. She was writing "Jewish" on the application, not waiting for his reply.

"Yes," croaked Boris, through a suddenly dry throat. He didn't want this card any longer. He didn't want these books. Again, he looked at his father beside him, but Nahum didn't interfere in any way, and seemed completely unperturbed.

"Address?" asked the librarian.

"Chernishevskaya 83, Apartment 5," answered Boris.

"Your new card and the books you requested will be ready in about twenty minutes," said the librarian, still smiling and looking at Boris above her huge glasses.

"Do you want to go with me to the third floor?" asked Nahum, as they walked away from the librarian's desk. "I'd like to see some medical books."

"No, Papa. I'll stay here and look through the catalogues. May I?" Boris wanted to be alone.

"Fine. I'll be back in twenty minutes. Stay in this room, though. I don't want to lose you."

Nahum went to the third floor and Boris sat at a table, staring blindly at the file cabinets.

He felt humiliated, even though the librarian hadn't done or said anything wrong or offensive. She had just done her job, filling out his application. But why? Why did she need to know whether he was Jewish or not?

They finally received their books, and Boris shoved his new library card deep into the pocket of his trousers. They walked about three blocks to the trolleybus stop.

"Papa," asked Boris, seriously, "why do you think she needed to know my nationality?"

Nahum put his arm around his son's shoulders. "I see it bothered you a lot. You couldn't bring yourself to say, "Jewish," could you? Let me tell you the truth. At your age, I had a similar reaction. How little has changed! I don't know why she or anyone else, for that matter, would need to know the nationality of a library patron, but," he sighed, "that question is on every application form, whether it's for a library card or a passport or employment. As I said, when I was a boy your age, I was stunned by it, as you were today. I didn't want to be Jewish. I didn't understand why I was Jewish. I didn't understand why I was relegated to a nationality different from everyone else in my class— well, from almost everyone else. We had a couple of Jewish kids in the class, and so do you. As you grow older, you'll understand why they do it. I hope you will. For now, though, you there's only one thing you need to know—you have to be better than the others in order to be accepted as an equal."

Reading began to consume most of Boris' free time. He immersed himself in adventures and science fiction, fairy tales and war stories, until he discovered the classics. He grew up with Tolstoy, Dostoevsky, Chekov, France, Zola, Balzac, Galsworthy and Dickens. He gobbled the poetry of Pushkin, Lermontov, Burns and Shakespeare.

But suddenly, a book by Thomas Mann, *Joseph and his Brothers*, fell into his hands. Jewish history, embellished by the masterful words of a great writer, was coming alive in front of his eyes. He couldn't put the book down. Even after he finished this masterpiece, he went back to it again and again, for a month, re-reading paragraphs and chapters.

A little later, his father suggested *The Jewish Wars*, by Leon Feuchtwanger, and Boris loved it. Now fifteen, Boris realized that the Jewish heritage went back to almost pre-historic times, tens of centuries before the known history of the Russian and other Slavic tribes.

He didn't want to compare, but the facts were so incredibly obvious that he was overwhelmed by his discovery. He became extremely proud of the long history of the Jewish people, and of his own heritage.

Yet, as he learned more and his initial pride and fascination grew, he stumbled on a couple of puzzling questions that remained unanswered despite his voracious reading.

"Papa," he asked, one day, "why are the traditions of the Jewish people so interwoven with the religion? How can we be true Jews and remain atheists? Is Judaism a race or is it a religion?"

These were the same questions that had gnawed at Nahum's mind on many occasions. Repeatedly and intentionally, he had pushed them away. Not that he tried to escape; he simply didn't want to deal with them. There was no need to know the answers. For years, during his adolescence, he had wished to assimilate into the Greater Russian culture that surrounded his daily life. When that had proved to be impossible, he had switched to his work and career. Thinking about being Jewish, and certainly about Judaism, could have undermined both. But now he had been asked these questions in a direct and specific way, and by his son, who was searching for answers.

Times had changed. People were no longer being arrested indiscriminately, the State of Israel existed and he, himself, had encouraged Boris to read books about Jewish history. Why had he done that, if he didn't want his son to find answers?

"You are very perceptive," he answered, slowly. "I have frequently thought of these questions myself. Not that I have an answer for you, but I can share some of my thoughts."

"That would be great!"

"The Jews have been persecuted throughout history, whether ancient, medieval or modern. This is a fact. Without getting into the causes of this persecution, I can tell you religion was the strongest tie, and the only one that kept the Jewish people together, prevented their extinction and helped them survive violent times. On the other hand, it was only when they escaped the boundaries of their religious life that they were able to enter and penetrate the upper layers of the societies in which they lived. Like the power of water breaking a dyke, the power of their intellect burst through the constraints of religion, and they swam to professional and political achievements in every culture they lived in.

"As with everything else in life, there is a price. For Jews and their incredible success, the payback came in two prongs: assimilation for some and anti-Semitism for others. They had to get away from their orthodox religion, but if they wished to remain Jewish, they had to keep traditions that are, in essence, the remnants of the religion."

"How can one learn more about traditions and about religion?"

"From books. I wouldn't recommend going any further than that. Going to the synagogues will ruin your professional career, at least in this country.

Communism is our official religion, and the Communist Party won't look approvingly at a flirtation with Judaism."

"Is there a happy medium?"

"Not yet. Maybe one day. As far as I can see, the Jews are trying to do that in Israel; to marry the Jewish religion with secular Zionism. It may or may not work."

"And how do people get to Israel?"

"Don't know that, either. I guess there are people who went there before the War. Also, some Polish Jews who became Soviet citizens during the War were allowed to go back to Poland, and many went from there to Israel. Here, our borders are locked. We are staying here, and must make the best of it."

"Isn't it crazy to live one life in society's eyes and another one in your own mind? It's like a split personality, isn't it?"

"And what's the alternative? To fight the system is useless. Bullets and labor camps are very persuasive. I'd rather live two lives and achieve some professional and creative satisfaction."

"I am not sure what I would rather do."

"I know what you should do if you are smart."

"What?"

"You'll do what I'm doing. If they jail you, they won't jail you alone. By becoming a fighter you would jeopardize the lives of your entire family; Mama's, your sister's and mine. I don't see how you have any right to do it. Your family and your creative life are the only two worthwhile things in your existence, anyway. It would be foolish to forget that. At the end, you might be left with nothing."

"But what's the point of existing as a prisoner of your own thoughts? So what that you became a professor, a respected man, when you know life here is so unfair; so unjust; so terribly oppressive and anti-Semitic?"

"I also know that I am arguably the best clinical endocrinologist in this country. I am one of the most creative medical scientists. I am one of the best teachers. And I still have many years to live and contribute. I am free to be creative in medicine and medical science. This is mine. No one can take it away from me."

"You hope. What if the arrests begin again? What would you do then?"

"I don't know, Boris. No one does. I must maintain my optimistic outlook. That is why I am talking with you so openly, as I would with my best friend, as with an adult. The future must be better than the past and the present. To be hopeful and optimistic is the only way to live, my son. The only way."

CHAPTER TWENTY-THREE

O n October 15, 1961, two weeks after Boris' sixteenth birthday, his high school, City School Number 13, held a fall dance. Practically every school in town held three such events a year, one in the fall, another in the second half of December, for the New Year's celebration, and the third in the spring, toward May Day. The dance at School Number 13 was held in the gymnasium on the ground floor of the school. Even though it was an event for seniors only, they were allowed to bring friends; younger students from the same school or even students from other schools. But the rules were fairly strict—the guests must be inside the school by seven-thirty p.m., a half-hour after the door opened. After that, only seniors of School Number 13 were allowed to enter. These rules, set in figurative stone, had been devised to keep rowdy guests away, and to maintain discipline inside.

Boris didn't particularly like attending school dances, but his best and probably only true friend at school, Yasha Ratner, loved dancing, and Boris reluctantly tagged along.

In the summer of 1961, bell-bottom pants had sprung into vogue among Minsk teenagers. Boris asked his mother to help him alter his pants, but she absolutely refused, saying that this was a terrible fashion, and he had a ridiculous idea, altering a perfectly nice pair of pants. So Boris and Yasha did it for themselves.

The night before the dance, they carefully opened the seams of their pants from the knees down, drew diagonal lines with a piece of chalk and sewed the pants along these new lines. The pants came out perfect—narrow in the thigh toward the knee, and wide at the ankle—just like the ones in the fashion magazines.

Their bell-bottom pants made them the stars of the dance. The girls watched them, clearly approving, and the boys were all asking them where they could get a pair of pants just like those.

The DJ played LPs of waltzes, tangos and foxtrots, or, occasionally, jazz and songs with good dance rhythms. The boys congregated along one wall of the gymnasium, and then crossed the floor, one by one, and invited girls to dance. The girls who had not been chosen formed pairs and danced together, figuring that that was better than leaning against the wall and waiting for someone to offer to dance with them.

Teachers assigned to keep an eye on discipline and morality walked among the students, convinced that, if they look hard enough, they'd find prohibited behavior.

At almost eight thirty, Yasha found Boris standing in the doorway. "Hey," he said, loudly, over the music, "I was told that there are three girls from School #20 outside, who came late and can't get in. Any thoughts on how we can help?"

"Uh. . . I assume our teachers are at the door?" asked Boris.

"Yep."

"So, we can't get them through, right?"

"Yep."

"I've got it!" exclaimed Boris. "We have painters working in the back hall of the second floor, haven't we? They have ladders. We can lower a ladder from the second floor classroom window that opens into the school yard, and they'll climb up."

"Brilliant!" Yasha confirmed. "Let's do it."

They raced upstairs and, sure enough, found a long ladder left by the painters in the back hall. They dragged it into a dark classroom and opened the window. Carefully, they lowered the ladder to the ground.

"Simply brilliant!" repeated Yasha. "I'll go down and find the girls. They should be in front of the school."

He went down the ladder, and Boris remained in the dark classroom, by the open window. Ten or fifteen minutes later, Yasha approached the ladder, accompanied by three girls. He wanted to hold the ladder below, sending the girls to climb ahead, but they were wearing wide skirts, and refused. After a little bickering, he climbed first. The girls followed, one by one.

Boris recognized the first one. He had seen her around the neighborhood. She recognized him, too.

"Marina," she introduced herself, jumping from the windowsill onto the classroom floor.

"Boris. Welcome to School #13," he joked.

The second girl to appear in the window was pale, but blushing from fear of falling down the unstable ladder and of this strange situation.

"Elena," she said, and extended her arm, counting on the boys' support as she prepared to jump down from the windowsill.

"Boris," answered Boris, and held onto her hand. "Welcome to School #13. How do you like our new entrance?" He laughed.

The third girl was tall, somewhat overweight and clumsy. As she climbed up, the aluminum ladder rattled, despite being held from above by Yasha and

Boris, and made a lot of noise. Also, she suddenly became afraid of falling, and refused to step from the ladder through the open window.

"I'm falling!" she screamed. "Help!"

Yasha and Boris, afraid of being discovered, grabbed her by the arms and tried to pull her in. She resisted, clinging to the ladder.

"Ina, let go!" shouted Marina. "Just get inside, stupid! Otherwise, you'll fall!" She also grabbed her friend and pulled.

The noise and screams coming from the back of the second floor of the school roused the interest of the headmaster, who decided to go upstairs to investigate. As he walked along the dark corridor, Ina, the last of the three girls, finally transferred herself from the ladder to the windowsill, and jumped to the floor with a loud thud.

"Who's there?" shouted the headmaster, and he began opening the doors of every classroom along the corridor.

"Down!" whispered Yasha. "Hit the floor behind the desks."

Boris and the girls spread out on the floor, while Yasha squeezed his tall, skinny body into the darkness of the corridor and ran downstairs, away from the approaching headmaster.

"Stop! Stop him! *Stop!*" shouted the headmaster, running along about fifty feet behind the shadow of the runaway boy.

But it was no contest. By the time the puffing, panting headmaster reached the bottom of the stairwell, Yasha was inside the gymnasium, among the crowd of students.

Meanwhile, Boris led the girls downstairs via the back stairs. They came to the first floor and stopped in the hallway, as if they had been standing there for a long time, chatting and laughing. They saw other teachers run upstairs in search of other intruders, summoned by the screams of the headmaster. Someone ran back, saying that he had discovered an open window and a ladder in one of the classrooms.

As Boris and the girls entered the gymnasium, the headmaster interrupted the music and announced through the mike, "Someone has broken into our school. There's clearly an intruder inside. We are going to call the police, but meanwhile we are evacuating the building. The dance is over. I ask everyone to leave through the main door. Everyone must leave in an orderly fashion."

Everyone did. Yasha, Boris and the three girls left the school with the other students, passing the headmaster, who stood at the door, trying to spot the intruder, but certainly not suspecting that Yasha, Boris or the accompanying girls might be involved.

"Good night," said Boris, as they passed through the door.

"Good night, Draznin," replied the headmaster, looking over Boris' head.

"It's all because of you, Ina," said Marina, angrily, when they were away from the school. "You were the first to agree to climb, and then you spoiled everything!"

"I'm sorry, but when I got up there, I froze."

"We noticed that," laughed Boris. He turned to Yasha. "You pulled a fast one. If you hadn't run away as you did, we would have been caught. Quick thinking. You saved the day."

"I didn't think," Yasha confessed. " It was just the instinct of self-preservation. Don't know what made me do it."

"It was certainly an exciting evening. Usually, dances are so dull," said Boris.

"It was too exciting for me," said Elena. "Can you imagine what would have happened if they'd caught us? I've never done anything even remotely that adventurous."

"You should hang out with us," said Yasha.

"No, thanks. That's enough."

It turned out that Marina and Ina lived about a block away from Yasha, and Elena lived a good fifteen-minute walk past Boris' apartment building.

"I'll walk you home," offered Boris, "if you don't mind."

"Thank you, not at all. It's not too far." Elena seemed glad, because she hadn't wanted to walk home alone.

"I haven't seen you in the neighborhood before," said Boris. "Have you moved here recently?"

"About four years ago. Not so recently, I guess. And you?"

"About the same time. When we first came to Minsk, we used to live close to the Opera."

"So you are not from Minsk, originally. How interesting. We moved to Minsk from Leningrad."

"And we came from Kharkov. In 1956. What's your last name?" asked Boris, curiously.

"Lerman. Elena Lerman."

"I'm Boris Draznin. My father is a doctor. He lost his job in Kharkov, and found one here."

"And both my parents are physicians, as well," laughed Elena. "What a coincidence!" She was truly amused.

"Maybe they know each other. What you think? I mean, our parents," suggested Boris.

"They might," Elena agreed. "Are you going to be a physician, too?"

"I'm not sure. I'm thinking about physics. Nuclear physics appears so interesting, but the physicists are awfully smart. Maybe it's not for me. I also like to write. Maybe I have the talent to be a writer; who knows? What about you?"

"I like medicine. Besides, I haven't detected any other talents in myself, yet," said Elena, gaily. "I think I'll stay with the family tradition."

"I'll make a decision by winter break," said Boris, more seriously. "If I go with medicine, I'll need to start preparing for the entrance exams. I hear they're tough. Until then, I still have time to think."

"That's what I've heard, too. The tests are really tough," said Elena. "Here's my house." She pointed at a five-story apartment building. "Our windows are on the second floor."

"Now that you know how to use a ladder, you can climb in and out."

They laughed.

Boris switched gears. "Do you want to go to the movies this weekend?"

"Sure. I'd love to."

"Shall I call you?"

"No, let's just pick a place to meet." Elena probably didn't want boys to call her at home.

"Fine. I'll meet you Sunday at six o'clock by the Pobeda movie theater. Do you know where that is?"

"I do. I'll be there."

And she left.

After that, they met many times. They saw movies together, walked hours in the evenings along the rainy streets of their neighborhood and in the center of town, and drank much coffee in the coffee shops. They applied to medical school and worried about getting in, as, by this time, the Jewish quota was back, albeit unofficially. They both did very well on their entrance exams, and were admitted to Minsk State Medical School.

In the summer of 1965, Boris proposed and Elena accepted. They got married on December 25, 1965. In atheist Russia, no one knew about Christmas. Besides, the Russian Orthodox Church celebrates Christmas by the Gregorian calendar, on January 7. For Boris, Elena, their families and almost everyone in Russia, December 25, 1965 was just another Saturday, a week before the New Year, the true national holiday.

On December 25, they had the first real wedding in the family in at least three generations. They were twenty years old, and aspiring medical students.

*   *   *

The Six Day War between Israel and her neighbors, Egypt, Jordan and Syria, shook and uplifted the Russian Jewish community as nothing had before. The brevity of war and the decisive victory of the Israeli Army made Russian Jews feel extremely proud.

At the end of the Six Day war, Israel occupied the Sinai Peninsula, the Golan Heights and the West Bank of the Jordan River, and had liberated East Jerusalem. Even though official Russian propaganda maliciously called Israel an aggressor and a puppet of World Imperialists, the scope and speed of the Israeli military victory were the most pleasant news Russian Jews had heard in decades.

Suddenly, many of these almost-completely-assimilated, secular people transformed their image as "rootless cosmopolitans" into that of noble defenders of their historical motherland. They found that the tiny foothold on the southeastern shore of the Mediterranean Sea, a little dot on the map, was more than capable of defending itself, proudly raising its white and blue flag with the Star of David on it.

Although it would still be a long time before freedom of expression arrived in the Soviet Union, a first puff of fresh air had entered Jewish homes, in a country where Jews were pitifully ashamed of their own identity.

Real news, particularly from abroad, was not easy to come by in the Soviet Union. All the Russian newspapers and television and radio stations were under the censorship of the Communist Party and the KGB. The only independent information that reached the Soviet citizen came from the Russian language broadcasts of the BBC, Voice of America and Radio Freedom. A good short-wave radio was a priceless possession in every home. People listened carefully to the news and commentaries that fought their way into people's kitchens and bedrooms, through the jamming devices and concrete walls of the apartment houses.

Nahum, Victor and Boris were glued to their short-wave radios nightly, catching every single word broadcast by the Voice of America and the BBC. Carefully adjusting the tuning knob in order to find a wave less affected by jamming, they listened, each in his own apartment, to the now-familiar voices of the announcers and commentators. With a knock at the door, they not only turned the radios off, but also, as an extra precaution, moved the tuning knobs away from the stations they had just listened to. The KGB was still too powerful, and no one was ready to play games with them.

Even though it was difficult, if not impossible, to follow entire broadcasts, what they heard made them extremely proud. Tiny Israel had defeated gigantic Arab countries in less than a week. The Sinai, the Golan Heights and Old Jerusalem were now in Israeli hands. A stunning victory by a small nation, born not quite twenty years before, over Soviet allies was the best news they could have hoped for.

"I wish we were there!" cried Boris, in Victor's apartment, as they exchanged news of what they had heard on the radio.

Victor, who was fluent in German and English, had much more information from foreign-language broadcasts, because they were not jammed. The authorities correctly assumed that almost no one in Russia knew foreign languages, and saved their jamming power for the Russian-language broadcast.

"And what would you do there?" asked Victor, provocatively.

"Almost anything!" Boris replied passionately.

"Not good enough. You must be able to contribute, not just be a pair of unskilled hands. You must be able to practice your profession and, for that, you need to know languages."

"I can learn Hebrew."

"English. English is the language you ought to master. English has become an international *lingua* in almost all professions. It has beaten out German and certainly French."

Boris, who was studying French as a foreign language in school, knew Victor was right. "I understand that, and I promise to handle it properly," he said, after a short pause.

Victor, remembering the challenges his father had imposed on him, replied, with a smile, "Don't think it's that easy. It's much more difficult than you think. Don't promise unless you intend to stand by your word."

Boris thought for another moment, and nodded, "I am going to handle it. I know I can do it."

Both of them turned out to be right. Boris bought many books for beginners, a textbook of English grammar and several dictionaries, and embarked on the self-teaching process with vigor and enthusiasm. Nevertheless, Victor's prediction also proved correct; it would be much more difficult than Boris had envisioned.

Elena gave birth to their first daughter, Julie, in September of 1967. The amount of time Boris could devote to the language began to be limited by the baby, their up-coming graduation in 1968 and uncertainty about future jobs. While taking care of little Julie was the most pleasant of the chores, worrying about jobs was clearly the most difficult.

In 1968, a new student transferred into Boris' class. His name was also Boris; Boris Dvogovsky. A tall, strong man, an amateur heavyweight boxer, he had transferred from Vilnius Medical School, in Lithuania, after marrying a young music teacher from Minsk. The two Borises met at a lecture, spoke briefly, and, at the end of the day, walked together to the bus stop. They clicked right away, and agreed to meet, with their young families, the next weekend. Their wives, Elena and Luda, also liked one another, and a friendship was born.

Boris Dvogovsky came from a strongly Zionist family. His father, Mikhail Dvogovsky, had been a member of the Lithuanian Zionist Organization before Lithuania was annexed by the Soviet Union as a part of its non-aggression pact with Nazi Germany, a move designed to divide Eastern Europe between the two giants. Before the Russian troops moved in, Mikhail Dvogovsky had been helping thousands of Lithuanian Jews to emigrate to Palestine.

The Iron Curtain that suddenly engulfed the three small Baltic Republics and locked them into the "happy family" of Soviet Nations prevented him from moving to Palestine, but it saved his life during the ensuing World War II. He and his friends in the Zionist movement were deported to Siberia within two months of annexation. They were free to live and work in their small Siberian town, but were not allowed to move away until the end of the War. The rest of his family perished in the Holocaust.

In 1946, Mikhail returned to Lithuania and, in 1948, he, his wife, little Boris and a small group of friends attempted to cross the Soviet border into Turkey, heading for Palestine. They were caught, and Mikhail, as a ringleader, received a twenty-five-year prison term and spent the next eight years of his life in jail.

He was released in 1956, but Palestine had to wait. He was not allowed to emigrate, and the annual applications that he filed routinely were as routinely denied.

His son, Boris Dvogovsky, had inherited his father's desire to reach the land of milk and honey. "One day, Boris," he used to tell his new friend, "we'll be there. One day, the door will open, the sun will shine and we'll be living in our own country."

Boris, who had never before met such a devoted Zionist, was enchanted by Dvogovsky's unwavering desire, enormous energy and unbeatable optimism about a seemingly unattainable future. Nothing appeared to stand in his way, except for the huge wall of the impenetrable borders of the Soviet Union.

"I have a profession that I can start using the day I arrive in Jerusalem," he used to say, as if he held an airplane ticket in his hand. "All I want to do is to treat my fellow Israelis; just to be an emergency physician for those who might need me."

"Where would you like to settle?"

"Doesn't matter at all," he replied convincingly. "Israel is a small country. I'd live anywhere. You see, I am not looking for big hospitals. I am not looking for a prominent career. I want to be a people's doctor; a worker bee; a simple Jewish physician for simple Jewish people."

There the two Borises parted in their ambitions. Boris Draznin had dreamed about a creative, academic life. His father and his father-in-law were far more convincing and attractive role models than the prospect of being "a simple doctor for simple folk." But the idea of living and working in Israel, no matter how far-fetched it seemed at that time, was incredibly appealing. If anything, these conversations with his friend instilled much-needed energy into his efforts to study English and to excel professionally. But then, quite unexpectedly, he learned something else . He learned to be patient.

"My father always taught me to be patient, flexible and pragmatic about my goals," said Boris Dvogovsky. "I know I'll be in Israel, and I'm prepared to wait until it happens. I am in no rush. I'm flexible enough to adjust to life here, while I'm waiting, and I hope to remain flexible enough to adjust to a new life in Israel, when I get there. I am moving step-by-step toward my goal."

"I am jealous," replied Boris Draznin. "I wish I had your discipline of mind. I want to do so many things in life, and I want them all right now. I wonder whether I'll ever have enough time to finish just a fraction of things I'd love to accomplish!"

Indeed, time seemed to be the hardest commodity to possess. Immersed in family, English and his research projects, he still managed to carve enough time from sleep to write a play about the life of King Herod, the ruthless ruler of Judea, builder of the Second Temple, and of Masada.

He finally finished his play in 1969 and, overcoming anxiety and shyness, took his script to the artistic director of the Minsk Drama Theater, who happened to be Jewish, as well.

"A Jewish play? You brought to me a Jewish play?" gasped the director, when they met after he read the manuscript. "With a Biblical theme! Mind-boggling!"

"No, no Biblical theme. An historical one. There is nothing from the Bible in the manuscript," Boris countered, quickly. "A mixture of history and fiction. Nothing else."

"Why can't it be a Roman play? Or Greek? Why does it have to be Jewish?"

Boris attempted to defend his choice of character. "I am just using a Jewish King as a tyrant protagonist; a despotic ruler who also wishes to go down in history as a prolific builder and a skilled politician."

The artistic director shook his head. "Young man, there are plenty of tyrants in the world. I am not about to glorify a Jewish one in my theater. You are not a bad writer, by the way." He handed Boris his manuscript. "But don't waste your time writing about Jewish history. It will lead you nowhere."

Boris took his manuscript home, and placed it at the bottom of the bottom drawer of his desk. "Pragmatism," he thought, "is a virtue. It tells me to stay with my profession. Oh, well; I'll be pragmatic. I'll do my best." He pulled a medical text from the shelf and opened it.

CHAPTER TWENTY-FOUR

The late sixties and early seventies in Minsk resembled the fifties in Leningrad, Moscow and Kharkov—Jewish physicians needed not apply for any academic or research-oriented positions. Boris finally obtained a position that afforded him some free time to do research, but the position itself was a dead-end job without any potential for academic appointment. This would have been fine, at least for a while; it was still early in his career and he could certainly wait for the right opportunity. A more troublesome fact was a complete lack of financial resources for advanced biomedical research.

Conceptually, Nahum, Victor, Dina and Boris had intriguing ideas, grandiose plans, inexhaustible energy and boundless enthusiasm. Practically speaking, however, they had no means of moving their research efforts to the next level. In the West, in the late sixties and early seventies, the biomedical sciences were making an unparalleled leap forward. Advances in technology, such as the catheterization of various vessels and computer tomography (known as CT scanning), along with new methods of hormone measurement and revolutionary developments in immunology and molecular and cellular biology were completely unavailable in the Soviet Union, at that time.

Biomedical technology cost money, a lot of it, and, for the Soviet government, the only spheres of science deemed worthy of capital investment were those that contributed to its military might. Medicine did not. Treating older people or those with chronic conditions who could not return to productive employment was considered by the socialist Soviet government a total waste of public resources.

Talented biomedical scientists and clinicians watched with frustration and jealousy the progress of medicine in the Western world, falling farther behind with alarming speed.

"At best, we are destined to re-invent the wheel," Nahum lamented. "Technology is changing medicine rapidly, and we have no means to participate meaningfully in this exciting process."

"A waste of brainpower," added Victor. "And the most appalling thing is that ordinary people, our patients, reap no benefit from these incredible advances."

"We'll just have to make do with what we have," Dina summed up, in her usual rational way.

And they did. They remained the most respected professors in Byelorussian medicine, the best physicians in their fields and the best teachers of the next generation of physicians.

Along with signs of fiscal instability, the country began showing tiny, barely perceptible clues to the administrative and moral decay of the Communists government and the entire system, which would eventually collapse during the nineties. At that time, however, the government itself had not yet foreseen the impact of the coming technological revolution on its totalitarian structure. The Communist leaders of the time thought they would be able to govern in their usual way, suppressing freedom of speech and freedom of expression among Soviet citizens.

To the government, the most frightening thing was the possibility of communication among citizens without government control. This was before the age of computers and the age of the Internet, and the government was attempting to control all means of communication as tightly as it could. Typewriters with memory and copying machines were few, and under the strict and restrictive control of the government.

One needed special permission to copy a document, to soothe the government's fear of citizens using copying devices to distribute unauthorized information. The uncontrolled and unauthorized distribution of information was considered a major threat to the government, and to the stability of the Communist regime.

It was against this background that the manuscripts of the books of Alexander Solzhenitsyn—*The First Circle* and *Cancer Ward*—were smuggled to the West, published and read over the radio. The BBC devoted prime time in their Russian language broadcast to readings of chapters of these books. These were "the sacred hours" for Russian intellectuals all over the country, who avidly gobbled up every word through the wall of noise of the jamming stations.

Solzhenitsyn's descriptions were the first eyewitness accounts of Stalin's concentration camps and the lives of the prisoners. The reality was frightening not only to the younger generation, Boris' contemporaries, but also to the generation of Nahum and Victor, who had known little of what had been going on behind the curtain of the Gulag.

"Did you know what was going on?" asked Boris, in astonishment.

"Yes and no," answered Nahum. "We knew people were taken away. We knew many were executed and many imprisoned. But I, for example, did not know anything about the lives of those prisoners. We could only guess how horrible it must have been."

"No one knew for sure what was going on at the Gulag," echoed Victor. "Once they were arrested, people didn't come back, and those few who did return preferred silence. Like many who returned from the Nazi death camps, people didn't want to discuss their horrific experiences."

In 1970, in what was arguably a somewhat political move, to the delight of Russian dissidents, Solzhenitsyn was awarded the Nobel Prize for Literature. Like Boris Pasternak before him (in 1958), Solzhenitsyn declined to attend the ceremony, fearing that he would not be allowed to return to Russia.

"They should be extremely proud to watch another great Russian author receive international recognition, but, instead, they wish to squash him. How typical of this government," said Victor. "Russia's governments have hated its intellectual citizens through the centuries, and Solzhenitsyn is no exception."

The mood in the country went from bad to worse. On December 16, 1970, a new trial opened in Leningrad. A group of Jews, including Edward Kusnetsov, Sylvia Zalmanson, her brother, Wolf Zalmanson, and Mark Dimshitz, were accused of trying to hijack an airplane in an attempt to emigrate to Israel. Mark Dimshitz, a former pilot, had been supposed to fly it.

Even though they were convicted and imprisoned, this time, a Jewish trial became a rallying-point for Jews around the world, helping focus attention on the plight of Russian Jews. The ancient slogan, "Let my people go!" became a pounding hammer, both inside and outside Russia. Instead of being frightened, Jewish and Russian dissidents raised their heads and opened their mouths. People were ready to go to jail or be exiled, in their fight for freedom of speech and freedom of emigration.

The next year, several famous Jewish professors of physics and chemistry in Moscow, Leningrad and Riga applied for exit visas to Israel. Their requests were denied; they lost their jobs and joined the ranks of the dissidents. Daily, the Voice of America and the BBC broadcast every detail of their fights with the Government. The fact that they were not arrested encouraged others to follow in their footsteps.

The wave of applications for exit visas grew. Every day, new people joined in the seemingly fruitless effort. But, in the end, their labor bore great fruit. Bowing to increased international pressure, Russian authorities allowed a large group of Jews to emigrate to Israel in 1972. The door had been cracked open, and was now ajar.

"Is this the right time?" pondered Boris.

Neither Nahum nor Victor thought so. The situation was not clear-cut. The number of people allowed to leave grew, but so did the number of people who were denied. The Government had created a new environment—an atmosphere of unpredictability. People applying for exit visas were simply gambling. They had no idea whether they would be the lucky ones who received permission or the miserable ones who were destined to lose their jobs and income and then be denied the visas for no obvious reason.

Nahum, Victor and Dina were close to their fiftieth birthdays. They were still in their prime, worrying about what they would do if their applications were rejected. At the same time, they had no idea of what they could possibly do in Israel. Would they find jobs? Would anybody need them there? What if the answer were "no?" Were they really ready to quit their reasonably stable positions in Minsk for an unpredictable outcome and a totally unclear future? They'd lived with their hatred of the Soviet system and its anti-Semitic environment for so long, they could certainly live there a little longer. Was the risk worth it? None of these questions had an answer. It was a pure-guess, gut-feeling, adventurous step that they couldn't quite make.

Boris and Elena did it for them. Realizing that their parents were fully behind them, but were tormented by fear of the unknown, Boris told his father that he was applying to leave the Soviet Union immediately.

Nahum though for a brief moment and said, "If we apply all together, as one big family with three professors in it, we may make a good target for them to set an example of by denying our request. If you think you are ready to do it, go ahead, and we will follow as soon as you leave. If they detain us, you will lead a campaign in the West in our support."

Victor agreed with the plan and, at the end of the spring of 1973, Boris and Elena submitted their applications for exit visas.

Minsk was shocked. Neither the Jewish nor the non-Jewish community had expected that children of such prominent families would do such a thing.

The Director of the hospital where Boris worked called a general meeting. It was held in the largest lecture hall, built as an amphitheater. The hall was packed. On the stage, there was a podium, a long table adjacent to it and a small table on the opposite side of the stage. The long table was covered with a red cloth, while the small one was bare. The Hospital Director, the Secretary of the Communist Party and the Secretary's deputy were sitting at the long table, looking at lonely Boris sitting at the small, bare table.

Boris was well prepared for this meeting. He had rehearsed this with his father more than once.

"Keep calm," Nahum advised. "Don't let them draw you into any controversy. Do not respond to provocative statements. Don't get upset or defensive."

"I know, I know, Papa. Don't worry. I am absolutely calm. Once I've made a decision to go ahead, I have full confidence and control over what I'm doing. They won't draw me into anything."

"The best strategy," offered Victor, "is to limit your answers to single phrases. And never, ever be sarcastic."

Nahum concurred. "I agree. Just tell them, 'I'm Jewish and I want to live in Israel.' No matter what they ask, stick to that answer."

And Boris did.

"How can you betray your motherland?" shouted the Hospital Director, angrily.

"I thank my motherland for everything I have," replied Boris, calmly. "But just as Russian people live in Russia and French people live in France, I am Jewish and I wish to live in Israel. I have nothing against the Soviet Union."

"We gave you a happy childhood and a free education, and you turn your back on us. You are going to live with capitalists and imperialists," replied the Secretary of the Communist Party.

"I only want to live in the Jewish state. I am Jewish and I wish to live in Israel," came the standard reply.

The meeting lasted for hour and a half. Numerous speakers accused Boris of treason and betrayal, predicted misery and disappointment in the West and denounced his moral character. To all this, Boris answered with the single objection—"I'm Jewish and wish to live among Jewish people."

After a while, it became predictable, and the spectators lost interest. Boris began examining the faces of the spectators. He knew a lot of doctors, among whom were several Jews, and quite a few nurses. They all watched him intently, but turned away when their eyes met. In the end, even the Hospital Director lost interest in the exercise. He ended the meeting, saying that he hoped Boris would be killed in a fight with Arab soldiers.

Boris was not fired from his position, and continued to work as if nothing had happened. No one among his colleagues and coworkers asked him a single question or addressed the matter in any other way. The only comment came about a month later, when one older Jewish doctor told him, when they met accidentally at the hospital entrance, "You'll be all right, Draznin. If I were your age, I'd do the same." He touched Boris' shoulder and moved away, not waiting for an answer.

The Draznins prepared for a difficult wait. There was no indication of whether their application would be considered positively or negatively. Not a word from the visa department of the Ministry of Internal Security. All they could do was wait.

On October 3, 1973, another war broke out in the Middle East. On the most Holy Day in Jewish tradition, Yom Kippur, the armies of Egypt and Syria attacked Israel from two directions. The Israelis had not anticipated the attack, and retreated. It appeared that the Arab countries were poised for a decisive victory.

On October 5, Boris received a phone call from the Visa Department—come tomorrow, at ten in the morning. He could only guess what that meant.

When he arrived at the door of the department, the next morning, he saw at least two dozen people already waiting in the corridor. They were all invited in at once.

At ten o'clock, the captain came out of his office and said, "The people whose names I am going to read out are granted permission to emigrate. You must leave the country within thirty days or change your minds." He added with a smile, "Your Israel may not exist by that time."

Boris's heart raced as the captain read the names. "Draznin," he heard.

Yes! he thought. *Yes!* He got the visas for himself, Elena and Julie, and ran home. So far, except for the stupid meeting at work, everything had been relatively painless.

The radio broadcasts were increasingly gloomy, however. Israel was on the defensive, retreating deep into her territory. The Russian government had granted an unprecedented number of exit visas, expecting many of the departing Jews to change their minds. Who in his right mind was going to emigrate to a war zone, particularly, when Israel appeared to be losing the war?

"First, we get to Vienna," said Boris. "Then we'll decide what to do. We are not staying here under any circumstances."

The situation was somewhat complicated because Elena was almost seven months pregnant, and the prospect of being homeless refugees in a foreign country was certainly frightening.

Boris attempted to joke. "My knowledge of French and English might become useful sooner than I thought." No one else found it funny.

Getting out of the Soviet Union turned out to be the prevailing priority among the Russian Jews, as no one among the holders of exit visas opted to stay. Also, the course of the war in the Middle East changed dramatically. In the third week of conflict, Israel emerged as the clear winner, threatening Cairo in the South and Damascus in the North.

Their train from Minsk to Brest to Warsaw and on to Vienna was leaving on November 7, 1973, the day of the National Holiday, the anniversary of the Communist Revolution. Both sets of parents, Nahum and Rosa and Victor and Dina, traveled with Boris and Elena to Brest, where, at the border between the Soviet Union and Poland, they were supposed to pass through Customs and Passport Control.

Everything was going smoothly, with tears and laughter over the separation, until they came to the narrow door of the departure hall.

A visibly drunk Captain of the local police force was standing at the door. He didn't seem to be paying any attention to the group of departing passengers and their families. Suddenly, when Nahum was hugging Elena goodbye, the Captain woke up from his apparent stupor and shoved Nahum away, screaming, "Enough! You Jewish traitors!"

His sudden push knocked Nahum off his feet, and he fell flat on his back on the dirty tiled floor. Before anyone realized what had happened, Boris leaped up and swung his fist into the Captain's open jaw. The Captain sagged to the floor, while two other policemen rushed in and pulled Boris away, twisting his arms behind his back.

"Take him to my office," ordered the Captain, getting back to his feet.

The family remained in shock as the policemen led Boris away. They realized that the repercussions could be terrible. The women stayed on the benches, while Nahum and Victor followed gravely behind the shuffling Captain to his office.

Boris was sitting on a plain wooden chair in front of the Captain's desk, where the policemen had left him. The Captain barely made it to his chair, and literally fell into it. He was so drunk and so confused by Boris' uppercut, he couldn't keep his head up. It fell forward and rested on the pile of papers on his desk. He was probably asleep or semi-conscious.

After five minutes of silence, Boris called, "Comrade Captain, Comrade Captain." Getting no answer, he leaned over the desk and touched the Captain's elbow. "Comrade Captain," he said, more loudly.

The Captain raised his head and looked at Boris, not understanding what was going on. "Who are you?" he asked.

"You wanted me to pay the fine," Boris replied, quickly.

"Twenty rubles," mumbled the Captain, and his head fell again onto the pile of papers in front of him.

Boris pulled a twenty-ruble banknote from his pocket and put it on the desk. "Here it is. Could you write me a receipt?" He couldn't believe his luck.

The Captain's hand reached for a pen. "Where is it?" he asked.

Boris grabbed a sheet of plain paper and scribbled, *Boris Draznin is released after paying a fine of twenty rubles.* "Here," he said, pushing it under the Captain's pen, "sign here, please."

The Captain, whose face was still on the pile of papers and turned away from the paper Boris had given him, scribbled his signature, not knowing what he was doing. Boris pulled the paper away, and carefully tiptoed out of the office.

He showed the paper to a puzzled policeman outside, and said, "The Captain told me to give you ten rubles. I have only twenty; share it with your colleague." He pulled out another twenty-ruble banknote, and gave it to the policeman.

"Good deal!" said the policeman, and stuffed the money into his pocket. "You can go. Keep this release, though."

Boris ran to his father and Victor, who stood fifty meters away, still looking terribly shocked. "Thank God this country has holidays!" smiled Boris, and he told them what had happened. They hurried to Elena, Rosa and Dina.

"You don't even know how lucky you were!" said Victor. "Get the hell out of here quickly, before he sobers up ."

But they had missed their train, and the next one to Warsaw was three hours later. The direct train to Vienna would not be until tomorrow, but they decided not to wait.

Nahum agreed with Victor. "Better wait in Warsaw, at the train station. Don't stay here even a minute more than necessary."

Three hours later, Boris, Elena, and Julie left the Soviet Union.

"We are going into a totally new life," said Elena, as the train departed. "Who knows what awaits us?"

Boris nodded. "Ignorance is bliss. That's all I can say."

EPILOGUE

hree weeks after their children left the Soviet Union, Nahum, Victor and Dina were fired from their academic posts. The reason was extremely simple—if they could not ensure the patriotic upbringing of their own children, they certainly could not be teachers in the Soviet system of education. They were fired effective immediately.

One zealous professor at Nahum's institution said, passionately, "If there were a war with the imperialists, and my son met your son on the battlefield, I hope my son would kill yours, and spill the blood of a traitor!"

Nahum was furious, but remained silent. He knew better than respond to provocation.

Rosa was the only one among the four parents who was still allowed to work. She was a simple dentist in a neighborhood clinic, and had not been fired from her job. A wait of unpredictable duration ended in June of 1974, when they were given exit visas, and told to leave the Soviet Union within two months.

Nahum spent a day at the grave of Rachel, who had died of a brain tumor in 1968, while Victor traveled to Zhitomir to visit the graves of his parents and Dina went to Leningrad to say goodbye to her father and plant a tree near her mother's grave. Rosa said farewell to her brothers and to her mother, who expressed a keen interest in leaving Russia with her daughter's family. Moshe, who was emigrating with Nahum's family, returned his red Communist Party membership card to the regional Party Secretary, who accepted it without a word.

In August of 1974, they boarded a train for Vienna. A week later, they landed at Ben-Gurion airport. In their early fifties, Nahum, Rosa, Victor and Dina were beginning new lives.